PHOTOGRAPHY AND SOCIAL MOVEMENTS

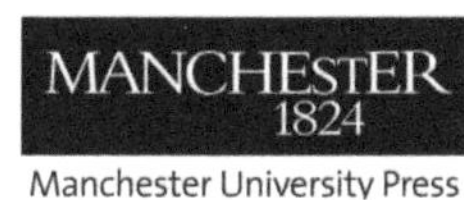

Manchester University Press

Photography and social movements

From the globalisation of the movement (1968)
to the movement against globalisation (2001)

Antigoni Memou

Manchester University Press

Published by Manchester University Press
Altrincham Street, Manchester, M1 7JA, UK
www.manchesteruniversitypress.co.uk

British Library Cataloguing-in-Publication Data
A catalogue record for this book is available from the British Library

Library of Congress Cataloging-in-Publication Data applied for

ISBN   978 0 7190 9999 1 paperback

First published 2013

This paperback edition first published 2015

The publisher has no responsibility for the persistence or accuracy of URLs for any external or third-party internet websites referred to in this book, and does not guarantee that any content on such websites is, or will remain, accurate or appropriate.

Typeset in Fournier and The Sans
by Carnegie Book Production, Lancaster

To my sister Chrysa Memou

Στην αδερφή μου Χρύσα Μέμου

Contents

List of plates

List of figures

Abbreviations

ATTAC	Art Tendency Against Capitalism
BB	Black Block
CAL	Comité d' Action Lycéens, (High School Action Committees)
CFDT	Confédération Française Démocratique du Travail, (French Democratic Workers Confederation)
CGT	Confédération Générale du Travail, (General Confederation of Labour)
CJA	Public Order Act
CND	Convención Nacional Democrática
CVB	Comité Viêtnam de Base, (Basic Committees on Vietnam)
CVN	Comité Viêtnam National, (National Committee On Vietnam)
EDT	Electronic Disturbance Theatre
ESU	Étudiants Socialistes Unifiés
EZLN	Ejército Zapatista Liberación Nacional
FAF	Fédération Anarchiste
FER	Fédération des Étudiants Révolutionnaires, (Federation of Revolutionary Students)
FONCA	Fondo Nacional para la Cultura y les Artes
GSF	Genoa Social Forum
ICC	International Criminal Court
JCR	Jeunesse Communiste Révolutionnaire, (The Revolutionary Communist Youth)
MST	Movimento dos Trabalhadores Rurais Sem Terra, (Brazil's Landless Workers Movement)

NAFTA	North American Free Trade Agreement
NGOs	Non-governmental Organizations
PCF	Parti Communiste Français, (French Communist Party)
PGA	People's Global Action
PRI	Partido Revolucionario Institucional, (Institutional Revolutionary Party)
RTF	Radio Television Française
RTS	Reclaim the Streets
SDS	Students for a Democratic Society
SNEsup	Syndicat National de l' Enseignemen Supérieur, (National Union of Higher Education)
UEC	Union des Étudiants Communistes
UJCML	Union des Jeunesses Communistes Marxistes-Leninistes, (Union of Marxist-Leninist Communist Youth)
UNEF	Union Nationale des Étudiants de France, (National Union of French Students)
WSF	World Social Forum
WTO	World Trade Organisation

Acknowledgements

M Y DEEPEST GRATITUDE goes to my sister Chrysa for her unconditional love, continuous encouragement, enormous psychological and financial support. This book is dedicated to her as it simply would not exist without her altruism and devotion. I would also like to thank very much my brother Christos for listening, sharing long discussions, giving me constant support, precious advice and continuous encouragement, but, most importantly, for showing me the way and for being a constant source of inspiration and hope. This journey would never have started without him. Special thanks to my parents for their love and devotion, and in particular to my mum who proves everyday that the 'true revolutionary is guided by a great feeling of love'.

Many people have generously contributed to this book in all kinds of ways. This book started as a Ph.D. project at the Courtauld Institute of Art and I would like to express my sincere thanks to my supervisor Prof. Julian Stallabrass for his invaluable advice and feedback on my thesis and my examiners Prof. Andrew Hemingway and Dr Steve Edwards for their precious insights. My thanks are also due to many people, for their advice and help at various stages of this project: John Jordan, George McKay, Nick Cobbing, Alex Macnaughton, Rossana Jaccavo and Françoise Blum at the Bibliotheque d' Histoire Sociale Du XXe Siècle (Université Paris I – Pantheon Sorbonne). For their help with copyright issues I would like to thank: Caroline Burghardt at Luhring Augustine Gallery in New York, Antonio Turok, Raúl Ortega, Marietta Bernstorff, Francesca Marzotto, Isabelle Martinon and Diego Berruecos. A special thanks to Dr Gregory Sholette for his constructive feedback on the latest version of the manuscript and to Dr Andrew Stephenson for his precious advice and constant support.

I gratefully acknowledge the Central Research Fund who funded my archival research in Paris (summer 2006), and the Art Historian Association for the award of the Image Cost Grant towards the copyright costs. An earlier version of the chapter 3 has been published in the journal *Third Text*, chapter 7 has appeared in the journal *Philosophy of Photography* and chapter 9 in the journal *Photographies*.

Last but not least, I would like to thank very much my editor and the team at Manchester University Press for all their support during the production of this book.

Introduction

T H R O U G H O U T its brief history, photography has had a close relationship to social movements. From the Commune of Paris in 1871, the first political uprising to be captured by camera, to the 1990s anti-globalisation movement, the photographic medium has played a crucial role in political struggles.[1] The camera's presence at very important moments of political resistance resulted in some of the best-known photographs in the history of twentieth-century photography. Some of these photographs transcended the historical and geographical boundaries of the particular struggle they depicted. As an example, the photograph taken by Charles Moore of a police dog attacking a black American during the events in Birmingham in the spring of 1963 came to stand as a quintessential image for the civil-rights movement. The publication of the photograph in the national newspapers raised public awareness about the civil-rights movement, provoked new demonstrations, sit-ins and riots and made the movement known worldwide.[2] Similarly, John Paul Filo's 'Kent-state girl screaming over dead body', taken on 4 May 1970 not only became the symbol of the American anti-war movement, but contributed to the revival of the movement with a new wave of demonstrations across the United States and Europe.[3] Equally recognisable is the image of a man stopping a tank, taken in Beijing in June 1989, which symbolised the Tiananmen Square protests and the subsequent massacre.[4]

Although all these pictures were taken in the era of television, and the last one especially owes its fame to a great extent to television broadcasting, it is the intrinsic qualities of the photographic medium, including its indexicality, reproducibility and memorability, that rendered these photographs as easily recognisable symbols of the struggles they stood for. Photography's ability to achieve a contemporaneity with the present and keep up with the speed of short-lived political events, repeats mechanically 'what could never be repeated existentially' and acts as a 'certificate of presence', as Barthes described it, for most of the activists.[5] Unlike the moving image, photography freezes an image within the photograph's frame, 'preserves a moment of time and prevents it being effaced by the suppression of further moments'.[6] At the same time, photographs are easily reproduced: in newspapers, magazines, on the internet, as well as in photobooks, academic books, institutional displays, archives or even family albums and with other photographs.

Within these contexts, photographs are juxtaposed with texts, headlines, advertising and other photographs attaining at times opposite interpretative meanings to those intended by the photographers or the people being photographed. For as Allan Sekula argued, it is not the maker alone who produces the meaning in photographs, but a matrix of external conditions on which photography depends for its readability.[7] Photographs acquire their meanings as they move through time, space and different contexts. Throughout this journey in time and space, the often contradictory interests of the photographers, the viewers, the people photographed and of those who use the photographs, emerge.[8]

Take the very early example of the documentary records of the Paris Commune. The posed and static photographs of the Communards, who had proudly posed for the camera – to a great extent a result of the limited technological means of photography in 1871 – confirmed their 'having been there'. The Communards' pride was related to both the actual privilege of being photographed (a privilege reserved to higher classes in these early stages of the medium) and the ability to confer on their achievements a kind of immortality.[9] Nevertheless, their pride of playing an active role in their history was not enjoyed for long, as the initial purpose of these photographs was subsequently subverted. After the suppression of the revolutionary government, the same pictures were used by the authorities and the Communards' prosecutors; many of the Communards who were arrested by the police and were shot dead were recognised from these earlier photographs of triumph.

From this very early example, it becomes evident that in photography it is not only important whether the photographer is an amateur or professional, who is photographed, who the viewers are, but even more importantly who has access to control the means of image production and dissemination. At moments of revolt, more than ever, a conflict takes place over the control of these means. On the one side of this conflict, mass media and state institutions, such as museums, libraries, archives and the police, have used photography to construct 'official' representations of protest events. Unlike police photographs – used as a means of surveillance in street demonstrations, as proof for prosecutions and arrests and as evidence in the courts, normally against protesters and activist groups – photographs published in mass circulation newspapers and magazines, exhibited in museums and published in photobooks are accessible to the wider public.[10] On the other side, activists have used photographs in their banners, posters and communication material, such as leaflets and newspapers, as a strategy of resistance to official mainstream representations. These photographic documentations, often contradictory, strive to prevail in the public domain, extending the political or economic struggle to a representational level.

This representational conflict is at the core of this book, which examines image production and dissemination at the time of political uprisings, examining the imagery of the political movements themselves in opposition to official representations of these moments. The book follows the 'currency' – to borrow John Tagg's term – of photographs of political movements within different contexts: the movements themselves and alternative media attached to them, including leaflets, magazines, newspapers and the Internet, as well as the mainstream press and subsequent photobooks and photographic displays. The analysis encompasses a wide range of photographic practices, professional and amateur, providing a sense of the original context of production, but mainly highlighting how photographs were used in different contexts and how their meanings were often reconstructed.[11] Thus, in considering contexts is not to think that photographic meaning is fixed, but it is rather to open up the discussion about photography's embeddedness within institutional and discursive contexts at times of social struggle.

Until recently, the role of photography in political movements has received little sustained criticism. This is presumably related to the unprivileged position of politically committed photography in academic photography history circles and the small emphasis that social movement theorists have given to the cultural aspects of the movements. In other instances, political and cultural movements have generated different academic literatures which functioned within disciplinary boundaries.[12] Recent scholarly work from different standpoints has brought to the fore important questions about the intersection of activism, protest movement and culture.[13] While these studies have been significant, none of them has focused on photography in particular. This book reflects critically on the theory of photography and the social movements themselves, drawing on a range of humanities disciplines, including photography theory and history, social movement theory, political theory, cultural history, visual culture, media studies and the history and theory of art.

The book takes as a starting point 1968 – a year that witnessed an explosion of social movements worldwide and has been repeatedly interpreted as a turning point for political practice and theory, but also for the culture as a whole – and as a finishing point 2001 — a signpost for international politics due to September 11 and a significant year for the movement because of the large-scale anti-capitalist protests in Genoa. Within these chronological limits, the book focuses on a selection of distinctive instances in which the photographic medium intersects with the political struggle. The three case studies are not the only pertinent examples, by any means, but they are important ones, not only historically and politically, but also iconographically. They are the student and worker uprising in France in May 1968 and two moments of the contemporary anti-capitalist movement, the indigenous Zapatista movement in Mexico and the anti-capitalist protests in Genoa in 2001.

The movement becomes global: from 1968 to 2001

The resurgence of a global movement against neoliberal globalisation in the late 1990s resonated with the global movement of 1968.[14] While these two movements appeared and evolved in different historical and spatial contexts and had particular and distinct political agendas, they shared ideological affinities, common ideas, strategies and tactics. Long before the coinage of the term 'globalisation', a chain of cross-border political mobilisations emerged worldwide in 1968, including the expansion of the anti-war movement in the United States and the subsequent workers' strikes and student occupations in France in May, the Prague Spring, and student demonstrations in Poland, Yugoslavia, Mexico, Germany and Italy in the autumn. Evidently, there was no organised global movement in 1968, but there were informal connections and close relations between the movements, which have been highlighted in the few comparative studies of the movements that took place in 1968.[15] Existing forms of international cooperation, rooted in the global movements of black people for freedom and rights in the 1960s, the international support for the anti-nuclear campaign, the transnational network of feminists and the growing anti-war movement following Che Guevara's calls to fight against capitalism and war with his slogan 'Create two, three, many Vietnams', prepared the ground for expansion of international networks between the movements.[16] These collaborative and communicative relationships were often reinforced by personal contacts, intellectual exchanges and collaborations between the protagonists of the movements and remained to a great extent informal.

The resurgence of these struggles, which challenged the framework of the post-war order 'exemplified in the climax of the US and Soviet Union confrontation' led historians and theorists to interpret 1968 as a turning point in the history of post-war Europe.[17] In France, the quite unexpected rebellion of middle-class students followed by a generalised strike in May 1968 paralysed the country, threatened to topple de Gaulle's regime and challenged the post-war period of capitalist growth and prosperity that France, along with other Western countries, was experiencing after the war. For many commentators, 1968 would be considered as a break between 'post-war' and 'contemporary'.[18] Immediately after the end of the events, Lucien Rioux and René Backmann asserted that 'from now on, French history will be divided into pre- and post-1968'.[19] Edgar Morin, Claude Lefort and Cornelius Castoriadis called May 1968 'une brèche' (a rupture with consumer society), while Alain Touraine saw in May the birth of a 'new social movement' and the 'birth of a new period in the social history of industrial societies'.[20]

What has been the core of May 1968 events was the emphasis on the critique of capitalist order, its mechanisation, mercanitlisation and reification, its social injustice and its growing focus on individualism. What appeared to be a crisis in the universities, stemming from the students' scepticism for the university system with its outmoded syllabuses and learning processes, bureaucratic and hierarchical structures, authoritarian professors and low career and life prospects for the students extended to a critique of authoritarian and hierarchal societal structure. The slogan in the protesters' banners stated it clearly: 'De la Critique de l' Université a la Critique de la Sociéte' (From the critique of the university to the critique of the society). The total questioning of any kind of guidance and power was only exemplified in the conservative government of General Charles de Gaulle and its morality. What was at stake was not only domestic affairs, but also international issues, such as the imperialist war in Vietnam, the invasion of Czechoslovakia and the liberation movements in the Third World countries. The rejection of power was all-encompassing: from the power exercised in the factory and the university classroom to the power over nations by great imperial states.[21]

In the years that followed − the end of the Cold War, the fall of the Berlin Wall, and the collapse of so-called 'actually existing socialism' − inaugurated a period in history when neoliberal capitalism became predominant in most countries of the World. The triumph of political and economic neoliberalism, infamously proclaimed as 'The End of History', seemingly showed a strong indication of the end of 'grand narratives' and ideologies and left no room for a systemic alternative.[22] The beginning of the 1990s signalled the opening of a new epoch, largely characterised by neoliberal globalisation, while the concept of 'globalisation' became the keyword of a 'new grand narration' 'with a universal and global pretension'.[23]

The Zapatista rebellion in Chiapas, Mexico on the 1 January 1994 challenged neoliberalism's famously celebrated triumph and its TINA ('there is no alternative') doctrine. The uprising of the Ejército Zapatista Liberación Nacional (The Zapatista Army of National Liberation – EZLN) against the Mexican army and the federal government was a 'cry of dignity' and demanded land, food, housing, health, education and work for the communities.[24] Their goals were not restricted to local or even parochial problems, but were more universal. Their demands for democracy and their concerns about neoliberalism and its subsequent economic injustices intersected with environmental issues, such as the destruction of the indigenous lands of Chiapas, women's and indigenous people's rights, the rights of labour and issues of inequality. Their declarations demanded a new society based on direct participatory democracy, freedom, dignity and justice.[25] The theory of the new movement, known as 'Zapatismo' and articulated mainly by the EZLN spokesperson Subcomandante Marcos, opposed 'the exclusionary consequences of economic modernization' and questioned 'the inevitability of a new geographical order under which capitalism becomes universally accepted'.[26]

The movement soon transcended the geographical limits of Chiapas and Mexico 'to insist that what was going on in Chiapas could not be written off as a narrow "ethnic" struggle, that it was universal'.[27] It became a constant source of inspiration and solidarity for another emerging movement, which started taking shape in the mid-1900s and targeted global powers, the policies they imposed and decisions they took in global meetings.[28] The movement became known as 'anti-globalisation movement', but given that this appellation did not reflect the movement's spirit, alternative terms such as, 'anti-corporate movement', 'anti-capitalist movement', 'global justice or fair trade movement', 'a movement for a globalisation of rights', or simply 'The Movement' have been adopted.[29] This global mobilisation became possible through anti-hierachical transnational networks, which brought together non-governmental organisations (NGOs), international and smaller national groups, more local protests and activists from diverse ideological backgrounds. These networks were facilitated by the use of the internet, as a tool for expression, mobilisation and organisation, as well as a forum for stimulating international awareness and support.

The diversity of causes championed by participants in the movement as well as their alternative visions, strategies and tactics indicate that this is 'a movement of many movements', a movement that brings together thousands of groups 'whose common thread is what might broadly be described as the privatisation of every aspect of life, and the transformation of every activity and value into a commodity'.[30] The calls for democracy, freedom, justice, women's and immigrants' rights and rejection of poverty and their slogans 'Abolish Capitalism Now' and 'WTO = Capitalism Without Conscience' – resonant of May 1968 demands – put in question the triumphalism of neoliberal globalisation and its foundational principles. 'The entering of the dread concept "capitalism" back into political speech' in the 1990s, when neoliberal politics enjoyed universal acceptance, was without doubt one of the biggest successes of the movement.[31]

The shape of the book

The principal aim of this book is a critical understanding of photography's interrelation with three instances of political struggle, namely the uprising of May 1968, the indigenous Zapatista movement in Mexico and the anti-capitalist protests in Genoa in 2001. Throughout these three case studies, the book examines the problematic of documenting social protest through photography taking into account diverse photographic practices, including photojournalism, amateur and professional photography. The book follows the circulation of these photographs in various contexts, and questions the function of photography within a complex indeological web of transmission of political ideas. It also examines how the meaning of photographs relates to the way these photographs have been used, considering different contexts and time.

As regards the mainstream press representations of political protest, the book examines the role of photography in shaping public perception and understanding of political movements by either constructing or challenging mainstream narratives about protest movements. When the focus shifts to photography in use by activists, photography's ability to act as a fundamental means for protesters to spread their messages among dispersed audiences and to resist dominant representations is examined. The book also looks at photography's contribution to the visibility and sustainability of the struggle and its role in raising international support and solidarity towards the movement. Finally, the book studies the publication of protest photographs in photobooks and their display in exhibitions, raising questions regarding the problematic of the display of these images and the images' function in challenging perceptions or reinforcing existing hierarchies.

From a more practical point of view, the relevant photographic material has been consistently and concertedly collated from a large number of photographs from different archives. As far as the May 1968 events are concerned, a considerable amount of archival research was required, especially in Paris, in the following archives: La Centre Historique des Archives Nationales, Bibliothèque de Documentation Internationale Contemporaine, Bibliothèque du Centre d'Histoire Sociale du XXe Siècle (Univerité Paris I, Panthéon, Sorbonne), Département des Estampes et de la Photographie (Bibliothèque Nationale de France) and Bibliothèque Historique de la Ville de Paris. In the case of the most recent movements, where 'official' archives are not available, online resources have proven valuable. The online photographic galleries of the Zapatista and the Reclaim the Streets (RTS) websites, as well as other online resources, such as organisations' websites, the World Social Forum (WSF) and European Social Forum (ESF) websites, Indymedia among others, have been central to my analyses. At times, the history of these events has been unwritten, so activists and their personal archives have also been useful source of information.

Regarding the photographs of the movements published in the mainstream press, the photographic material was drawn from the British Library archive of newspapers. The focus from the particular case studies has been on the British and Italian press, while supplementary material from the French, Spanish and Greek press enhanced the discussion where necessary. In terms of British press, the book drew on the *Daily Telegraph*, *The Guardian*, *The Independent*, *Evening Standard*, *The Times*, *The Sunday Times* and *The Observer* as well as the tabloid papers *The Sun* and *The Daily Mail*. As for the Italian press, the book drew in particular on newspapers with some national circulation, such as *Il Corriere della Sera*, *La Stampa* and *La Republicca*. When French, Spanish and Italian literature has been quoted, all translations are the author's, unless otherwise indicated.

The book is divided into three parts, each one focused on a particular thematic topic concerning the three case studies. This thematic organisational structure highlights the common threads and perspectives between the different movements and contributes to drawing conclusions about the different levels of interaction of photography and social struggle.

Part I examines the official representations of these movements in the mainstream press, drawing upon examples from British, French and Italian newspapers. It studies how photographs of social protest find their way into the mainstream media and investigates the mechanisms used by the mass media in order to produce newsworthy stories attractive to a wide audience. This part focuses on photojournalistic images and their intersection with journalistic writing, attempting to reveal the role of photography in constructing or reinforcing hegemonic narratives of social protest. Finally, this first part analyses how photojournalistic coverage of protest events shapes public perception about protest movements and considers the cases when the movement found ways to self-consciously manipulate the mass media and construct an image for the media spectacle.

Part II studies the function of photography within the movements' networks of communication, namely the movements' newspapers, leaflets, newsletters, banners and websites. It examines the use of photography as circulated within and by the movement, considering whether the photographs chosen by activists to reflect their political praxis might act as an alternative narrative to the official discourse. The photographs used by activists in these cases, often a blend of professional and amateur images, are not chosen on basis of their aesthetic or technical qualities, but they are selected from their ability to bear realistic information, to tell an alternative story believed by the activists to be overshadowed or ignored in the mainstream media. Consideration is given to the role of these photographs in arousing international support and sympathy towards these movements and, at the same time, in revealing the movements' failings, weaknesses and antinomies.

Part III examines subsequent institutional displays and photobooks that took as their subject matter photographs of revolt that is a commemorative photographic exhibition of 1968, Antonio Turok's photobook of the Zapatistas and the photographic project of the protests in Genoa by Joel Sternfeld. The possible different audiences that these displays and photobooks address and their long lives – in the case of the photobooks – open up the discussion about how the movements have been thought of, discussed and remembered in the aftermath of the protests. Photography's close interrelationship with these institutions as well as with mechanisms of memory and forgetting are under scrutiny.

Notes

1 For the use of photographic camera in the Commune uprising, see: G. Doy, 'The Camera against the Paris Commune', in T. Dennet and J. Spence (eds), *Photography/Politics: I* (London: Photography Workshop, 1979), pp. 13–26. Also, see information about an exhibition of photographs of the Paris Commune at www.musee-orsay.fr/en/events/exhibitions/in-the-musee-dorsay/exhibitions-in-the-musee-dorsay-more/article/photographs-of-the-paris-commune-4293.html?tx_ttnews%5BbackPid%5D=649&cHash=db17556944 (accessed 10/03/2012).

2 For a discussion of the role that photographs played in the civil-rights movements, see: V. Goldberg, *The Power of Photography: How Photographs Changed Our Lives* (New York, London, Paris: Abbeville Press, 1991), pp. 203–11; S. Kasher, *The Civil Rights Movement: A Photographic History, 1954–68* (New York, London, Paris: Abbeville Press, 1996).

3 For a discussion of the photograph's emotional power, see: R. Hariman and J. L. Lucaites, *No Caption Needed: Iconic Photographs, Public Culture and Liberal Democracy* (Chicago and London: The University of Chicago Press, 2007), chapter 5.

4 For a discussion of the Tiananmen Square photograph, see: Hariman and Lucaites, *No Caption Needed*, chapter 7.

5 R. Barthes, *Camera Lucida: Reflections on Photography* (London: Vintage, 2000), pp. 4 and 87–8.

6 J. Berger and J. Mohr, *Another Way of Telling* (New York: Pantheon, 1972), p. 89.

7 A. Sekula, *Photography Against the Grain* (Halifax: Press of the Nova Scotia College of Art and Design, 1984), p. 17.

8 Berger and Mohr, *Another Way of Telling*, p. 7.

9 Doy, 'The Camera Against the Paris Commune', p. 16.

10 The use of different photographic practices by the police force has been discussed by John Tagg via a thorough analysis of a whole set of assumptions about the relationship of photography to realism and the truth. See: J. Tagg, *The Burden of Representation: Essays on Photographies and Histories* (London: Macmillan Education, 1988), pp. 66–102.

11 The theoretical writings that reconnected photography to the wider ideological forces of society and were developed mainly in Britain in the late 1970s and 1980s, and have largely informed this book. See: A. Sekula, 'On the Invention of the Photographic Meaning', first published in *Art Forum*, 13: 5 (1975); V. Burgin (ed.), *Thinking Photography* (London: Macmillan, 1982); Sekula, *Photography Against the Grain*; M. Rosler, 'In, Around and Afterthoughts (On Documentary Photography)', in R. Bolton (ed.), *The Contest of Meaning: Critical Histories of Photography* (Cambridge, MA: The MIT Press, 1992); Tagg, *The Burden of Representation*.

12 R. Eyerman and A. Jamison, *Music and Social Movements: Mobilizing Traditions in the Twentieth Century* (Cambridge: Cambridge University Press, 1998), p. 8.

13 Recent studies of the interaction of the political movements and culture from different standpoints, include: H. Johnston and B. Klandermans (eds), *Social Movements and Culture* (Minneapolis, MN: University of Minnesota Press, 1995); T. V. Reed, *The Art of Protest: Culture and Activism from Civil Rights Movement to the Streets of Seattle* (Minneapolis, MN: University of Minnesota Press, 2005); G. Raunig, *Art and Revolution: Transversal Activism in the Long Twentieth Century* (Cambridge, MA: MIT Press, 2007); B. Stimson and G. Sholette (eds), *Collectivism after Modernism: The Art of Social Imagination after 1945* (Minneapolis, MN: University of Minnesota Press, 2007); W. Bradley and C. Esche (eds), *Art and Social Change: A Critical Reader* (London: Tate, Afterall, 2007).

14 Activists Christophe Aguiton and Susan George have pointed out the resemblance, as cited in A. Callinicos, 'Where Now?', in E. Bircham and C. John (eds), *Anti-Capitalism: A Guide to the Movement* (London: Bookmarks Publications Ltd, 2001), p. 387. For a similar point from social movements theory, see: D. della Porta and M. Diani, *Social Movements: An Introduction* (Oxford: Blackwell, 2006), p. 2.

15 G. Katsiaficas, 'Introduction', in *The Imagination of the New Left: A Global Analysis of 1968* (Boston, MA: South End Press, 1987). C. Fink, F. Gassert and D. Junker (eds), *1968: The World Transformed* (Cambridge: Cambridge University Press, 1998).

16 Fink *et al.* (eds), *1968: The World Transformed*, p. 18.

17 E. Hobsbawm, '1968: A Retrospect', *Marxism Today*, 22 (1978), pp. 130–1.

18 Editors, 'The legacy of May '68', *New Left Review*, 115 (May/June 1979), p. 1.

19 L. Rioux and R. Backmann, 'L' Explosion de Mai: Paris, 1968', as quoted in M. Seidman,

The Imaginary Revolution: Parisian Students and Workers in 1968 (New York and Oxford: Berghahn Books, 2004), p. 2.

20 E. Morin, C. Lefort and C. Castoriadis, *Mai 1968: La Brèche* (Paris: Éditions Complexe, 1998); A. Touraine, *The May Movement: Revolt and Reform* (New York: Random House, 1971), p. 26.

21 R. V. Daniels, *1968: The Year of the Heroic Guerrilla* (Cambridge, MA: Harvard University Press, 1989), p. 5.

22 F. Fukuyama, *The End of History and the Last Man* (London: Hamilton, 1992).

23 B. Stråth, '1968: From Co-determination to Co-worker: The Power of Language', *Thesis Eleven*, 68 (2002), p. 79.

24 J. Holloway, 'Dignity's Revolt', in J. Holloway and E. Peláez (eds), *Zapatista!: Reinventing Revolution in Mexico* (London: Pluto Press, 1998), p. 159.

25 The declarations from the Lacandon Jungle have been published in Ž. Vodovnik (ed.), *Ya Basta! Ten Years of the Zapatistas Uprising* (Oakland and Edinburgh: AK Press, 2004), pp. 643–81.

26 M. Castells, *The Power of Identity* (Oxford: Blackwell, 1997), p. 77.

27 N. Klein, 'The Unknown Icon', in T. Hayden (ed.), *The Zapatista Reader* (New York: Thunder's Mouth Press/Nation Books, 2002), p. 119.

28 The movement was opposed to treaties with global effect, such as the North American Free Trade Agreement (NAFTA) and to global meetings such as the G7, G8, IMF and World Bank meetings, European Union summits, the World Economic Forum meetings and conferences of North American and Pacific organisations.

29 D. della Porta, M. Andretta, L. Mosca and H. Reiter (eds), *Globalization from Below: Transnational Activists and Protest Networks* (Minneapolis, MN: University of Minnesota Press, 2006), p. 8. This book adopts the term anti-capitalist movement as the most appropriate appellation, but sometimes the term anti-globalisation is also used.

30 'A Movement of Movements' is the title of a collection of writings on the movement. The quotes are from an essay published in the collection, see: N. Klein, 'Reclaiming the Commons', in T. Mertes, *A Movement of Movements* (London: Verso, 2004), p. 220.

31 Retort, *Afflicted Powers: Capital and Spectacle in a New Age of War* (London and New York: Verso, 2005).

Part I

1

Toute la presse est toxique: May 1968 in the mainstream French press

LTHOUGH the events of May 1968 occurred in the age of television, the transistor radio was the most popular means of information for both the general public and the protesters themselves.[1] Despite the introduction of television into a great number of French households by 1968, the reports from the occupied Latin Quarter reached the wider public in Paris and the rest of the country via two radio transmitter vans, which had a central role in the barricades.[2] The most significant reason for this was not only the clearly greater accessibility of the public to the radio, but, most importantly, the lack of coverage of the events on French television. A characteristic example of French television's downplaying of the events was the television programme 'Panorama', a weekly review of events, which initially 'ignored' the growing demonstrations and occupations in Paris and in the rest of the country which began on the 6 May.[3] Under the pressure of events, the programme, scheduled to broadcast a documentary on the events on the 10 May, was eventually censored.

This noticeable lack of coverage became more striking given the acceleration of the street fighting on the night of the 10 May, famously known as the 'night of the barricades'. The first report followed the demonstrations and clashes between students and police which took place outside the Sorbonne on the 3 May and the subsequent arrest of 500 students. Events culminated on the 10th, when students and workers constructed barricades in the Latin Quarter. The students were protesting against the established social order and the oppressive power of the police, and wanted space to express their demands.[4] The symbolic value of the barricades – a revival of a technique used in earlier moments of popular uprisings in French history, namely in 1830, 1848 and in the Paris Commune – and the contrasting brutal violence performed by the police generated support of students and the mobilisation of other social groups – mobilisation as a response to the government's repression.

The poor reporting was an inevitable result of a 'governmental model' of broadcast organisation, in which public broadcasting equates with state broadcasting, since it is directly under the control of the government. This was clearly the case with French broadcasting under de Gaulle.[5] In France, the staff of Radio Television Française (RTF) was 'appointed directly by the Minister of Information until 1964' and was 'under the tight political control even later'.[6] This governmental control over French television and radio was only reaffirmed, if not intensified, during the events. It was only international radio, in particular Europe 1 and Radio Télé Luxembourg (RTL), that were available and willing to report from the heart of the barricades and demonstrations, and which became the central means of information for the French citizens.[7]

The transmission of images of the events was then left to the printed media, in particular the illustrated magazines and the mainstream newspapers. Popular illustrated magazines were the dominant visual news medium in the pre-television era and the platform for serious photojournalism, especially from the 1930s onwards. French *Paris Match*, which was very popular in France and covered many daily events in the 1960s in colour photo-stories, covered the events briefly in their two issues on the 11th and 18th, becoming 'conspicuously unavailable' between the 18 May and the 15 June.[8] It was, therefore, through the mainstream press, and the communication institutions that served the student and worker movement, that images of the events reached the wider French public. It is worth noting that civic growing mistrust towards the mainstream mass media raised confidence in the movement's own publications, including the journals published by the various groups, enragés the leaflets circulated within the ranks and the Atelier Populaire posters hung on the walls of the Sorbonne and disseminated in the streets of Paris.[9]

This chaper provides an analysis of the photographic material published in the mainstream press during the events of May of 1968, drawing upon the French dailies published in Paris, that is *Le Figaro* and *L'Humanité* and the weekly *Le Nouvel Observateur*. *Le Monde* does not constitute a good example given it rarely included any photographs in its editorial until 1972, and it did not feature photographs on its front page until 1983.[10] It is a fact that photography was seen as more suitable for popular illustrated magazines rather than for the serious press. The chapter examines the use of photographs covering the events during May and June and studies whether photojournalism contributes to constructing stereotypes of the events, which informed the construction of subsequent dominant narratives.

The old image for a new struggle

The failure of television to report the 'night of barricades' was heavily criticised by *Le Monde*, which reported 'La Grande Muette' (The Great Silence) in a special weekend edition.[11] Nevertheless, the coverage did not include any photographs in accordance with Le Monde's policy towards photographs. *L'Humanité* and *Le Figaro* covered the accelerating violence after the 7 May. Both published photographs of policemen attacking students on their front pages, although the students were hardly visible in the background. Quite expectedly, their headlines had an absolutely different tones. *L'Humanité* directly accused the government of being responsible for the escalation of the violence in the Latin Quarter with the headline 'Escalade de la violence policière au Quartier latin: Le Responsible c'est le gouvernmement' (Acceleration of Police Violence in Latin Quarter: The Government is Responsible), while *Le Figaro* presented the events in a rather neutral tone with the headline 'Violents Accrochages Hier jusqu'a 23 Heures' (Violent Clashes Yesterday Until 23.00).[12]

It is interesting, therefore, to see how photographs of seemingly similar content are anchored to a different commentary to fit the political orientation of each newspaper. *L'Humanité*, the official organ of the Communist Party was initially at odds with the student mobilisation and their demands. The introduction of new social groups into the struggle against capitalism, in particular students, as opposed to the working class and capital, brought confusion to the ranks of the Party. *L'Humanité* described the students' actions as 'opportunistic and bourgeois'.[13] 'These false revolutionaries', the newspaper reported:

> ought to be unmasked, because, in fact, they serve the interests of the Gaullist state ... It is necessary to combat and completely isolate the extreme leftist 'groupuscules' who want only to harm the democratic process drowning it in talk.[14]

Similarly, the major workers' unions, the Confédération Générale du Travail (General Confederation of Workers – CGT) and Confédération Française Démocratique du Travail (French Democratic Workers Confederation – CFDT) distributed leaflets in the factories warning workers against young subversives. This did not necessarily bring the desired effects. When younger workers joined the students and went on strike without their unions' support, the CGT, which was not in favour of the student—worker coalition, was left with no choice. As Reader explains, 'there was little' the unions 'could do but belatedly endorse the movement and try to assert the authority over it'.[15] Therefore, the events proved the inadequacy of the Communist Party to lead the working-class struggle and brought to light the vast split between these new struggles, the Party and the trade unions.[16]

The difficulty of the trade unions in embracing the students' demands for the transformation of everyday life and culture was manifested in the spatial separation between workers and students. Since the mass strikes had begun on 14 May, the workers had occupied their factories which meant that students and workers remained separated. This enabled the government to deal with each group individually and thus more effectively.[17] Ross questions whether the practice of 'factory occupation' was favoured by the government in that it prevented dialogue between the different social groups involved in the struggle, or whether it was reinforced by the trade unions in their efforts to control a general strike that had been initiated without their motivation.[18] The symbolic practice of 'factory occupation' was not an imitation of the students occupying the Sorbonne, but a rebellion against the factory director's authority, and an appropriation of a 'non-neutral space', which could be seen as analogous to the barricades in that the 'occupation, like the barricade, *reveals* class conflict, the relation to the adversary'.[19] Although it had a symbolic function, the occupation also kept the workers within a controllable space and prevented them from joining the large street demonstrations, where they could be in contact and exchange ideas with the students and other social groups. As Ross argues 'with workers still safely in the workplace – even if non-functioning – occupation may have lessened any extension via coordination between different factories; it may have blocked communication at variance with the union leadership's representation of the strike'.[20]

This spatial isolation found its visual equivalent in the photographs published in *L'Humanité*, in which photographs of the striking workers in their occupied factories became customary during May and June. In such a photograph published in *L'Humanité* on the 26 May, the workers are depicted gathered in front of the Citroën factory. Some of them had climbed on the fences and the main gate of the factory (figure 1). The snapshot seems rather amateurish, with the banner hung on the gate clearly illegible. The workers are seemingly captured unaware of the camera's presence and noticeably inactive. The photograph could have been taken on a normal working day, but the absence of chronological and geographical cues

PREMIERE ENTREVUE
SYNDICATS-PATRONS-GOUVERNEMENT

Benoît FRACHON :

« Les travailleurs ne cesseront la grève que lorsqu'ils seront certains de bénéficier des avantages substantiels qu'ils escomptent »

A l'ouverture des négociations, Benoît Frachon, président de la CGT, a fait la déclaration suivante :

« Au moment où s'engagent des discussions dont l'importance n'échappe à personne, la C.G.T. considère comme indispensable de les situer dans le cadre exact où elles vont se dérouler.

Pour les travailleurs, les choses ne sont plus comme elles étaient hier. Le gouvernement et le patronat doivent en tenir compte sous peine de prendre la responsabilité de provoquer un mécontentement encore plus profond.

La C.G.T., pour sa part, ne saurait en aucun cas négliger les aspirations des millions de salariés qui lui accordent leur confiance.

Nous nous trouvons aujourd'hui en présence d'un mouvement de grève et d'occupation des entreprises qui n'a jamais connu d'égal dans notre pays, même en 1936.

Que de huit à dix millions de salariés se soient en quelques jours rejoints dans la lutte pour imposer la réparation des torts dont ils sont victimes depuis de nombreuses années, témoigne de la profondeur de leur rancœur accumulée et de leur volonté d'obtenir des changements substantiels.

Pour sa part, la C.G.T. était convaincue que la politique anti-sociale de l'Etat et l'opposition systématique du C.N.P.F. à régler avec les centrales syndicales par voie d'accords contractuels des problèmes parmi les plus urgents, comme l'augmentation des salaires, traitements, pensions et retraites, la réduction du temps de travail sans perte de salaire, la garantie de l'emploi, les libertés syndicales dans les entreprises, les administrations et les services publics et d'autres revendications de leur ressort, aboutiraient à un affrontement comme celui devant lequel nous nous trouvons aujourd'hui.

Depuis l'été dernier sont venues s'ajouter à cette longue liste les ordonnances sur la Sécurité sociale, prises unilatéralement par l'Etat et qui ont largement contribué à pousser ce mécontentement jusqu'à l'exaspération dans la majorité de la population.

Depuis deux ans et demi, après l'accord conclu entre la C.G.T. et la C.F.D.T., les manifestations et des arrêts de travail à l'échelle nationale se sont déroulés, comme des mises en garde, pour rappeler qu'il était temps de faire droit à des demandes justifiées.

Ni au gouvernement ni au C.N.P.F. on n'a voulu tenir compte de ces coups de semonce.

Le résultat, vous le connaissez. Toutes les branches de l'économie nationale sont touchées par la grève et, ce qui est plus impressionnant encore, c'est le calme, l'esprit de responsabilité et la détermination qui animent ces millions d'hommes, de femmes et de jeunes gens, convaincus de leurs droits et fermement décidés à les faire triompher.

La politique du gouvernement et du C.N.P.F. a abouti à ce résultat, que tous les censés ne pouvaient manquer de prévoir. Au moment où les discussions s'engagent, aucun des travailleurs participant au mouvement ne peut avoir la moindre confiance dans les nouvelles promesses qui pourraient leur être faites. Ils ne cesseront la grève que lorsqu'ils seront certains de bénéficier des avantages substantiels qu'ils escomptent. Ils attendent les résultats de nos délibérations.

A la C.G.T., nous avons pris l'engagement devant tous les salariés de rendre publiques toutes nos délibérations et de leur soumettre les résultats que nous aurons obtenus, les garanties qui seront consenties pour préserver leurs nouvelles conquêtes des aléas ou des manœuvres qui peuvent surgir dans un système économique où ils ne disposent encore d'aucun pouvoir ou de moyens d'intervention efficaces, afin qu'ils puissent se prononcer en connaissance de cause sur la cessation ou la poursuite de leur action. Nous tiendrons fidèlement nos engagements.

Je laisse à notre camarade Séguy, secrétaire général de la C.G.T., le soin d'exposer succinctement les revendications que nous avons l'intention de défendre et de faire triompher lors de nos confrontations que nous désirons conduire avec la plus grande célérité, la population attendant avec la plus vive impatience les décisions qui seront prises.

Il était trois heures moins cinq, hier après-midi, lorsque M. Pompidou a franchi les marches d'un ministère qui ne lui était pas trop familier : le ministère des Affaires sociales. C'est ici, rue de Grenelle, que doivent se dérouler les négociations entre le gouvernement, le patronat et les syndicats ouvriers et enseignants, dont l'issue peut apporter un règlement à la grève qui paralyse le pays.

Les délégations syndicales avaient précédé de quelques minutes le premier ministre, MM. Jeanneney, ministre des Affaires sociales, et Chirac, sous-secrétaire d'Etat à l'emploi. Chaque fois que l'une d'elles arrive, elle est entourée d'une nuée de photographes et de journalistes.

Celle de la C.G.T. notamment est très entourée. Nul n'ignore que le poids du mouvement repose essentiellement sur elle. Benoît Frachon, souriant, tranquille comme à son habitude ne lâchant pas sa pipe répond à quelques questions. « Ça vous rajeunit de trente ans », blague un journaliste en évoquant 1936 et les accords de Matignon. Benoît Frachon ne le nie pas.

Georges Séguy, secrétaire général de la C.G.T., paraît un peu fatigué, mais retrouve toute sa vivacité lorsque les journalistes l'interrogent.

André Berteloot, René Buih, Henri Krasucki et Jean-Louis Moynot, sûrement le plus jeune des syndicalistes présents, font également partie de la délégation C.G.T.

La délégation C.F.D.T. est conduite par son secrétaire général Eugène Descamps ; celle de Force Ouvrière, par André Bergeron, secrétaire général, et celle de la C.F.T.C. par son président J. Sauty. La F.E.N. participe aussi à l'entrevue, elle est représentée par une délégation conduite par James Marangé, secrétaire général.

Les Petites et Moyennes Entreprises (P.M.E.) sont également présentes, leur délégation comprend MM. Gauthan, Delleau, d'Oiron. Quant au C.N.P.F. sa représentation comprend sept membres : MM. Huvelin, Pollet, Faure, Emery, Paquet, Peugeot, de Préricourt.

Sollicité de toutes parts par les journalistes, M. Huvelin : « Ne m'obligez pas à une défense fous animaux. » C'est pourtant un peu ce qui l'attend à l'intérieur.

17 heures : première suspension de séance. On ne l'attendait généralement pas si tôt. Le président du ministère est envahi par les journalistes. Des interviews se poursuivent dans la cour. La délégation de la CGT a fait connaître à la presse la déclaration faite par Benoît Frachon et exposé des revendications formulées à la réunion par Georges Séguy. Ce dernier résume la séance : « La CGT, FO, la FEN, la CFDT ont exposé les grandes lignes des revendications des travailleurs ; le patronat et le gouvernement ont fait une déclaration liminaire et M. Pompidou a demandé une suspension de séance pour examiner un ordre du jour possible. Dans nos exposés nous avons repris les demandes déjà formulées (abrogation des ordonnances contre la Sécurité sociale, etc.) et insisté spécialement sur le paiement des jours de grève. Il y a, poursuit-il, une grande similitude entre les revendications formulées par les syndicats. Nous sommes prêts, a-t-il conclu, à discuter sans désemparer jusqu'à conclusion d'un accord ».

Eugène Descamps, de la C.F.D.T. s'étonne de l'attitude des patrons : « ils n'ont pas l'air de réaliser que la France compte neuf millions de grévistes et que leurs usines sont occupées. »

La séance reprend à 17 h 30. Après « ce premier tour de piste » comme dit Joseph Sauty de la C.F.T.C., les discussions vont aborder maintenant le fond du problème.

18 h 35. Nouvelle suspension de séance. C'est le CNPF qui a sollicité cette interruption pour examiner la réponse à donner à la demande des syndicats du salaire minimum mensuel à 600 F (Le SMIG porte actuellement la rémunération minimum mensuelle à 385 F).

Un ordre du jour a déjà été mis au point. Un salaire mensuel garanti constituera un premier test. On examinera ensuite les salaires, l'emploi, les droits syndicaux, la fiscalité.

Il a été convenu d'examiner globalement chacune de ces questions.

Ensuite, les discussions se poursuivront en deux groupes : l'un chargé des revendications qui ressortent des pouvoirs publics ; l'autre concernant celles à régler avec le patronat.

20 h 10 : Nouvelle suspension de séance. Les délégations se séparent pour aller dîner. Les discussions vont se poursuivre sur le salaire minimum. La séance doit reprendre à 21 h 15.

Pierre CAMES.

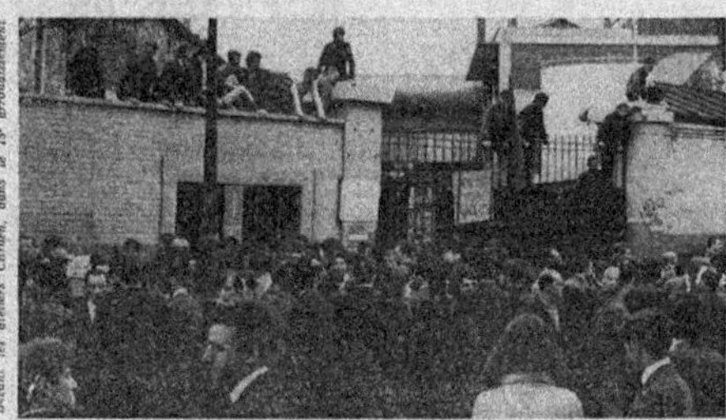

GEORGES SEGUY : VOICI NOS REVENDICATIONS

Georges Séguy, secrétaire général de la CGT, a déclaré, s'adressant au gouvernement :

« L'une des raisons essentielles de l'accumulation du mécontentement général des salariés réside dans la promulgation des ordonnances antisociales, en particulier celles qui ont gravement mutilé le système de la Sécurité sociale par la diminution des prestations, de l'augmentation des cotisations ouvrières et la suppression des élections démocratiques des administrateurs.

Pour édicter ses ordonnances, le gouvernement n'a pas demandé leur avis aux organisations syndicales ; afin de faciliter les négociations qui s'engagent et d'éviter toute perte de temps, LA CGT LUI DEMANDE DE DECIDER IMMEDIATEMENT, COMME PREMIERE MESURE SOCIALE L'ABROGATION DES ORDONNANCES Nos 67.706 - 707 - 708 et 709 du 21 août 1967.

A l'époque où les progrès des sciences et des techniques permettent un accroissement considérable de la productivité du travail, il est naturel que les travailleurs, les cadres, techniciens et ingénieurs, bref, ceux qui produisent les richesses nationales en soient les principaux bénéficiaires.

De longue date, et depuis deux ans avec la CFDT, la CGT demande l'ouverture de discussions avec le gouvernement d'une part et le Conseil National du Patronat Français, d'autre part, des revendications générales essentielles des travailleurs des secteurs privé, nationalisé et public en vue de les régler par voie d'accords contractuels.

Ces propositions se sont systématiquement heurtées à un refus intransigeant aussi bien de la part du gouvernement que du patronat, de sorte qu'un lourd contentieux s'est accumulé entre les parties syndicales, patronales et gouvernementales. Les négociations doivent le résorber de telle façon que l'amélioration des conditions de vie et de travail qui en résulteront soient garanties, pour l'avenir par des dispositions appropriées, ce qui suppose notamment l'extension des droits syndicaux, en particulier dans les entreprises et tous autres lieux de travail.

Cette extension implique qu'il soit définitivement mis un terme aux mesures de discrimination diverses qui frappent, depuis vingt ans, la principale centrale syndicale nationale.

Dans l'esprit de qui précède, nous demandons, en tout premier lieu, que les parties en présence se prononcent en faveur du paiement des jours de grève, revendication sur laquelle la majorité des grévistes s'est déjà prononcée, et que la négociation porte sur les chapitres essentiels suivants :

Augmentation générale des salaires

retraites et pensions

— Pas de salaire minimum inférieur à 600 F par mois et relèvement proportionnel du pouvoir d'achat des familles, des personnes âgées, invalides, etc. ;

— Suppression des disparités régionales de salaires ;

— Suppression des abattements d'âge et autres discriminations salariales qui affectent notamment la main-d'œuvre juvénile, féminine et immigrée ;

— Clause d'échelle mobile des salaires liée à l'évolution du coût de la vie.

Garantie des ressources et sécurité de l'emploi

Réduction progressive de la durée du travail

sans diminution de salaire, et abaissement de l'âge du départ en retraite.

Extension et garantie des droits syndicaux

— Reconnaissance de la section syndicale d'entreprise, impliquant notamment :

— l'octroi d'heures payées pour la participation aux assemblées générales de syndiqués ;

— La mise à disposition de locaux dans les entreprises à l'intention des syndicats et sections syndicales ;

— Le droit de réunion, d'affichage, de collectage des cotisations et de diffusion de la presse syndicale au sein des entreprises ;

— L'immunité syndicale des délégués et représentants syndicaux.

— Extension des pouvoirs des Comités d'entreprise.

Ces dispositions supposent l'abrogation de toutes les mesures restrictives du libre exercice du droit syndical et de grève.

Ces revendications doivent s'accompagner :

— d'une réduction des dépenses improductives en vue de l'accroissement des investissements productifs et publics répondant aux besoins de logement, d'instruction et de santé de la population ;

— d'une réforme démocratique du système d'enseignement et de formation professionnelle ;

— d'une refonte démocratique de la fiscalité ;

— des mesures mettant un terme aux privilèges fiscaux qu'alors consentis aux grandes sociétés privées.

Une fois les accords conclus à l'échelle gouvernementale et patronale sur les revendications générales ci-dessus exposées, il conviendra de les poursuivre sans délai à tous les autres niveaux : patronal, professionnel, gouvernemental, ministériel et à l'échelle des entreprises nationales, afin qu'ils puissent être précisés et complétés dans le cadre des conventions collectives et des statuts, étant entendu que la procédure Toutée-Grégoire est caduque.

La CGT se déclare prête à siéger, au niveau le plus élevé, sans désemparer, afin que les conclusions de la discussion lui permettent, au plus tôt, de consulter les travailleurs en grève. »

1 *L'Humanité*, 26 May 1968, p. 5.

leaves the viewers to rely on the extended textual information for its meaning. In fact, the text capturing the opinions of the CGT president Benoît Frachon and CGT general secretary Georges Séguy equates the workers' demands with their delegates' views. The headline underneath the picture reads 'Georges Séguy: Voici Nos Revendications' (Georges Seguy: These Are Our Demands), while on the top of the page Benoît Frachon's statement reads 'Les travailleurs ne cesseront la grève que lorsqu'ils seront certains de beneficier des avantages substantiels qu'ils escomptent' (The workers will continue the strike until they receive the significant benefits they expect).[21] The union's delegates become the voice of the movement, reducing this unique and diverse movement to basic salary demands. It is not accidental that the paper is dated 26 May when CGT negotiated with the government the settlement called the 'Grenelle Accords', which offered a small increase in minimum salary and extension of union rights in the factories, but which was initially rejected by the workers.[22]

The largest strike that affected every sector in French society and the unique alliance among all the different social groups was, therefore, reduced to just another strike that needed to be negotiated between the unions and the government. In terms of visual representation, this found its equivalent in *L'Humanité*, where the photographs that portrayed the workers in the occupied factories resembled the photographs of old labour movements in both their subject matter and their contextualisation. A photograph published on the front page of *L'Humanité* on the 28 May depicts a meeting of workers at Renault being addressed by the president of the CGT (figure 2). The focus is on the speaker, while the workers on strike are listening passively to their union delegate. The existing hierarchy and the separation between the party representatives and the public not only resemble older representations of the labour movement, but also remind us of the representation of mainstream politics. The photograph is divided into two levels: the upper stage where the delegate addresses the crowd and the lower level where the mass of workers stand. As the photograph was taken from a high viewpoint, this division becomes even clearer; the delegate occupies a significant proportion of the image directing the viewer's attention towards the speaker and not to the massed workers. In contrast to the delegate, who is clearly seen in the photograph, the crowd is represented as a mass and it is difficult to distinguish the individuals' faces. This clear hierarchy is not only spatial but also ideological, a large discrepancy between the movement's critique of conventional Leftist perceptions of revolutionary practice and denunciation of the mainstream political status quo.

What is also striking in this photograph is the representation of the individual as indistinguishable from a homogenised mass. This is a common characteristic

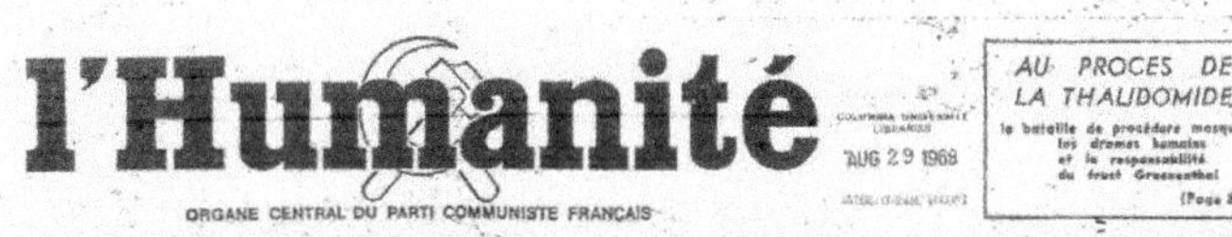

l'Humanité

ORGANE CENTRAL DU PARTI COMMUNISTE FRANÇAIS

MARDI
28 MAI 1968

0,30 F
4, boul. Poissonnière
PARIS-9e

AU PROCÈS DE LA THALIDOMIDE

la bataille de procédure masque les drames humains et la responsabilité du trust Gruenenthal

(Page 8)

Des concessions patronales et gouvernementales, mais des revendications essentielles en panne

ÇA NE FAIT PAS LE COMPTE

DISENT LES GRÉVISTES.

La C.G.T. : resserrez votre unité dans la lutte

- Les travailleurs consultés décident de continuer l'action
- Nombreuses manifestations en province

[Pages 2, 4, 5, 6 et 7]

Le Parti Communiste propose une rencontre immédiate à la F.G.D.S.

Waldeck ROCHET,
secrétaire général du Parti Communiste Français.

La réponse de François Mitterrand

François MITTERRAND.

Le temps presse

René ANDRIEU.

Communiqué de la Commission Administrative de la C.G.T.

PARIS, le 27 mai, 16 heures.

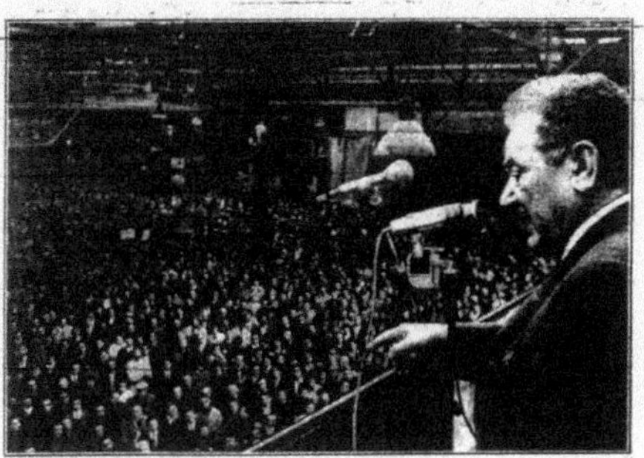

LA VÉRITABLE FORCE RÉVOLUTIONNAIRE

CONTRE TOUTE MANŒUVRE

- SATISFACTION DES REVENDICATIONS
- GOUVERNEMENT POPULAIRE ET D'UNION DEMOCRATIQUE

LE BUREAU POLITIQUE
DU PARTI COMMUNISTE FRANÇAIS

Paris, 27 mai 1968.

ILS MENTENT !

2 *L'Humanité*, 28 May 1968, p. 1.

PARIS : jamais vu depuis dix ans !

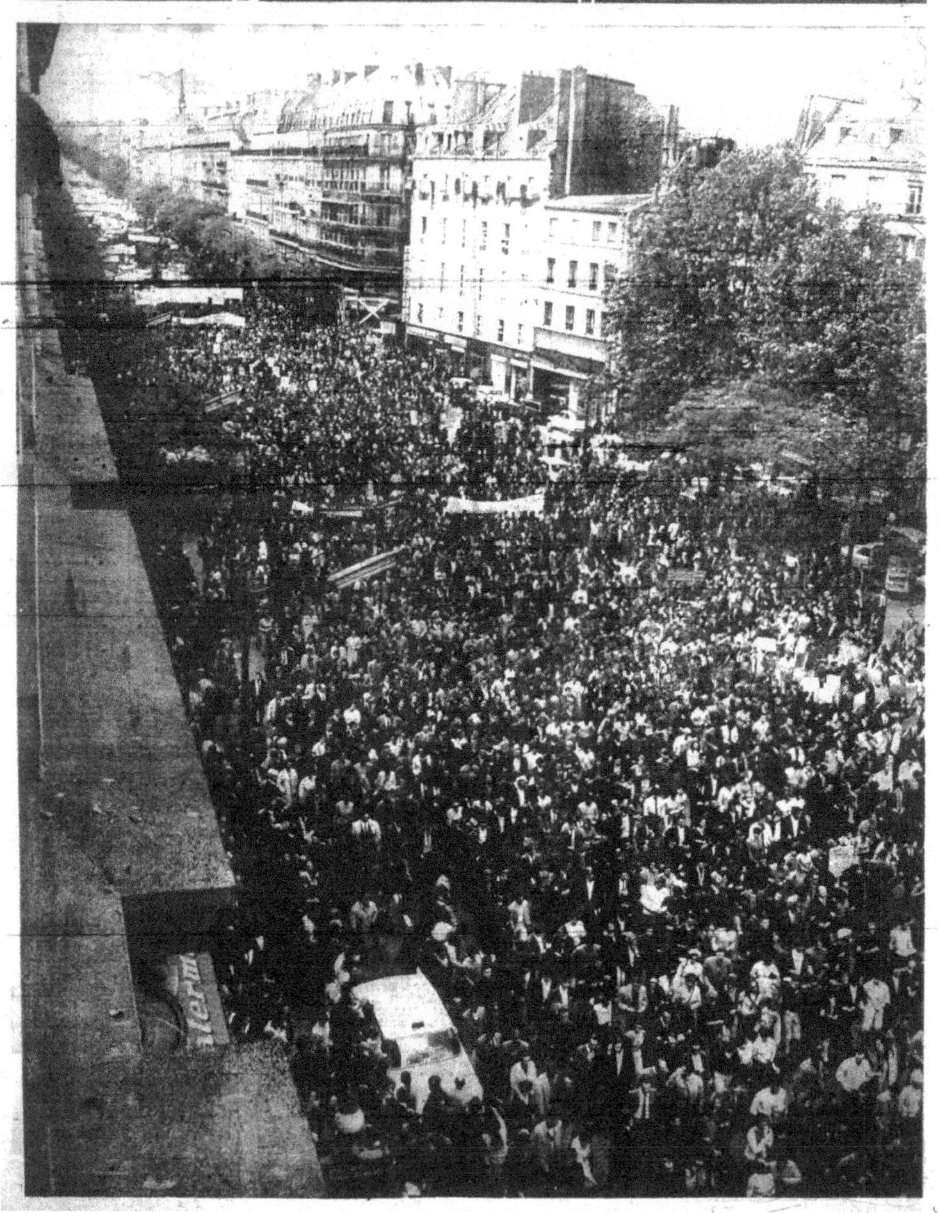

3 *L'Humanité*, 30 May 1968. N.p.

with the other habitual photographs published in *L'Humanité* during May and June, which is emblematic photographs of the crowd on the street (figure 3). These oceanic photographs of the crowd on the street are ordinary in the history of the labour movement in the twentieth century, pointing to the use of these photographs as an objective measurement, but most importantly highlighting the complex problem of visually representing the crowd in a mass demonstration'.[23] Uroskie's reading of oceanic photographs of the crowd is significant in this respect in pointing to the limitations of the photographic representation of the crowd, but also in highlighting the detachment of the viewer from the demonstration, given the elevated point of observation from which the homogenised crowd is viewed.[24] This is crucial in the representations of the large demonstrations of May 1968 since these photographs reduce the diversity of the movement to a homogenous crowd, at the cost of losing the specificity of the participants. Such a perspective fails to encounter the street as the meeting space for the demonstrators, the police and the bystanders, a failure heightened by the fact that the May 1968 demonstrations were an unprecedented intermingling of different social classes, genders and age groups.

Collectivisation in *L'Humanité* was associated with either photographs of static workers taken in the occupied factory or photographs of a crowd without particular characteristics. The latter photographs are even more problematic when one looks at the representations of pro-Gaullist demonstrations that preceded de Gaulle's electoral victory at the end of the month in the Right-wing *Le Figaro*. *Le Figaro*, in contrast with the student press and *L'Humanité*, covered the demonstrations in support of the General. In particular, the first demonstration in support of the government, which took place in Paris on the 30 May 1968, made the front page of *Le Figaro*. On that day, General de Gaulle called for elections, announced the dissolution of the National Assembly and asked French civilians to 'undertake "civil action" against subversion and the threat of "totalitarian Communism"'.[25] As a response, some thousands of his supporters marched up the Champs-Élysées holding national flags. The photograph published on the front page is of an oceanic crowd, taken from a very high standpoint similar to photographs of the movement published in *L'Humanité* rendering such a representation even more problematic.

From the crowd to the individual

While the absence of photographs of students in *L'Humanité* was striking, the rest of the mainstream press covered the student mobilisation, often focusing on one individual who stood for the rest of the movement. The mass media played a significant role in selecting a 'spokesperson' to exemplify and personify the entire movement, that is Daniel Cohn-Bendit. Cohn-Bendit's recognition within broader French society was due to mass media attention, since the French media treated him as the leader of the movement from the beginning of the events. Photojournalists Bruno Barbey and Serge Hambourg took photographs of Cohn-Bendit among the students and published them in the dailies and weeklies during May and June.

A characteristic example is the coverage of the events in the weekly French magazine *Le Nouvel Observateur*, one of the most popular general magazines. On the 15 May, in their first issue after the acceleration of the events, *Le Nouvel Observateur* covered the events with a story by Daniel Cohn-Bendit. The first page of the cover story featured a photographic portrait of him taken by the well-known photojournalist Serge Hambourg. The portrait is a close-up of Cohn-Bendit casually dressed and relaxed. Seemingly posing for the camera, his gaze does not look at the camera, but it is directed outside of the frame. The portrait resembles fashion and lifestyle magazines' photographs of celebrities photographed in close-up, in particular as it is printed to cover the largest part of the page. What is also important about the coverage is that as early as the 15 May, Cohn-Bendit was selected by the magazine among the numerous students to represent the movement. The text, entitled 'Notre Commune du 10 mai' (Our Commune of 10 May), is an account of the 'night of the barricades', narrated by Cohn-Bendit. It becomes clear that this is a projection of his own views and the groups he represented in the movement. In his own words:

> Dans la nuit de mercredi, le 'Mouvement du 22 mars' s'est réuni et nous avons dit: 'Nous ne pouvons plus en rester là, le movement a sa dynamique propre, les jeunes sont decidés à se battre, il faut leur donner quelque chose.'[26]

> (On Wednesday night, the 22 March movement met and we said: 'We will not stop there, the movement has its own dynamic and the young people are determined to fight, we should give them something.')

This early focus on him to stand for a whole movement can be thought of as a response to the media's appetite for a charismatic individual, a leader of the movement, and it is indicative of many other photographs that focus on Cohn-Bendit, either as an individual or part of the student body, but always in a distinguished position. These images added to his recognisability to a wider

French and international audience and rendered him a 'celebrity', although he personally denied that he held such a role.

Daniel Cohn-Bendit initially belonged to the group known as the 22 March movement, which denounced the necessity of leaders for the movement and 'considered its more prominent members as simply spokesmen for the rank and the file'.[27] Unlike Jacques Sauvageot, vice-president of UNEF and Alain Geismar, general secretary of SNEup, who had emerged as the most outstanding leaders of the movement by the 7 May, Cohn-Bendit was not the official leader of an organised group.[28] The 22 March movement he was part of was an amalgamation of Trotskyists and anarchists, who came together at Nanterre against 'the outmoded authoritarianism of de Gaulle on the one hand and the PCF on the other' and rejected 'established political styles and organisations'.[29] Cohn-Bendit was seen as an 'irresponsible amateur', compared to Sauvageot and Geismar, 'political revolutionaries in training'.[30]

Nevertheless, the 22 March movement and its refusal of any attachment to a party or a line remained the acknowledged initiator and theoretical inspiration of the emerging mass movement. In fact, what was 'new' in the movement was not an abolition of 'leadership', but a looser organisation which greatly differed from the bureaucratic structure of the old labour movement.[31] Within these looser networks, which consisted of small groups of students responsible, as we have seen, for the occupations of the Sorbonne and other university campuses, new forms of collective organisation emerged. The larger numbers of students who were finally attracted to the occupations, the assemblies, the sit-ins and the barricades were not necessarily members of any organised political groups. Therefore, 'more decentralized networks of activists and leaders without strong offices, organized around particular campaigns and claims' emerged.[32]

Cohn-Bendit's ironic attitude and his spontaneity had drawn the attention of the media as early as 8 January 1968 when he confronted the minister of youth and sports, François Missoffe. During the minister's visit to the campus of Nanterre to inspect a new swimming pool, Cohn-Bendit accused him of not having included the sexual problems of young people in his recent book on French youth. When the minister's reply implied that Cohn-Bendit take a dip in the swimming pool, the latter responded: 'That's the kind of answer you would get under a fascist regime.'[33] The importance of the incident resides, to a large extent, in the style of confrontation, which inaugurated Cohn-Bendit's celebrity as a 'verbal provocateur'.[34]

These qualities were also partly responsible for Cohn-Bendit's prominence in the movement, within which his popularity grew gradually and accelerated towards the end of May. A turning point for his recognition in the movement was 21 May, when the Counsel of Ministers prohibited Cohn-Bendit's re-entry into France.[35] In its effort to devitalise the movement, the French government succeeded the opposite. The vibrant demonstrations in solidarity with Cohn-Bendit were simultaneous with the government's prohibition and brought thousands onto the streets, under the slogan 'Nous Sommes tous des Juifs Allemands!' (We are all German Jews).[36] Reader explains that the expulsion brought to the centre of the students' attention de Gaulle's nationalism, which was at odds with the movement's internationalism, and the students' slogan expressed international solidarity and hostility to anti-semitism.[37]

This solidarity was visually represented in the movement's posters. After the expulsion, the Atelier Populaire produced a poster of Cohn-Bendit's portrait followed by the text 'Nous Sommes Tous Indésirables' (We are all undesirables).[38] Cohn-Bendit was the only living individual – beside General de Gaulle – whose face came to be used on posters. In contrast with de Gaulle, who was becoming an object of ridicule, Cohn-Bendit gained admiration.[39] The poster's popularity became evident in the circulation of different versions of it. One version of the poster was divided into parts, bearing on the one half Cohn-Bendit's image and on the other Che Guevara's Guerrillero Heroico, showing Cohn-Bendit's status in the movement and the movement's tendency to adopt the iconographical modes imposed by the mass media. There are many more photographs that depict Cohn-Bendit inseparable from the other students, taking part in assemblies or demonstrations. The student newspapers *Action*, *Tribune Socialiste* and *Le Monde Libertaire* published photographs that depict Cohn-Bendit in the first row of the demonstration clenching his fist, often focusing on his expressive and angry face, a personification of the movement's calls for negation of the state and its organs of authority.

While most of the photographs in student publications represented Cohn-Bendit as an integral part of the demonstration, the reproductions of these photographs along with the photojournalistic shots decidedly contributed to his face becoming gradually recognisable and appearing separately from the student body. Cohn-Bendit's image never reached the personality cult of Che Guevara, neither was it lionised to appear on demonstrators' banners and posters. Nevertheless, the recurrence of his image and Che Guevara's along with the other Leftist leaders shows the difficulty of the movement to overcome the deeply rooted tradition of an iconography of leadership. Although the seeds of a critique of leadership cult and hierarchical structures existed in the movement, this critique did not extend to the photographic representations of the movement, not only in the mainstream press, but also within the movement's own means of communication.

Constructing mainstream narratives

There are two different approaches to the events of May 1968 reflected in the principal images chosen to portray the events in contemporary French mainstream media. These two approaches represent the two principal narratives that dominated the theoretical discourse after the end of the events. The first is exemplified in *L'Humanité*'s configurations of the crowd and the representation of the struggle as strictly rooted in the factory space, guided by the trade unions and their delegates. The second is reflected in the fascination with the photograph of the students' leader, Cohn-Bendit, chosen to stand for a rather complex movement and its association with issues of youth and spontaneity.

In alignment with the first approach, one can also consider the ways that Orthodox Marxists failed to 'recognise the working-class character' of May 1968, and as a consequence in the elimination of its importance.[40] The problem, here, arises from a definition of the working class and, as a result, a definition of the struggles that this working class is involved in.[41] In fact, if one takes as given that the 'working class' consists of workers in factories, the so-called industrial and urban proletariat, it can easily be concluded that the class struggle has been in decline and that the new struggles in the form of student, feminist and ecological movements cannot be explained under this term. Attempting to locate the participants of May '68, namely young people, students, women and the unemployed – to name but the most important – in this 'pigeonhole' gave rise to continuous discussions about 'class and non-class movements, class and "other forms" of struggle, "alliances" between the working class and other groups, and so on'.[42] The limitations of orthodox Marxist approaches to the 'working class', according to which this class consists only of the waged industrial workers, leave out of the schema a wide range of unwaged workers such as students, housewives, children and peasants 'whose work under capitalism consists primarily of the production and reproduction of the ability and willingness to carry out activities (including industrial work) which contribute to the maintenance of the system'.[43]

This 'vulnerable old orthodox definition of working class' became 'a convenient target of critique' for new social movement theorists, who saw in May '68 the eclipse of the old labour movement.[44] The heterogeneity of the social groups that participated in May '68, namely students, workers, professors, professionals and women among others, and the plurality of their immediate demands did not only raise hopes for a society where capitalist exploitation would be destroyed, but also aspirations for equality of the sexes and sexual liberation. Slogans such as 'Qui Parle de l' Amour Détruit l' Amour' (Whoever Speaks of Love Destroys Love), 'Ouvrez les Fenêtres de Votre Coeur' (Open the Windows of your Heart), 'Sexe: C'Est Bien, A Dit Mao, Mais Pas Trop Souvent' (Sex: It is fine, Said Mao, But not Too Often), 'Je Jouis Dans les Paves' (I Find my Orgasms Among the Paving Stones), 'Vivez Sans Temps Mort, Jouissez Sans Entraves' (Live Intensively, Have Orgasms without Restraint), were undeniably related to these concerns.[45]

These new circumstances led theorists, contemporary to the movement, to argue that the importance of class struggle was diminishing. Sociologist Alain Touraine, taking into account these new societal groups, argued that the May movement could not be perceived as class struggle. Instead, he interpreted the May movement as a new kind of conflict which was not principally opposed to capitalism. In his book *The May Movement*, Touraine wrote:

> The May movement ushered in a new form of class struggle. More than any other collective action in the last few decades, it exposed and simultaneously formed part of the basic social conflict of our society ...
>
> It is not an economic conflict; it does not activate opposition between selfish profiteers and exploited wage earners ...
>
> French students, like their counterparts in Berlin or Berkeley, clashed with the apparatus of integration, manipulation, and aggression. These words, rather than exploitation, best define the nature of the conflict. It was social, political, and cultural rather than exclusively economic.
>
> The struggle was not against capitalism, but first and foremost against technocracy.[46]

According to Touraine, the events of May set before us a new type of conflict where the working class was no longer at the centre of the revolutionary process. May '68 was then described as a 'new social movement' and as such the 'beginning of new struggles'. May '68 was seen as a product of new values and forms of action created by changes in an emerging society, defined as 'postindustrial'. In his book, Touraine held out the hope that in the 'programmed society', new social classes would replace the ruling and working classes as the central actors of the conflict.[47]

Similarly, Claus Offe and Alberto Melucci analysed the principal innovations of the new social movements, such as an emphasis on lifestyle, 'identity' and culture in contrast to the past movements and their focus on economic issues.[48]

According to 'new social movements" theories, the movements that emerged in the 1960s were fundamentally different in ideology, goals, tactics, structure and participants from the older labour movement. Therefore, labour relations and class conflict were of decreasing relevance and the working class was not the key agent of change. It seemed to many theorists, then, that the emphasis that the new social movements were putting on lifestyle, 'identity' and culture, not only differentiated them from older movements that were mainly focused on economic and class issues, but also rendered the Marxist model of interpretation of social conflict largely inappropriate. These two different lines of thought reflected in the coverage of the events point not only to the limits of mainstream coverage of protest, but also to dominant subsequent narratives which weakened the breadth of the public support for this extraordinary coalition between students, the various Leftist groupuscules, the professionals, the workers and their trade unionists. Photographs published in the mainstream press failed to represent the movement's novelty, focusing on stereotypical configurations of the workers occupying their factories, or reducing the movement to an amorphous crowd or an individual.

Notes

1 K. A. Reader, *The May 1968 Events in France: Reproductions and Interpretations* (New York: St Martin's Press, 1993), p. 94.

2 C. Fink, F. Gassert and D. Junker (eds), *1968: The World Transformed* (Cambridge: Cambridge University Press, 1998), p. 261; Reader, *The May 1968 Events in France*, p. 94.

3 A. Feenberg and J. Freedman, *When Poetry Ruled the Streets: The French May Events of 1968* (Albany: State University of New York Press, 2001), p. 42.

4 A. Touraine, *The May Movement: Revolt and Reform* (New York: Random House, 1971), p. 176.

5 D. C. Hallin and P. Mancini, *Comparing Media Systems: Three Models of Media and Politics* (Cambridge: Cambridge University Press, 2004), p. 30.

6 Ibid., p. 106.

7 V. H. F. Scott, 'May 1968 and the Question of Image', *Rutgers Art Review*, 24 (2008), p. 5.

8 Ibid.

9 The centrality of photography within these crucial sites of production and distribution of the movement's ideas will be discussed in part II. For May 1968 posters, see: M. Albin, *Paroles de Mai: Affiches de l'Atelier Populaire des Beaux-Arts* (Paris: A. Michel, 1998); Atelier Populaire, *Posters from the Revolution, Paris, May 1968* (Paris: Usines Univerisités Union, 1969); Biblioteque de Mai, *Atelier Populaire* (Paris: Usines Univerisités Union, 1968); V. Gasquet, *500 Affiches Mai 68* (Paris: Aden, 2007).

10 *Le Monde* did not publish photographs until February 1972, when it published a cartoon for the first time. A photograph on its first page appeared only in December 1983. See

K. Willsher, 'Le Monde Lightens Up', *The Guardian* (Tuesday, 8 November 2005), www. guardian.co.uk/media/2005/nov/08/pressandpublishing.france (accessed 07/05/2010).

11 Scott, 'May 1968 and the Question of Image', p. 5.

12 *L' Humanité* (7 May 1968), p. 1. *Le Figaro* (7 May 1968), p. 1.

13 D. Star (ed.), *Beneath the Paving Stones: Situationists and the Beach, May 1968* (Edinburgh: AK Press, 2001), pp. 88–9.

14 G. Marchais, *L' Humanité* (3 May 1968), p. 10, as quoted in Feenberg and Freedman, *When Poetry Ruled the Streets*, p. 9–10.

15 Reader, *The May 1968 Events in France*, p. 13.

16 H. Cleaver, *Reading Capital Politically* (Edinburgh: AK Press, 2000), p. 36.

17 K. Ross, *May '68 and Its Afterlives* (Chicago and London: The University of Chicago Press, 2002), p. 69.

18 Ibid.

19 Ibid., p. 71 (emphasis in the original).

20 Ibid., p. 72.

21 *L' Humanité Dimanche* (26 May 1968), p. 5.

22 Ross, *May '68 and Its Afterlives*, pp. 67–8.

23 A. V. Uroskie, 'Far Above the Madding Crowd: The Spatial Rhetoric of Mass Representation', in J. T. Schnapp and M. Tiews (eds), *Crowds* (Stanford, CA: Stanford University Press, 2006), p. 309.

24 Ibid., p. 317.

25 D. Caute, *Sixty-Eight: The Year of the Barricades* (London: Hamish Hamilton, 1988), p. 218.

26 *Le Nouvel Observateur* (15 May 1968), p. 32.

27 D. Singer, *Prelude to Revolution: France in May 1968* (Cambridge: South End Press, 2002), pp. 16–17.

28 Feenberg and Freedman, *When Poetry Ruled the Streets*, p. 15.

29 Reader, *The May 1968 Events in France*, p. 9.

30 Ibid.

31 D. S. Meyer and S. Tarrow, *The Social Movement Society: Contentious Politics for a New Century* (Lanham: Rowman & Littlefield, 1998), p. 17; C. Barker, A. Johnson and M. Lavalette (eds), *Leadership and Social Movements* (Manchester and New York: Manchester University Press, 2001), p. 2.

32 Meyer and Tarrow, *The Social Movement Society*, p. 17.

33 Reader, *The May 1968 Events in France*, p. 7.

34 M. Seidman, *The Imaginary Revolution: Parisian Students and Workers in 1968* (New York and Oxford: Berghahn Books, 2004), p. 60.

35 Feenberg and Freedman, *When Poetry Ruled the Streets*, p. 50.

36 Ibid., p. 52; Reader, *The May 1968 Events in France*, p. 14.

37 K. Reader, 'Three Post-1968 Itineraries: Regis Debray, D. Cohn-Bendit and M. Karmitz', *South Central Review*, 16: 4 (1999–2000), p. 93.

38 Mésa, *Mai '68: Les Affiches de l' Atelier Populaire de l' Ex-École des Beaux-Arts* (Paris: Mésa, 1975), p. 124.

39 Seidman, *The Imaginary Revolution*, p. 138.

40 Cleaver, *Reading Capital Politically*, 2000, p. 16, footnote 13.

41 J. Holloway, 'Class and Classification: Against, In and Beyond Labour', in A. C. Dinerstein and M. Neary (eds), *The Labour Debate: An Investigation into the Theory and Reality of Capitalist Work* (Farnham: Ashgate, 2005), pp. 33–4.
42 Ibid.
43 Cleaver, *Reading Capital Politically*, p. 23.
44 Ibid., p. 16, footnote 13.
45 M. Rohan, *Paris '68: Graffiti, Posters, Newspapers and Poems of the Events of May 1968* (London: Impact Books, 1988).
46 Touraine, *The May Movement*, pp. 27–8.
47 Ibid.
48 A. Melucci, 'Ten Hypotheses for the Analysis of New Movements', in D. Pinto (ed.), *Contemporary Italian Sociology* (Cambridge: Cambridge University Press, 1981), p. 179.

2

The Zapatistas and the media spectacle

ALMOST from the beginning of the struggle and, more particularly, when they decided on a ceasefire in 1995, the Zapatistas' emphasis shifted from the use of arms to the use of words.[1] Through declarations, reports, letters and communiqués, they sent out their message to national and international media and thus to the world. Subcomandante Insurgente Marcos, one of the spokespersons of the movement, with his captivating communiqués, combining stories, poetry, philosophy, satire, romanticism and political analysis, sent to the world a strong message from the indigenous communities in insurrection. The communiqués unsurprisingly were not reproduced in the mainstream mass media with the exception of published excerpts from the EZLN declarations, which were occasionally published.[2] These excerpts, either very short or taken out of context, did not allow the wider public to understand the Zapatistas' ideas and goals. A rare exception was the Leftist Mexican newspaper *La Jornada*, which more than any other daily Mexican newspaper published Zapatista communiqués in full and provided analytical reports on the struggle. The communiqués had a great impact both in Mexico and internationally and were reproduced endlessly on activists' websites and blogs across the world.

The unknown Marcos, a masked Zapatista with a secret identity, gained prominence within the movement, despite his efforts to remain an unknown member of the struggle. Marcos encouraged secrecy about his identity and his life before moving to Chiapas and repudiated any kind of leadership within the EZLN. He called himself Subcomandante (subcommander) acting upon the orders of the EZLN's Comite Clandestino Revolucionario Indigena-Comandancia General (Indigenous Revolutionary Clandestine Committee), the General Command. Nevertheless, his genuinely poetic language and his political and philosophical writings rendered him the spokesperson of the movement, for both the movement itself and the media.

Along with his letters addressed to 'the peoples of the world', photographs

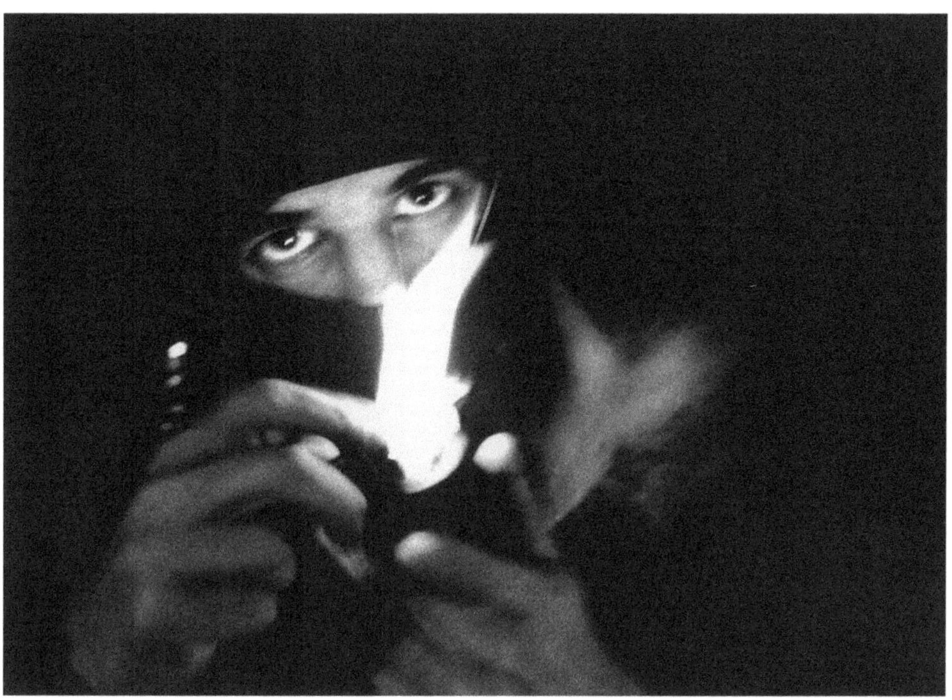

4 Raúl Ortega, Subcomandante Marcos, La Realidad, Chiapas 1995 (© Raúl Ortega)

of Marcos were published in the mainstream media and were circulated on the internet. Marcos soon became the favourite subject of many activists, journalists and photojournalists, who travelled to Chiapas during the months that followed the outbreak of the uprising, and whose photographs contributed to converting his image into the landmark of the EZLN struggle. The plethora of photographs of Marcos varies, both in styles and motifs. The most recurrent themes either depict Marcos as a guerrilla fighter on a horse or focus on his masked face and his pipe. The numerous variations of photographs around the latter theme have been widely circulated and have established him as an easily recognisable figure. The majority of these close-ups focus on Marcos's masked face, highlighting the photographability of his eyes. The black mask and the pipe have become the most distinguishable characteristics, reproduced in graphics and posters based on the photographs. A very well-known photograph taken by photojournalist Raúl Ortega, focuses on Marcos lighting his pipe (figure 4). The photograph was obviously taken at night without a flash, so that the light of the pipe contrasts strikingly with the black background of the photograph. The shot is central and

Marcos looks directly at the camera. The focus and lighting draw attention to his eyes, the only uncovered part of his face. Ortega's photograph, published initially in *La Jornada* and reproduced widely, is only symptomatic of the wide media attention that Marcos received in the months after the break up of the uprising, which resulted in an obsession with his hidden identity.

Unmasking Marcos

This obsession seemed to be coming to an end on 9 February 1995, when the Mexican federal government unmasked the 'Zapatista leader' at a press conference in Mexico City. During the press conference 'the black-and-white photograph of a Milquestoatsy-looking young man with a beard and large, dark eyes' was displayed in front of the reporters and photographers for observation.[3] The photograph, according to the Mexican intelligence service, portrayed Rafael Sebastián Guillén Vicente, which was believed to be Subcomandante Marcos's real identity. The governmental aide superimposed a slide of a balaclava on the old photograph attempting to establish the resemblance between the man shown in the photograph and the famous revolutionary.[4] More details were soon revealed: thirty-seven-year-old Rafael Guillén was from a middle-class family from Tampico, he studied philosophy in the National Autonomous University of Mexico in Mexico City and later became a professor at the Autonomous Metropolitan University's Xochimilco campus. Guillén was remembered by his university colleagues as one of the most brilliant, hard-working and congenial teachers in the radical Department of Theory and Analysis.[5]

The timing of the unmasking of Marcos was not accidental. Almost thirteen months after the beginning of the uprising in south-eastern Mexico, Zedillo's government began a new offensive against the Zapatistas, violating the terms of the ceasefire agreed between the rebels and the previous government of Carlos Salinas, and issued arrest warrants for Marcos. The economic recession that affected the country due to poor financial decisions by the Salinas government, manifested in the devaluation of the Mexican currency and the withdrawal of foreign investment in Mexico, was attributed by the government to the impact of the conflict in Chiapas on Mexico's economic policy.[6] The new governmental offensive was proof to the United States, which contributed decisively to the Mexican economy's stabilisation with a large bailout loan, that Zedillo's government was in full control of its national territory, and unmasking Marcos was a well-staged act for the media spectacle.

In Mexico City, the response was immediate. More than 100,000 people demonstrated in solidarity with Zapatistas, chanting the slogans 'Todos somos Marcos!' (We are all Marcos!), 'Todos Somos indios!'[7] (We are all Indians). The slogan was in accordance with the basic Zapatista principle of facelessness and anonymity. The Zapatistas had covered their faces with balaclavas and bandanas since the early days of the uprising, becoming anonymous and refusing any notion of leadership. Marcos emphatically pointed this out during the first days of the uprising:

> the one who speaks is a more collective heart, not a caudillo [a charismatic, personalistic leader]. That is what I want you to understand, not a caudillo in the old style, in that image. The only image that you will have is that those who make this happen are masked. And the time will come when the people will realize that it is enough to have dignity and put on a mask and say: Well then, I can do this too.[8]

It was exactly the image of the masked collective body in uprising and not the image of one charismatic leader that was promoted from the Lacandon Jungle to the world. And it is true that even after the unmasking, the image that stayed with most of the people was the image of the masked Zapatista, often reduced to the image of masked Marcos in the media coverage, and not the old ID photograph of Guillén. The failure of the unmasking became evident in the eagerness to become Marcos, to become a Zapatista, which characterised activists in Mexico and in the rest of the world alike. It was exactly the strong presence of Marcos's image in the social imaginary that rendered any effort of the Mexican government to defeat the Zapatistas' continuous creative forces totally unsuccessful. Marcos's mockery of any effort of the government to reduce the Zapatista movement into a 'fixed' identity was evident in his communiqué:

> I heard that they discovered another Marcos and he is very tampiqueno [very much from Tampico.] It does not sound bad, the port is beautiful. I remember when I was working as a bouncer in a brothel in Cuidad Madero during the times in which LA Quina did to the regional economy what Salinas did to the stock exchange: to inject money to hide poverty. I left the port because humidity makes me sleepy, and seafood makes the sleepiness go away.[9]

Desemanscarar (unmasking), an ancient ritual deeply rooted in the nation's soul, can mean to destroy or, quite the contrary, to elevate to a higher status.[10] It seemed that the Mexican government clearly failed to undermine Subcomandante's fame and unwillingly contributed to adding to his myth.

The resurrection of an old image

In all revolutions, the dead are resurrected for the 'purpose of glorifying the new struggles', Marx wrote once.[11] So are their images. The appeal of Marcos's image within and outside Mexico is not totally unrelated to the visual resemblances the image bears to two of the most reproduced photographs in Latin America. The first is the full-body portrait of Emiliano Zapata wearing a sombrero and carrying a rifle in his right hand taken by the German photographer Hugo Brehme and initially published in Mexico in 1913.[12] The photograph of Zapata has created an archetype of the revolutionary and has served as a model for Mexican filmmakers.[13] The iconic photograph of Zapata is well known to the people of Chiapas, who, like other Mexican citizens, learn about Zapata through the educational system and mass media commemorations.[14] In a 1994 letter, Marcos narrates an encounter with 'el Viejo Antonio' (the old Antonio) (an elder from the Indian communites who is the protagonist in a series of his stories) to whom he explains who the Zapatistas are and how their struggle links with the Mexican revolution, including an account of Zapata's trajectory from Anenecuilco to Chinameca. Old Antonio narrates his long true story about Zapata, talking about two gods, Ih'al and Votán, who walked together but also separated, highlighting that they chose the longer path, and they moved along asking questions.[15] Antonio said:

> It's that Zapata that appeared here in the mountains. He wasn't born here, they say. He appeared just like that. They say that he is Ik'al and Votán, that they came here to end their long journey … And this Zapata said that he had arrived here and here he was going to find that answer to where the long road led. And he said that sometimes there would be light and sometimes there would be darkness, but that they were all the same, Votán Zapata, Ik'al Zapata, white Zapata, and black Zapata, and that the two were the same road for all real men and women.[16]

Zapata is gradually transformed into Votán Zapata, a constructed figure by the Zapatistas, a fusion of the indigenous god and the mythical revolutionary.[17] Marcos approaches the iconic figure of the revolutionary through the eyes of old Antonio, that is through the local myths and traditions of the indigenous people.

It was through a rereading of Mexican history and the past revolutionary projects that the EZLN placed Zapata at the centre of their creation myth, with him standing for all the marginalised, the oppressed and the indigenous communities deprived of basic rights.[18] Antonio, then, pulled out a small black-and-white photograph of Zapata, the one taken in 1913, and kept on with a detailed description of the photograph, showing clearly that he knew it well.[19] It is, in fact, the old Antonio who gives Marcos lessons on how to look at images:

> Old Antonio said to me, 'I have asked this picture (Zapata's portrait) a lot of questions. That's how I got this far'. He coughed and flicked the ashes off his cigarette. He gave me the photo. 'Take it', he said, 'so that you can learn to question … and to walk.'[20]

The story indicates Marcos's understanding of the importance of this archetype of Mexican revolutionary. From the very early days of the uprising, Marcos appeared in public as a guerrilla fighter on horseback with his chest crossed with cartridge belts in an X, exactly like Zapata. Many black-and-white photographs of him in these early stages available on the EZLN website (figure 5) evoke the easily recognisable revolutionary symbol of Zapata for the majority of the Mexican population, and even more for the indigenous people in Chiapas. The links with the Mexican revolution were not only evident in the direct reference to Emiliano Zapata in their name, in the conscious return to the Mexican revolution's aims for agrarian reform, but also in the appropriation of its dominant iconography.

In her study of the photographic production of the Mexican revolution, Andrea Noble demonstrates that there is an element of performativity in the EZLN appropriation of the famous photographs of the Mexican revolution. Through interesting examples Noble demonstrates how the Zapatistas referenced directly iconic photographs of the Mexican Revolution by staging photo-opportunties.[21] In August 1994, the EZLN organised the first Convención Nacional Democrática (CND) in the jungle of Chiapas, calling Mexican and foreign delegates to discuss the issues of democracy, justice, civil rights in Mexico and, in particular, the rights of the indigenous communities. The poster that promoted the event entitled 'De La Selva de Concreto a La Selva Lacandona' (From the Concrete Jungle to the Lacandon Jungle) was an appropriation of *Villa en la Silla Presidencial*, an iconic photograph of the Mexican revolution depicting a smiling Pancho Villa siting on the presidential chair and Emiliano Zapata beside him staring into the camera with his sombrero on his knee. The photograph – more accurately,

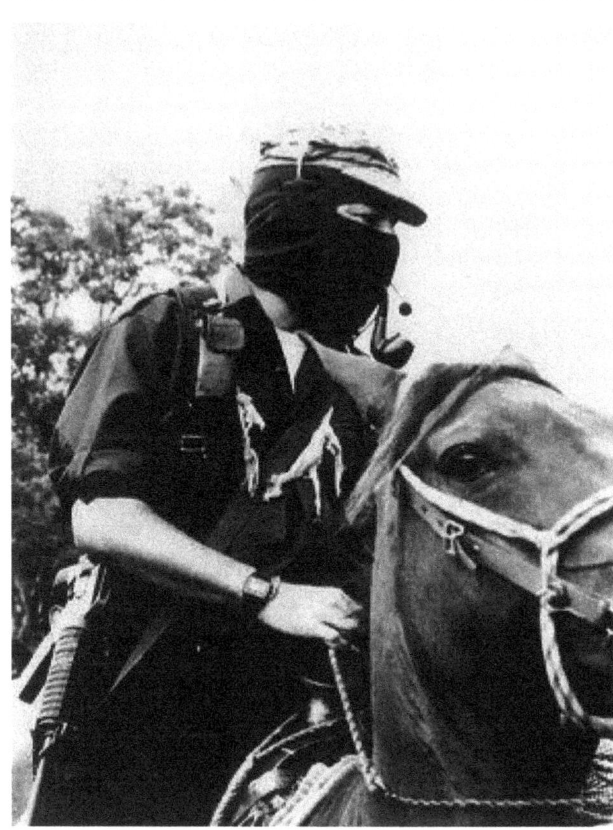

5 Photographer Unknown, Subcomandante Marcos, EZLN website

the photographs, as four versions of this image are in circulation – was taken during the brief occupation of Mexico City by Zapatista and Villista troops in December 1914. The significance and recognisability of this photograph was established through endless reproductions within Mexico.[22] The importance of the occupation of Mexico City by the revolutionary troops is only one of the reasons why the photograph joined other iconic images, such as the famous image of Emiliano Zapata, in standing as a symbol of the revolution and impacted upon post-revolutionary discources of memory.[23] It comes as no surprise therefore that the poster was an appropriation of this iconic image, superimposing Marcos's head right at the centre of the composition, in the position of Zapata. Subcomandante in his usual ski-mask holds a sombrero, while next to him, the social activist Superbarrio Gómez, in his wrestling costume, sits in the place of Villa. The poster was disseminated in the streets of Mexico City where the image would be easily recognisable. Through this appropriation the

Zapatistas created a visual link between the past and the present and contested the use of this symbolic image by the Mexican state. In another instance, on 16 March 1999, eight Zapatistas entered the famous restaurant of Sanborns in Mexico City in order to take light refreshment at the bar. The resulting photograph taken by several waiting photojournalists was to all intents and purposes a recreation of the 1914 photograph of Zapatista troops with their cartridge belts across their chests partaking of light refreshment in the same bar.

It becomes clear from this performative appropriation of the images of the Mexican revolution that the Zapatistas consciously use these symbols in their struggle. The image of Zapata, omnipresent in the murals in the villages in Chiapas, is part of the everyday life of the indigenous communities. It is the portraits of Zapata and Che Guevara, arguably the most reproduced images in the history of Latin America, which have attained symbolic function both in the struggle and the indigenous communities' everyday life. Many times, these murals became the background for photographs of the indigenous people. Subcomandante Marcos has also been photographed in front of a huge colourful mural of Zapata, establishing the historical as well as the iconographical link between the two (plate 1).

Is Marcos the Che Guevara of his generation?

The images of Che Guevara are equally present within the movement. In the Caravana de la Dignidad Indígena (Caravan for Indian Dignity), which took place between February and April 2001, the Zapatistas marched through the Mexican countryside visiting several communities along the way.[24] On these visits, the Zapatistas merged with the local communities, participated in their rituals and shared ideas, encouraging a dialogue with civil society.[25] In a symbolic gesture, this march of indigenous people outside Chiapas, also known as Zapatour, led by twenty-four Zapatista commanders including Marcos, followed the route that Zapata took in 1914. Zapatour culminated in Mexico City, where Marcos addressed the people of Mexico in the Plaza Zócalo.[26] Zapatista delegates claimed the right to enter to the Federal Congress to explain to legislators their positions about indigenous rights and culture. Although the subsequent revision of the constitution was far from what the indigenous people had initially hoped for, the appearance of the delegation in the Congress and the speeches of four delegates were without doubt of historical importance for Mexico. It is, therefore, not accidental that along with many other references to local history and culture, banners with Che Guevara featured on the march.

This direct reference to a past revolutionary intentionally highlights the historical continuation between the Zapatistas and the older historical Mexican and Latin American revolutions, projecting the continuities in their struggle. The Zapatistas perceived their uprising as a part of Latin American history of oppression, exploitation, resistance and uprisings. This continuity connects the Zapatistas not only with the Mexican revolution but with all other revolutionary projects on the continent, including Simón Bolívar's, Manuelita Saenz's and Che Guevara's. It is Che Guevara's revolutionary dream that transcends geographical and historical limitations to connect with earlier revolutionary moments in the continent. As Marcos wrote:

> thirty years ago, el Che dreamed and dreamed again of a transformed new, better reality: the dream of rebellion. That dream crossed the time and the mountains of the Mexican Southeast. The dream that summons us together today is one of rupture and continuity with Che Guevara's dreams, just as his dream was one of rupture and continuity with the dream that kept Simón Bolívar and Manuelita Saenz.[27]

Marcos clearly points to Che Guevara's legacy and the significance of his struggle for a contemporary revolutionary project. While it is almost certain that Subcomandante had read Che Guevara's writings, it is the latter's oft reproduced image that Marcos directly refers to. *The Guardian Weekend* on 3 March 2001 featured a photograph of Subcomandante Marcos in the easily recognisable red-and-black poster of the style of Che Guevara (plate 2). The cover line reads 'Why Marcos is the Che Guevara of his generation', while the cover story by Naomi Klein provides an analysis of the theory of Zapatismo and the position of Marcos within a non-hierachical democratic indigenous community in insurrection.[28]

The photograph of Marcos with his masked face and pipe without doubt resembles the famous portrait of Che Guevara based on Alberto Korda Díaz's photograph of Ernesto Che Guevara. The photograph was taken on 5 March 1960 at a mass funeral service called for by Fidel Castro for the Cubans who were killed during an explosion in Havana. Although it has not been proven, Cubans strongly suspected that the explosion was most probably planned and carried out by the Americans or by Cuban exiles supported by the CIA.[29] The second of the two snapshots taken that day of the revolutionary, taken by Korda, was destined to become probably one of the most reproduced and appropriated pictures of the late twentieth century.[30] The photograph remained in Korda's studio until 1967, when an Italian publisher, Gian-Giacomo Feltrinelli, produced posters using two prints of the image given as a gift to him by Korda.

Although Che Guevara's image as a whole was reproduced a few times before 1967, it was not until his death that the image's wide dissemination began.[31] From the Plaza de la Revolución, where the image appeared on a huge banner to accompany Castro's speech on Che Guevara's death, to the various versions of posters starting with the ones by Cuban Niko (Antonio Pérez González) and by the Irish artist Jim Fitzpatrick, the image took on its own life.[32] In 1968, the Che Guevara poster was converted into an emblem of revolution hung on the wall of the occupied Sorbonne in May, and in October it was carried by the demonstrators in the massive student protest in the Plaza Tlatelolco in Mexico City, often accompanied by the slogans 'Hasta la Victoria Siempre!' (Until victory always) and 'Unidos Venceremos!' (United we will win).[33] Jim Fitzpatrick maintained that it was Daniel Cohn-Bendit who introduced the image to the street demonstration in May '68 and that it was through the May events that the image was passed on to other groups, such as the Dutch group *The Provos*.[34]

Feltrinelli's poster version, almost contemporaneous with the poster boom of the late 1960s and the growing international youth audience interested in the political struggles for justice and freedom, gave to the image its iconic status. Che Guevara's young face, his long hair, the beard, the beret with the star and his aggressive gaze embodied the romanticism of his ideas and appealed to the young students in revolt. Despite the fact that he was a leader of a revolutionary vanguard and a senior figure in the Cuban government, Che Guevara was not associated with mainstream politics, but he was seen as an uncompromising radical. His fight for the liberation of the Third World and his militancy and anti-capitalist struggle was appealing to the revolutionary youth in Western capitalist societies.[35] Che Guevara's fight against exploitation, imperialism and capitalism, his vision for a new man, his fight in solidarity with the Third World was embraced by the '68 radicals. The romantic figure of Che Guevara that appeared on the walls and posters in Paris in 1968 and inspired students and protesters all over the world captured the imagination of millions of people at moments of social and political unrest in the following decades.

Marcos consciously plays with Che Guevara's image, an image that has been reproduced repeatedly, even refashioned to serve other causes in different cultures since the 1970s. In particular, in Latin America the image has been ascribed holy virtues and has been frequently displayed next to images of Christ and the Pope.[36] Despite this frenetic commercialisation from T-shirts to an outstanding example of state kitsch in Cuba, Che Guevara's image has been used by many contemporary Latin American political movements in a straightforwardly inspirational way, maintaining to a certain extent its primitive innocence. In the small towns of Chiapas, Che Guevara's image appears in most of the paintings on walls and banners that are made either collectively or by single artists.[37] In the photographic exhibition '69 Miradas Contra Polifemo' organised by the Zapatistas to celebrate ten years of struggle, many photographs depict Zapatistas posing for the camera in front of a mural with Che Guevara. This is the case in Rafael Sequí Serres's photograph of the young students in front of their school, the Escuela Emiliano Zapata (School Emiliano Zapata) situated in the autonomous province of San Pedro in Chiapas, and Raúl Ortega's photograph of a young female Zapatista in front of a house. Che Guevara's image prevails in murals in both buildings, accompanied in the latter case with the writing 'Nuestra America: Con el Soldetu Bravura Comandante Ordene!' (Our America, with the sunshine of your courage, at your orders, Commandante!). Che Guevara's image seems to be an integral part of the Zapatistas' everyday visual experience and it is used extensively in buildings.

Subcomandante Marcos followed the example of Che Guevara, sharing the material conditions of the indigenous people and winning the allegiance of their communities.[38] Even more, the EZLN in its early days understood itself to be the 'revolutionary vanguard' which was to initiate and lead the 'prolonged popular war'. In reality, they understood their tasks in terms of the 'implantation' of an armed *foco* (nucleus of guerrilla fighters) using practices and tactics analogous to those promoted by Ernesto Che Guevara.[39] Che Guevara's ideas were built on the basic humanistic, philosophical, ethical, economic, sociological and political premises of an anti-dogmatic Marxism, which transcended Stalinism and reformism and attempted to use Marxist thought as a guide to action, going back to the living sources of living communism.[40] Che Guevara developed a *revolutionary* humanism, which differs greatly from any bourgeois, Christian or philanthropic humanism, since it is 'above all ... expression in his conception of the role of men in the revolution, in his communist ethics, and in his vision of the new man'.[41]

The Zapatistas, on the other hand, shunned guerrilla warfare, denounced the necessity of a vanguard party leading an armed struggle as a central part of their political praxis and announced that they were not a *foco* movement.[42] Soon an extensive emphasis on local aspects of the rebellion took precedence over the class struggle, which had been particularly emphasised by Che Guevara. The terms used in previous revolutions by Che Guevara, such as 'proletariat', 'socialism' and 'vanguard' were not highlighted any more. In contrast, there was an extensive emphasis on 'other categories previously dismissed as being irrevocably compromised by their liberal use, such as "freedom", "democracy", "justice" and new categories such as "dignity"'.[43] Their demands for a radical and democratic movement, an 'organisation of self defense for excluded people', were realised in various political initiatives aimed at strengthening the democratic qualities of their movement, namely national and international encounters against neoliberalism and for democracy, freedom and justice.[44]

Despite the ideological differences, the recognisability of the portrait of Marcos and its reproducibility across the globe bears similarities with that of Che Guevara. The fact that the Zapatista struggle transcended their national and local barriers played a significant role in this. The Zapatistas quite successfully linked with activists globally to such a degree that many accounts recognised that their movement should not be seen as merely local, but as a 'part of the largest globally interconnected social movement of our time'[45] or even as the beginning of a global movement.[46] Images of the Zapatistas were used by activists worldwide and were circulated within the wider movement. In the demonstrations of Seattle, there were many graffiti borrowing the Zapatista motto 'Ya Basta!', many protesters wore T-shirts with the red star-the symbol of the EZLN struggle-and Subcomandante Marcos, while many leaflets with the image of a masked Zapatista were circulated.[47] As Jen Couch observes, there were protesters who wore a Zapatista style black ski mask, while 'various political leaflets, advertising everything from teach-ins to the upcoming protest, and seminars portrayed the image of a ski-masked face of a Zapatista'.[48] This is not only an immediate reference to the Zapatista struggle and a confirmation of the Western activists' solidarity with their movement, but also evidence of the strong ideological, strategic and tactical links between the movements, which share many ideological beliefs, swap ideas, strategies and tactics, and struggle against the same 'enemies'.

The popularity of Marcos's image exceeded the geographical limitations of Mexico and the political circles of activists to reach the broader society via mainstream media. Amongst the multiple reasons for this success, one should not forget to add Marcos's self-conscious interaction with the media and the construction of an image for media spectacle. From the very beginning of the struggle, Marcos seemed to be completely aware of the power of the mass media and their importance for the struggle's sustainability and continuation. Marcos attracted many Western journalists, who travelled to Chiapas to interview Subcomandante, many times being denied access through the Zapatista checkpoint or being made to wait for him.[49] In July 1994, Subcomandante sent out a communiqué, which was only revealing of how well he understood the dominant logic that underpins contemporary media: 'Everything You Wanted to Ask About El Sup [Marcos's nickname] but Were Afraid to Ask'.[50] The communiqué supplied the journalists with multiple choices:

> At last we arrived at (a valley/a forest/a clearing/a bar/a Metro station/a pressroom) … there we found (El Sup/a transgressor of the law/a ski mask with a pronounced nose/a professional of violence). His eyes are (black/ coffee/gren/blue/red/honey-colored/oatmeal-colored/yogurt-colored/ granola colored). He lit his pipe while he sat on a (rocking chair/swivel chair/throne …).[51]

Photography has been central to Marcos's self-conscious decision to interact with the media. In December 2007, Marcos agreed to be photographed for *Gatopardo*, a mass circulation magazine in Latin America, which persuaded Marcos to pose for Ricardo Trabulsi, a fashion photographer. The photograph of Marcos, which appeared on the cover of *Gatopardo*, plays with these characteristics that rendered him a recognisable figure. Marcos is depicted in his military uniform, masked, smoking his pipe (plate 3). In a mode similar to that in fashion photography, Marcos posed in a straightforward position against a white background. The story conveys Marcos's deep understanding of the power of visual imagery for the sustainability of the struggle and the immense impact of this imagery when it is reproduced within mainstream media. Replying once to a question about him being turned into an attraction, he stated:

> This is nothing very special, don't you think? And then, after that? Marcos will lose his image but the indigenous will gain security. That is the main point. They will have more chances to eat and fewer threats over their heads. So we say, welcome to celebrities. We have to hold out until the rainy season. Another month and we will be saved until next year.[52]

Max Horkheimer's statement that the 'mass media assimilate the revolution by absorbing its leaders into their list of celebrities' seems to be subverted in this case by Marcos's effort to construct an image for media spectacle.[53] This image is of a radical intellectual who becomes a poor peasant, a guerrilla who uses words instead of weapons, a Zapatista who needs to hide himself in order to be seen. When will he remove his mask? Marcos responded to Régis Debray: 'The day when an Indian will enjoy the same rights as a white person in every corner of the republic; the day when the party-state is finished and when election will no longer be a synonym of fraud.'[54]

Notes

1 For more on the ceasefire, see: J. Holloway, 'The Zapatista Uprising', *Common Sense*, 17 (1995), p. 6.

2 H. Cleaver, 'The Virtual and Real Chiapas Support Network: A Review and Critique of Judith Adler Hellman's "Real and Virtual Chiapas: Magic Realism and the Left"', at www.eco.utexas.edu/~hmcleave/anti-hellman.html (accessed 18/05/2006).

3 A. Guillermoprieto, 'The Unmasking', in T. Hayden (ed.), *The Zapatista Reader: Thunder's Mouth* (New York: Press/Nation Books, 2002), p. 33.

4 Ibid., p. 33.

5 Ibid., p. 36.

6 J. Ross, *The War Against Oblivion: The Zapatista Chronicles* (Monroe, ME: Common Courage Press, 2000), pp. 97–8.

7 Ibid., p. 109.

8 Subcomandante Marcos, 'Testimonies of the First Day', in Hayden (ed.), *The Zapatista Reader*, pp. 209–10 (originally published in *La Jornada*, 19 January 1994).

9 Subcomandante Marcos, 'The Zapatistas Hike Up the Price of the Indigenous Mexican Blood', in Ž. Vodovnik (ed.), *Ya Basta! Ten Years of the Zapatista Uprising* (Oakland, CA: AK Press, 2004), p. 86.

10 I. Stavans, 'Unmasking Marcos', in Hayden (ed.), *The Zapatista Reader*, pp. 391 and 386–95.

11 K. Marx, 'The 18th Brumaire of Louis Bonaparte', in K. Marx and F. Engels, *Collected Works*, Vol. 11 (London: Lawrence & Wishart, 1979), p. 101.

12 A. Noble, *Photography and Memory in Mexico: Icons of Revolution* (Manchester and New York: Manchester University Press, 2010), p. 146; J. Mraz, *Fotografiar La Revolución Mexicana: Compromisose Iconos* (México D.F.: Instituto Nacional de Anthropología e Historia, 2010), p. 221, footnote 7.

13 E. Rajchenberg and C. Héau-Lambert, 'History and Symbolism in the Zapatista Movement', in J. Holloway and E. Peláez (eds), *Zapatista!: Reinventing Revolution in Mexico* (London: Pluto Press, 1998), p. 19.

14 S. Brunk, *The Posthumous Career of Emiliano Zapata: Myth, Memory and Mexico's Twentieth Century* (Austin, TX: University of Texas Press, 2008), p. 228.

15 Marcos Letter, 13 December 1994, in *EZLN: Documentos y Cominicados*, 2 vols. Era (Mexico City, 1994).

16 EZLN as cited in Noble, *Photography and Memory in Mexico*, pp. 145–6.

17 Ibid., p. 146.

18 Brunk, *The Posthumous Career of Emiliano Zapata*, p. 234.

19 Noble, *Photography and Memory in Mexico*, p. 146.

20 EZLN cited in Noble, *Photography and Memory in Mexico*, pp. 145–6.

21 Noble, *Photography and Memory in Mexico*, p. 154.

22 Ibid., p. 58. S. Brunk, 'The Eyes of Emiliano Zapata', in S. Brunk and B. Fallaw, *Heroes and Hero Cults in Latin America* (Austin, TX: University of Texas Press, 2006), pp. 109–27.

23 Noble, *Photography and Memory in Mexico*, p. 61.

24 N. Klein, 'The Unknown Icon', *Guardian Weekend* (3 March 2001), www.naomiklein.org/articles/2001/03/unknown-icon.

25 M. Mentinis, *Zapatistas: The Chiapas Revolt and What It Means for Radical Politics* (London: Pluto Press, 2006), p. 26.

26 I. Ramonet, 'Marcos Marches on Mexico City', in Hayden, *The Zapatista Reader*, p. 133.

27 Subcomandante Marcos, 'Today Eighty Years Later, History Repeats Itself', in Subcomandante Marcos, *Our World Is Our Weapon: Selected Writings* (New York: Seven Stories Press, 2002), p. 104.

28 Klein, 'The Unknown Icon'.

29 S. Lens, *The Forging of the American Empire* (Sterling, VA, London: Pluto Press, 2003), p. 407.

30 The story of how Korda took these photographs at the moment that Che Guevara briefly stepped forward was recorded by many writers. For a detailed description of the event and of Feltrinelli's later version of this image, see: T. Ziff, 'Guerrillero Heroico', in Trisha Ziff (ed.), *Che Guevara: Revolutionary and Icon* (London: V&A Publications, 2006), pp. 15–22; D. Kunzle, *Che Guevara, Icon, Myth and Message* (Los Angeles, CA: University of California, Fowler Museum of Cultural History, 1998).

31 T. Ziff claims that the image was produced before Che Guevara's death only in *Revolución* in 1961 and in an issue of *Paris Match* in July 1967. Ziff (ed.), *Che Guevara: Revolutionary and Icon*, pp. 16, 18.

32 Fitzpátrick claims that it was he and not Feltrinelli who reproduced the first poster of Che Guevara before Che Guevara's death. For relevant discussions, see: Ziff (ed.), *Che Guevara: Revolutionary and Icon*; A. Mir and J. Fitzpatrick, 'Not Everything Is Always Black or White', in G. Watson, G. van Noord and G. Everall (eds), *Make Everything New: A Project on Communism* (London and Dublin: Book Works and Project Arts Centre, 2006), pp. 10–23.

33 F. D. Garzia and Ó. Sola, *Che Images of a Revolutionary* (London: Pluto Press, 1997), p. 205.

34 Mir and Fitzpatrick, 'Not Everything Is Always Black or White', p. 20.

35 M. Löwy, *The Marxism of Che Guevara: Philosophy, Economics, and the Revolutionary Warfare* (New York and London: Monthly Review Press, 1973), pp. 113–18.

36 In Latin America, peasants believe that he performed miracles. In La Higuera in Bolivia, where he died, the people pay homage to San Ernesto de la Higuera, who is one of the two patron saints of the town. For relevant discussions, see: V. Goldberg, *The Power of Photography: How Photographs Changed Our Lives* (New York, London, Paris: Abbeville Press, 1991), pp. 156–61; P. J. Dosal, 'San Ernesto de la Higuera: The Resurrection of Che Guevara', in L. L. Johnson (ed.), *Death, Dismemberment and Memory in Latin America* (Albuquerque: University of New Mexico Press, 2004), pp. 317–41.

37 J. Stallabrass, 'The Dead, Our Dead, Murals and Banners the Zapatistas', *Third Text*, 38 (Spring 1997), p. 58.

38 O. Paz, 'The Media Spectacle Comes to Mexico', in Hayden, *The Zapatista Reader*, p. 52.

39 L. Lorenzano, 'Zapatismo: Recomposition of Labour, Radical Democracy and Revolutionary Project', in Holloway and Peláez (eds), *Zapatista!: Reinventing Revolution in Mexico*, p. 127.

40 M. Löwy, *The Marxism of Che Guevara*, pp. 13–14.

41 Ibid., p. 17.

42 Lorenzano, 'Zapatismo', p. 130.

43 Holloway and Peláez (eds), *Zapatista!: Reinventing Revolution in Mexico*, p. 7. Indeed, these three terms are strongly emphasised in Subcomandante Marcos's speeches. Many of his speeches end with the triptych: 'Democracy! Liberty! Justice!' See: Subcomandante Marcos, *Our World Is Our Weapon: Selected Writings* (New York: Seven Stories Press, 2002).

44 R. Debray, 'A Guerrilla with Difference', in Hayden (ed.), *The Zapatista Reader*, p. 129.

45 Notes from Everywhere (ed.), *We Are Everywhere: The Irresistible Rise of Global Capitalism* (London: Verso), p. 21.

46 N. Klein, 'Reclaiming the Commons', in T. Mertes, *A Movement of Movements* (London: Verso, 2004), pp. 81–7.

47 J. Couch, 'Imagining Zapatismo: The Anti-globalisation Movement and the Zapatistas', *Communal/Plural*, 9: 2 (2001), p. 244.

48 Ibid.

49 J. Simon, 'The Marcos Mystery: A Chat with the Subcommander of Spin', in Hayden (ed.), *The Zapatista Reader*, p. 45.

50 Ibid., p. 47.

51 Ibid., p. 47.

52 R. Debray, 'A Guerrilla with Difference', p. 342.

53 M. Horkheimer, 'The Authoritarian State', in A. Arato and E. Gebhardt (eds), *The Essential Frankfurt School Reader* (New York: Urizen Books, 1978), p. 112.

54 Régis Debray, 'A Guerrilla with Difference', p. 347.

3

'When it bleeds, it leads': death and press photography in the anti-capitalist protests in Genoa 2001

AN international protest was organised to coincide with the G8 summit taking place in Genoa from the 19 to 22 July 2001. The decision to mobilise an international protest was taken a year before at the World Social Forum (WSF) in Porto Allegre in Brazil, and was put into practice by the Genoa Social Forum (GSF) and over 800 international organisations and various groups.[1] The protest events gained their significance, if not their notoriety, not from the numbers of protesters, but from the intense preparations of the Italian government to keep the protesters away from the summit, the violence of some protesters and, more importantly, from the culmination in police violence with the shooting of a young protester by a member of the carabinieri, the Italian military police force.

The afternoon of 20 July 2001, when the young protester, Carlo Giuliani, was shot dead, was arguably a turning point for the anti-capitalist movement. Dylan Martinez and Sergei Karpukhin of Reuters, Italo Banchero and Luca Bruno of the Associated Press and Jess Hurd were among the photographers who gave the world the picture of his death. These photographs are undoubtedly the most oft-reproduced photographs of the events in Genoa in 2001.[2] Photography's ability to confer on the event immortality, which it would not have had if photographers had not been present at the event, is confirmed in this case.[3] Photography not only documented Giuliani's death but it also transformed it into a symbol of the anti-capitalist protests in Genoa.

Dylan Martinez took a series of eleven pictures that depict not only the dead body but also the moments before and during his shooting. In the first pictures,

Carlo Giuliani is photographed from the back, holding a fire extinguisher and wearing a balaclava.[4] The protester seems to have lifted the object in the air and pointed it at the police's vehicle. The following pictures show Giuliani lying on the street and a police vehicle reversing over his body. The final image is of Giuliani's lying dead within a pool of blood (plate 4). Many photographers took photographs of Giuliani's dead body, but Martinez was the only photographer who also took pictures of the moments preceding his death.

David Perlmutter and Gretchen Wagner, writing on Dylan Martinez's Death in Genoa argue that the picture of Carlo Giuliani aiming a fire extinguisher at the police's vehicle, rather than the later pictures of his death or of his dead body, was the one mainly selected by the American mass media. In their own words:

> Rather than feature the scene where Giuliani lies contorted on the ground in a pool of his blood or even an image where the police jeep has backed over his body, the mainstream popular press selected the suggestive image of Giuliani.[5]

According to them, the US mass media chose this picture to represent the man's death without actually showing it. As this picture was reinserted in various newspaper contexts, often completing 'a simple narrative of protester violence, not police violence', it was open to specific interpretations.[6] This particular visual emphasis highlighted the protester's violence and not the police violence.[7] Therefore, according to Perlmutter and Wagner, the image of the young protester in conflict with the police was accorded international notoriety and acted metonymically for the greater event and the anti-capitalist movement as a whole.

The American mass media choice, which merges four days of protests in Genoa, illustrates a well-known media policy. European press coverage is strikingly different. In clear contrast with the American press, the Italian and European mainstream newspapers did reproduce the image of Giuliani's dead body endlessly. The centrality of such a photograph raises interesting questions about the reasons for this publicity, and its relationship to issues of censorship, aesthetics and the politics of the media.

An image of death

As one would have expected, the protests made the front pages only the day after Giuliani's death, on 21 July 2001, when almost all the leading national

European papers covered the protests in Genoa, and many of them chose the picture of the dead protester for their front page. Indicatively, the picture made the front page of the British newspapers *The Guardian*, *The Times* and the *Daily Telegraph*, the Spanish *El País* and *El Mundo*, the French *Libération*, the Greek *E Kathimerine* and the Italian national paper *La Stampa*.[8] It was also repeatedly reproduced in their cover stories, often as part of the series of pictures taken by Martinez.[9]

This fact should make us reconsider issues of censorship on the images of tortured and dead bodies in the Western mass media. Even in our image-saturated society, discussion in media circles and in society as a whole about what should or should not be seen by the public continues. Images of tortured and dead bodies have an uneasy position in the mass media, and are often subject to censorship. The photographs of the dead and of people jumping from the World Trade towers on 9/11 constitute an indicative example of such an act of censorship. The most important reasons for their prohibition were the maintenance of good taste along with respect for the survivors and the relatives.[10] The argument that such censorship is imposed in order to respect the relatives' rights did not apply to the photograph of the dead young protester.

On which criteria and under which circumstances, then, do contemporary mass media decide which pictures of dead people are insensitive? As Susan Sontag observes, there has always been a restriction on showing dead bodies, and, even when shown there has been an interdiction on showing their faces.[11] Abigail Solomon-Godeau argues that the prohibition of photographs of slaughtered bodies has historical links to bodily exposure and censorship.[12] While this constraint seems to have always been applied to our dead, 'this is a dignity not thought necessary to accord others'.[13] Pictures of victims of violence in remote and exotic continents or pictures of enemy dead bodies do not conform to the same rules as pictures of our own victims. The Western media tends to represent enemy casualties far more often than our own.

A recent example is the war in Iraq, where images of the bodies of enemy soldiers were transmitted and reproduced, but US soldiers' dead bodies were out of sight.[14] This contradiction became glaring when snapshots of atrocities taken on digital and mobile phone cameras were publicly circulated. Photographs of the tortured Iraqi prisoners in Abu Ghraib taken by American soldiers, which surfaced in the mass media and on the internet, contrasted with the Pentagon's policy to ban the media from taking photographs of returning American military coffins, a policy that the Bush administration reactivated just before the war in Iraq started in March 2003.[15]

But, the issues of the Third World people being depicted by the Western media and the role of media in the visual representation of pain in war, as have been discussed in the context of the wars in Iraq and Vietnam, cannot be applicable to the photograph of a dead Western protester in the anti-globalisation protests that took place in an Italian city.[16] The first self-evident difference is that torture and death at this point is not the result of an appalling war, but of a public demonstration in a democratic society. In theory, any of the Western citizens who travelled to Genoa to protest could have been in Guiliani's position. This therefore urges us to think how the European mass media represent political protest, and whether press representation of the anti-G8 protests in Genoa are indicative of a wider mass media policy.

The publication of Giuliani's photograph should be seen along with the imagery of violent protesters, increasingly dominant in the mass media. It comes as no surprise to notice that the majority of the press focused on two basic issues in their coverage of Genoa: the death of the young protester and the violence that was performed by the protesters. While in none of this coverage is the death of Giuliani directly linked to the violence of some of the protesters, the way that the photograph of his body is represented along with iconic images of burning cars and street battles between masked protesters proposes a specific reading. Snapshots depicting this violence framed Giuliani's photograph and provided the context within which the image of a young protester should be seen and understood.

Indicative is the coverage of the Italian newspaper *Il Corriere della Sera*, on 21 July. Martinez's photograph of the young man carrying an extinguisher was chosen for the front page (figure 6).[17] The photograph is a cropped version of Martinez's original picture, so that only Giuliani is seen. This version focuses more on the action of the protester rather than the police jeep in the background of the photograph. The headline 'Battaglia a Genoa, muore giovane di 23 anni' (Battle in Genoa, 23 year old young man dies) is strengthened by the subtitle 'Violenti Scontri Provocati dagli Anarchici. Carabiniere Assediato Fa fuoco, Ucciso un Manifestante' (Violent clashes provoked by anarchists. Siege policeman fires, a protester dead.)[18] What is striking is that the policeman's firing and the death of the protester are associated with the violent actions of the anarchists. On page 12 of its coverage, *Corriere della Sera* offers extensive accounts of the protester's death and the violence that occurred.

On the pages referring to Giuliani's death, Martinez's photograph of his dead body is published twice.[19] The second time, the photograph is seen along with the other five pictures of Martinez. On the next page, a report on Black Block (BB) is accompanied by photographs of hooded protesters acting violently

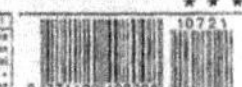

CORRIERE DELLA SERA

Fondato nel 1876

SABATO 21 LUGLIO 2001 — ANNO 126 — N. 172
Lire 2.000* Euro 1,14 (*con «la stampa»)

Saccheggi, auto in fiamme, centinaia di feriti per il vertice dei Grandi. L'angoscia di Berlusconi e Ciampi. Oggi nuovo corteo dei contestatori

Battaglia a Genova, muore giovane di 23 anni

Violenti scontri provocati dagli anarchici. Carabiniere assediato fa fuoco, ucciso un manifestante

IL GIORNO DOPO
di FERRUCCIO DE BORTOLI

Il pomeriggio di sangue genovese lascia sgomenti. Quella giovane vita spezzata sul marciapiede di una città tanto bella quanto spettrale agita nelle nostre menti antichi fantasmi, ricordi brucianti dell'inutilità di ogni violenza. Sfugge il senso delle cose davanti alle immagini di tanti volti feriti, coperti da fazzoletti e passamontagna o celati da caschi e visiere d'ordinanza. Giovani della stessa età che si sono confrontati in un'assurda guerriglia urbana, ragazzi che probabilmente, fuori da questo surreale teatro di violenza, avrebbero intrecciato amicizie, condiviso sentimenti, convenuto su molti dei temi all'ordine del giorno del vertice del G8, dalla lotta alla povertà, alle campagne contro l'Aids, alle disuguaglianze sociali. E che invece oggi di nuovo schierati gli uni di fronte agli altri, speriamo senza ulteriori conseguenze, coltiveranno nei loro animi altre incomprensioni, risentimenti, persino odio.

re incidenti e disordini. Guerrieri fanatici nel loro credo antiglobale più interessati alla riuscita delle loro inconsulte azioni che alle sorti dei poveri e degli oppressi che ambiscono a rappresentare. Mischiati a tanti altri giovani — la stragrande maggioranza, oggi ugualmente sconvolti e schiacciati dalle emozioni — che avevano l'unica legittima aspirazione di gridare la loro voglia di un mondo migliore. E per questo sono stati ascoltati e sono diventati protagonisti di un summit globale che mostra tutti i limiti di una formula ormai logora. La ragione ha anfitto, per fortuna, le organizzazioni di protesta più responsabili a prendere subito le distanze dalle frange violente che [...]

GENOVA — Sangue e morte a Genova nel primo giorno del G8. Un ragazzo di 23 anni è rimasto ucciso dopo che un carabiniere ha fatto fuoco negli scontri che hanno devastato la città, mentre a Palazzo Ducale il presidente del Consiglio, Silvio Berlusconi, accoglieva i leader stranieri arrivati per il vertice dei Grandi. Pesantissimo il bilancio: circa 180 feriti tra manifestanti, forze dell'ordine e giornalisti, 22 le persone ricoverate, un centinaio i fermati, di cui la metà di nazionalità straniera.

● Gli scontri. I violenti disordini sono stati provocati dai circa 400 anarchici del Black Bloc («blocco nero»), infiltratisi nel corteo di Cobas, centri sociali e Network per i diritti globali, aderenti al Genoa Social Forum. I militanti anarchici, armati di bastoni e spranghe, e preceduti da un altro gruppetto di estremisti francesi, hanno compiuto atti di vandalismo e saccheggi nell'area di piazza Giusti, piazza Manzoni, via Canevari. Auto rovesciate e bruciate, vetrine sfondate, cassonetti dati alle fiamme, lanci di pietre contro polizia e cronisti. Agenti e carabinieri caricano con idranti, lacrimogeni e manganelli. Un cellulare dei carabinieri viene «catturato» dai manifestanti violenti e dato alle fiamme.

● La tragedia. Poco prima delle 17, dopo quasi due ore di lotta, il portavoce del Genoa Social Forum invita i suoi manifestanti a lasciare le strade. Ma la battaglia riprende, e il ventitreenne Carlo Giuliani, romano residente a Genova, rimane ucciso dopo aver tentato di assaltare con alcuni compagni una jeep dei carabinieri. «Uno dei militari ha sparato, centrandolo», accusano i testimoni. Il ministero dell'Interno replica: è stata legittima difesa.

● I leader. Il presidente della Repubblica, Carlo Azeglio Ciampi, e Silvio Berlusconi hanno espresso la loro angoscia per la tragedia che ha sconvolto la prima giornata del G8. E oggi i contestatori torneranno in piazza con un nuovo corteo annunciato.

■ Da pagina 2 a pagina 9 — CONTINUA A PAGINA 2

La testimonianza
Ho sentito due colpi, è caduto poi mi hanno trascinata via
di FIORENZA SARZANINI

GENOVA — Ero con i contestatori mentre dalla camionetta dei carabinieri sono partiti due colpi di pistola. Ho visto Carlo Giuliani, quel giovane con l'estintore in mano, avvicinarsi al fuoristrada e poi cadere. Sono caduta anche io, trenta metri più in là, e i carabinieri hanno cominciato a picchiare. Un ragazzo che era con me è stato ferito alla testa, aveva il sangue che gli colava sugli occhi. Ma questo non li ha fermati. Ci colpivano con i manganelli, tiravano certi, ci sbattevano gli scudi in testa, urlavano «bastardi». Accecati dai lacrimogeni, con la gola che bruciava, non ci siamo accorti subito che per quel ragazzo dietro di noi non c'era più nulla da fare. Gli altri erano già andati via, spaventati dagli spari che sono arrivati all'improvviso.

Un fazzoletto bagnato sulla bocca, il limone spremuto sugli occhi per cercare di resistere a quel fumo che ti blocca il respiro, fino a stordirti, ciao si è cercato di fronteggiare le «cariche». Confusa tra i No Global mi sono tolta la pettorina che identifica i giornalisti per vedere quello che succederà dall'altra parte della barricata. Alle 17.30, mentre il corteo delle Tute Bianche è bloccato in via Tolemaide dallo sbarramento della polizia, [...]

CONTINUA A PAGINA 2

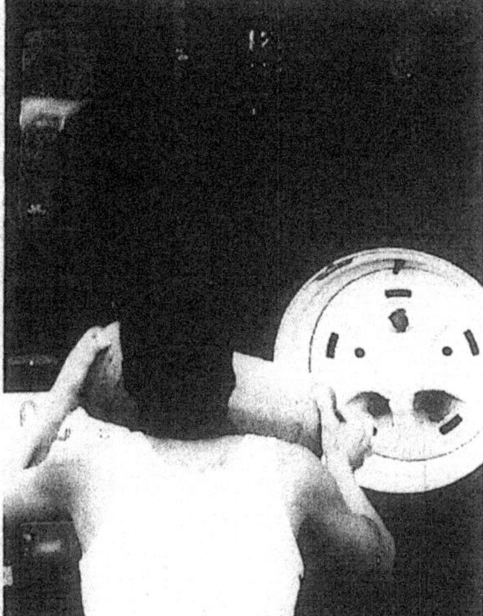

Carlo Giuliani, 23 anni, pochi istanti prima di morire. Dalla jeep un carabiniere punta la pistola (D. Martinez/Reuters)

Carlo, un corpo disteso tra bastoni e manganelli
di FABIO CAVALERA

GENOVA — Ai piedi della Chiesa del Rimedio c'è il corpo di un ragazzo su cui fari in faccia, sotto la lapide è scritto: Carlo, di vent'anni, caduto qui. Un colpo di pistola alle cinque e poco più di un giorno terribile. È inutile. Per strega? Per follia? Per paura? Pietà. L'ultima pietà, ma è stata consumata a un metro dai poveri senza possibilità alcuna di offendere. Raccontano tutti i testimoni, il fotografo porgeva Bruno Abile, Siletti e le altre foto danno che erano alla finestra del numero 4 di piazza Alimonda. Il barista Nicles per due volte ha comandato dai carabinieri e passata sopra a quel corpo. [...]

CONTINUA A PAGINA 3

«Blocco nero» all'attacco Devastata mezza città
di MARCO IMARISIO

GENOVA — Comincia tutto con un ragazzo vestito di nero che spunta dai tuffi nei giardini di piazza Da Novi. Dietro, altri seguiti a lui.

Sono le 11.30. Tirano fuori le mazze e iniziano a spaccare le piastrelle del selciato. Le raccolgono e le tirano sui cassonetti che hanno appena finito di rovesciare. Sotto un albero, tre ragazzi confezionano una ventina di molotov. «Voi chi è... siete?», chiedono quelli dei Cobas che in quella piazza hanno fissato il loro raduno. Non rispondono. [...]

CONTINUA A PAGINA 5

Duello tra i Poli dopo la tragedia. Fini: il ministro resterà al suo posto

«Hanno sparato per difendersi»

Scajola giustifica le forze dell'ordine. L'opposizione: si dimetta

GENOVA — «Sono stati attaccati e si sono difesi». Con il Viminale, annuncio che il giovane manifestante è stato ucciso da un carabiniere, racconta la dinamica dell'episodio. È la morte del ventitreenne militante anti-globalizzazione diventa un elemento che investe il governo. «Bisogna se ne deve andare», proiestano sia in molte Bifurcazione e Verdi. «Il ministro dell'Interno risarcì al suo posto: qui manifestanti volevano linciarlo e il carabiniere si è difeso, e la risposta immediata del vicepremier Gianfranco Fini. Gli fa eco il ministro degli Esteri Renato Ruggiero. «Siamo stati attaccati, ci siamo difesi. Se gli agenti hanno usato la forza lo hanno fatto perché non stati aggrediti». L'Ulivo chiede che il vertice dei Grandi venga sospeso. I Ds impongono che non partecipano alla manifestazione di oggi. Il ministro dell'Interno ha riferito saltato lunedì e Violante e Mancino insorgono: basta. È troppo serio. Il ministro, verrà oggi a raccontare che cosa è successo.

■ Alle pagine 10 e 11

LE TUTE E LE DIVISE
di GIAN ANTONIO STELLA

GENOVA — «Potevo essere tuo fratello! Giuliano! Giuliani di tutti poteva essere vostro fratello». Urlavano le sei di sera, il corpo del ragazzo morto era steso a terra, c'era tanti fili di bruciato e immondizia c'era amore e lacrimogeni e giovani piombati sulla piazza in silenzio spaventoso e incredulo. Resto solo da un singhiozzo, un lamento, un grido isolato. Di più, spaventati e scossi, i ragazzi venuti a urlare contro il G8. Di là, spaventati e scossi, i ragazzi in divisa. Faccia a faccia.

Annientati torti dall'enormità di ciò che era appena successo. Eppure abissalmente lontani. [...]

CONTINUA A PAGINA 6

I leader annunciano uno stanziamento di 2.600 miliardi di lire, per Kofi Annan serve molto di più

«Un fondo dei ricchi per la lotta all'Aids e alle malattie»

GENOVA — Un fondo di un miliardo 200 milioni di dollari (oltre 2.600 miliardi di lire) per «la salute e la lotta all'Aids», disponibile subito. Lo stanziamento, al quale l'Italia contribuirà con 440 miliardi di lire, è stato reso noto dai Grandi nel primo giorno del G8 ed è stato l'annuncio politicamente più significativo nel programma del vertice, dove per la prima volta sono stati invitati al summit leader di Paesi in via di sviluppo. Di fronte all'emergenza del virus che ha devastato l'Africa e molte altre aree del Pianeta — ma anche di fronte ad altre malattie come malaria e tubercolosi — i Paesi del G8 (Canada, Francia, Germania, Giappone, Gran Bretagna, Italia, Russia, Usa) sono pronti a integrare il fondo fino a raggiungere i 4 mila miliardi di lire entro la fine dell'anno. Di fronte al dramma dell'Aids la comunità internazionale si è data come obiettivo garantire che tutti i malati possano evitare l'infezione; evitare la trasmissione del virus tra la madre e il feto; fornire una terapia a tutti i malati; raddoppiare gli sforzi di ricerca per un vaccino; assistere le vittime indirette, come gli orfani. Ma per tutto questo, dice il segretario generale dell'Onu, Kofi Annan, occorre molto di più: fino a 10 miliardi di dollari all'anno.

Per il resto, nel documento economico che deve riassumere le conclusioni del G7 fra prima parte della riunione, servono la Russia) non ci sono state novità significative nei confronti dei Paesi in via di sviluppo. I Grandi non hanno preso nuovi impegni sul fronte della riduzione del debito di là di quelli già assunti in precedenza. Niente di concreto anche per due Paesi che stanno attraversando in questo momento una difficile crisi finanziaria: l'Argentina e la Turchia. Il comunicato finale si limita a indicare le dure misure di austerità adottate in quelle nazioni «rappresentano passi positivi nella buona direzione».

■ Alle pagine 12 e 13

IMPEGNI E ILLUSIONI
di SERGIO ROMANO

Sembra che i contestatori del G8 abbiano già ottenuto un primo successo. Agenda sulle preoccupazioni e, forse, sulla novità dei suoi membri si hanno comunci a considerarsi «povero del mondo» e a concentrarsi sul loro ordine del giorno sui temi «globali» per cui si manifesta nelle strade e nelle piazze di Genova: cancellazione dei debiti, lotta contro l'Aids e altre grandi malattie del continente africano, programmi di sviluppo [...] luppo. Anziché replicare che il G8, nella migliore delle ipotesi, è soltanto un club delle maggiori potenze industriali, con responsabilità e poteri limitati, i grandi hanno assunto un impegno e hanno accettato di essere giudicati, alla fine dei lavori, per il modo in cui avranno affrontato quegli temi. Potrebbe essere un passo sulla strada della globalizzazione governata.

CONTINUA A PAGINA 13

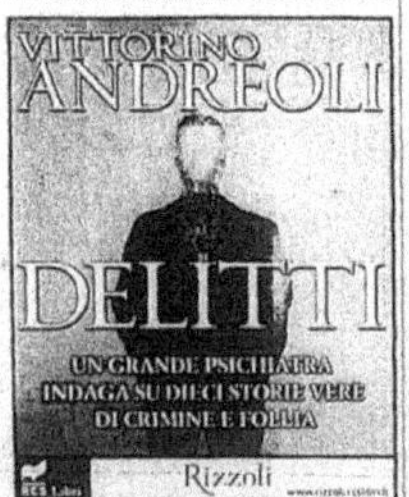

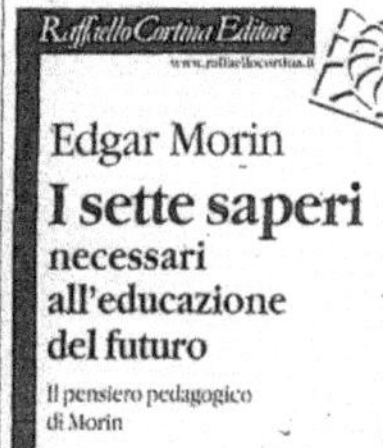

6 *Il Corriere della Sera*, 21 July 2001, p. 1 (© RCS Media Group)

and clashing with the police. The first photograph, which depicts a member of the BB throwing a stone, is a frequent stereotypical photojournalistic snapshot. The second photograph shows the arrest of a protester who is lying on the ground surrounded by policemen. The long article explains their actions, while a third photograph of a BB member is followed by a detailed description of the group, under the titles: 'Black Block', 'How They Move', 'The Formation', 'The History', 'Where They Are'.[20]

In total contrast to this extensive coverage of the BB, a very short article on the non-violent groups was published on the next page.[21] Entitled 'Pallottole Contro i Non Violenti, Indisturbati i Duri' (Bullets Against the Non-Violent, the Tough Undisturbed), the article provides the views of Luca Casarini and Vittorio Agnolleto, spokespersons of Tute Bianche (White Overalls) and Social Forum respectively. They confirmed that the BB used weapons that were banned by the central organisation of the protests. Unlike the full page coverage of the Black Block, the article only occupies one third of the page, while the Genoa Social Forum and the Tute Bianche are very briefly introduced. Interestingly, the photograph published alongside this article shows a nude protester wearing a mask, posing in front of an unclear background, while the smoggy atmosphere is reminiscent of turbulence. The other two photographs published on the same page depict moments of arrests of protesters by the police.

This explicit difference between the coverage of the BB and the non-violent groups can be more easily understood if we decipher the role that these groups played in the organisation of the protests. The BB is not an organisation, but a small group of young protesters, who dress in black and wear black masks in a militant style, and campaign violently against symbols of capitalism. Consisting of very young people, mainly members of groups that focus on radical forms of conflict, such as the Autonomen in Germany or the Basque borrokas, the BB targets cars, shops and especially banks and transnational stores as a symbolic act. According to BB protesters, property destruction as a protest tactic:

> brings the media to the scene and it sends a message that seemingly impervious corporations are not impervious. People at the protest, and those at home watching on TV, can see that a little brick, in the hands of a motivated individual, can break down a symbolic wall. A broken window at Nike Town is not threatening to people's safety.[22]

In this context, violence is perceived as a form of interaction, of communication and cultural expression in the most visually powerful way. Writing about how protest violence can be seen as meaningful, anthropologist Jeffrey Juris called this violence 'performative' and defined it as:

> a mode of communication through which activists seek to effect social transformation by staging symbolic confrontation based on the representation of antagonistic relationships and the enactment of prototypical images of violence.[23]

While some theorists may regard 'performative violence' as meaningful, the majority of participants in the anti-capitalist movement consider it senseless and irrational, since they prefer 'nonviolence as both an option of value and a strategic choice'.[24] Moreover, according to interviews conducted during the Genoa events, 90 percent of the protesters in Genoa denied any involvement in violent tactics.[25] Instead, references to Martin Luther King and Gandhi are recurrent in various groups that seek to develop non-violent methods.[26] Among hundreds of other groups, Rete Lilliput, ATTAC and Tute Bianche define their direct actions and their civil disobedience as non-violent.

All these groups, under the central organisation of the GSF, decided on many different repertoires of action during the G8 summit in Genoa. They planned an International Forum to take place from the 15 to 22 July, a march in support of the rights of migrants for the 19 July and a mass demonstration for the 21 July.[27] Rete Lilliput members painted their hands white to demonstrate the non-violent nature of their actions, while ATTAC, along with Left-wing political parties and trade unions, held balloons, banners, eggs and music, which echoed the RTS Global Street Parties.

While in the beginning these groups tolerated BB actions in the name of pluralism, the negative coverage that their protests received urged activists to rethink their principles. This had the result that within the movement:

> violent repertoires have become increasingly stigmatized both in principle (seen as a form of accepting the violence of the system and even more as a behaviour akin to war) and for their practical effects in isolating protest.[28]

As a result, this denunciation of violence was synonymous with the deterioration of the relationship between the BB with other groups before the Genoa protest. Even more specifically, some BB group members stayed outside of the GSF.[29] Studies of the events showed that the isolation of the BB affected the movement negatively:

Isolating the BB, however, has meant that the non-violent demonstrators were left with less negotiating power over the more radical groups. Characterised by a very loose coordination and increasingly hostile to the movement, the BB have often spurned even minimal non-belligerent pacts (and in Genoa sometimes attacked demonstrators as well as trying to invade the headquarters of GSF).[30]

BB direct action did not target only symbols of capitalism in Genoa, but also small shops, private cars or in extreme cases even other demonstrators.

The point is that the majority of the images published in the Corriere della Sera depicted protesters in clashes with the police, throwing stones and Molotov cocktails, breaking shop windows, or under arrest. Most of these pictures depicted BB actions, which means that they represented a small and marginalised group of a large diverse movement. None of the press coverage made clear the distinction between the BB and the rest of the movement. This identification of the BB with the movement as a whole reflects the governmental view. The day after the raid on Diaz School, Prime Minister Berlusconi declared that it was not possible to distinguish between the GSF and the BB.[31] All the demonstrations and other events that were organised by the central organisational committee, the GSF and other non-violent groups, were not even mentioned in the coverage, nor were they depicted photographically.

Nor were there any depictions of the excessive police violence in Genoa. A typical example is the violent raid on Diaz School, a dormitory for peaceful activists, and the Indymedia centre on the evening of 21 July. The police burst in with the ostensible purpose of searching for weapons and confronting the BB. Instead, they wielded truncheons, beat half-alseep and helpless activists, kicked and humiliated them in a performance of extraordinary violence. Most of the activists, detained and arrested in the building, were injured, some of them seriously. In the Indymedia centre, computers and videos were destroyed and printed material was taken away. The injured were taken to the San Marino hospital and the rest of them arrested and taken to the detention centre in the city's Bolzaneto district. The injured and the arrested were mistreated by the police, and especially the latter who were humilated, sprayed with irritants, forced to stand for hours and compelled to sing fascist slogans and songs.

According to most of the arrested activists, all this was an exercise in creating fear, a rather successsful one. As Davies writes, 'In statements, prisoners later described their feeling of helplessness, of being cut off from the rest of the world in a place where there was no law and no rules.'[32] All of them were charged with 'aggressive resistance to arrest and conspiracy to cause destruction'.[33] Seven years later, activists and public prosecutor Emilio Zucca are still seeking justice. Zucca and Mark Covell, one of the victims, have collected 5,000 hours of video, thousands of photographs and hundreds of witness reports in their effort to shed light on the events. Police officers, however, were unable to evade discipline or criminal charges, and, finally, in June 2008, police officers were put on trial for their part in the raids of 21 June 2001. The politicians responsible for the police never made any apologies.

This story never made mainstream news coverage; only a few distorted accounts were published. Davies highlights how Covell, one of the victims of police violence that night, was presented on the *Daily Mail* front page 'as having helped mastermind the riots' – a false report for which the newspaper 'eventually apologised and paid Covell damages for invasion of privacy', though only four years later.[34] Activists' efforts to make the story known can be found on activist webpages and blogs on the internet. Joel Sternfeld photographed the aftermath of the police raid on Diaz School, and his published book offers an alternative view, as it will be discussed in Part III.[35]

Similarly, *La Stampa* on 21 July focused on the same two issues: the death of Giuliani and the violence of the BB protesters. The coverage, shorter than *Corriere De La Sera*'s, is divided into equal parts: a page is devoted to Giuliani, illustrated with Martinez's photographs, and another to the BB, illustrated with photographs of destruction. The only other photographs in both newspapers are photographs of politicians. On *La Stampa*'s first page a photograph of Italian Prime Minister Silvio Berlusconi and Italian banker and politician Carlo Azeglio Campi are printed just underneath three photographs by Martinez.

An example from the British press reveals similarities in the way the Genoa protests were covered. In the *Daily Telegraph*, on 21 July, Martinez's photograph is on the front page with the title 'Protester pays with his Life' and followed with the subtitle 'Police open fire as violence erupts at Genoa' (figure 7).[36] In the two pages of coverage that follow, the first is covered with a photograph of protesters 'ready for a battle' and the other one with four photographs of the Martinez's series. The protesters depicted wear helmets and masks, carry shields and look ready for conflict and damage. The caption accompanying the picture refers to an anarchist's opinion: 'It's like being with a Roman legion'.[37] The four pictures show the murder of the protester in four stages. The caption informs us about the stages: 'A shot is fired, he falls to the ground, and then the vehicle reverses over him.'[38] Although the death of the young protester is shown as a result of the protesters' preparation to be involved in a 'battle' with the police,

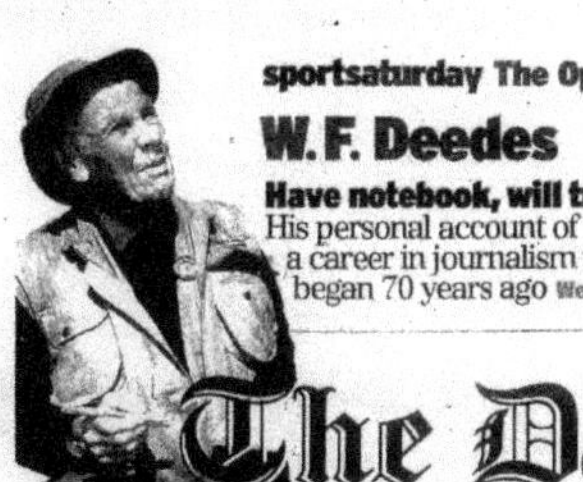

Protester pays with his life

● Police open fire as violence erupts at Genoa ● Future of 'rich club' summits thrown into doubt

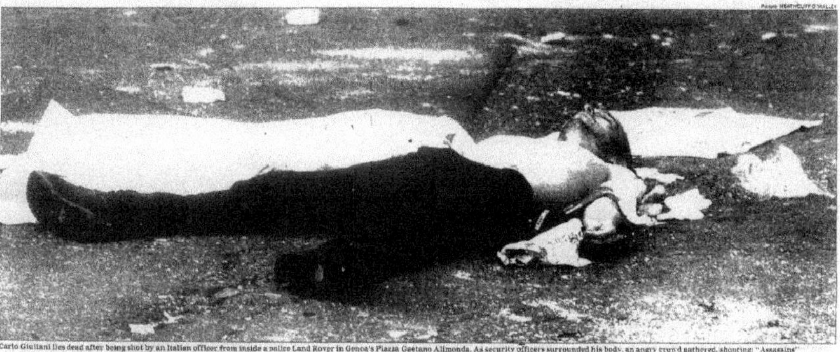

Carlo Giuliani lies dead after being shot by an Italian officer from inside a police Land Rover in Genoa's Piazza Gaetano Alimonda. As security officers surrounded his body, an angry crowd gathered, shouting: "Assassins"

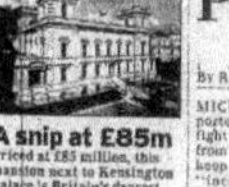

Portillo supporters to fight on

By Rachel Sylvester

Widdecombe happy to be out in the cold

By David Millward

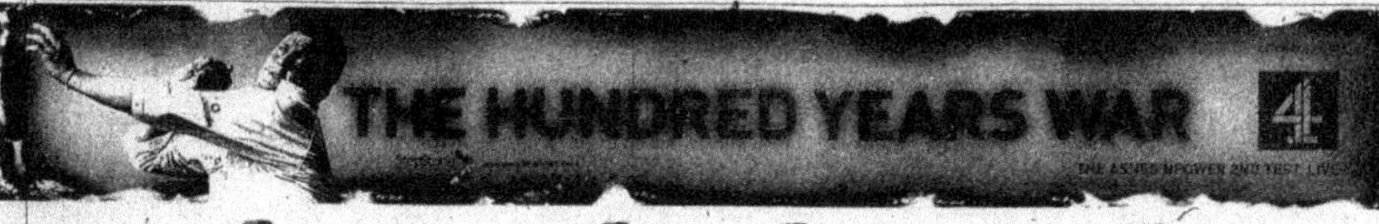

7 *Daily Telegraph*, 21 July 2001, p. 1 (© Telegraph Media Group Limited 2001)

no evidence is given that Giuliani was part of the specific group, neither was he dressed as the BB protesters were. The article seems to imply: 'this can happen to any one of these protesters', linking their preparation for a conflict with the death of one of them. That is the implicit message in the article, while in the same pages a more secure alternative is proposed. The advertisements at the bottom of the pages suggest another way of life. You can plan your summer holidays now, save money for this reason. You can also register for more television channels and spend peaceful and serene family moments distant from any violence and risk to yourself.

A vulgar juxtaposition of a photograph showing BB members and the prime ministers Tony Blair and Silvio Berlusconi, expresses the recurrent themes in the coverage of the protests. The photographs in the *Daily Telegraph* are followed by an article which reports on the initiatives taken by the leaders to increase the funds to combat AIDS and other diseases in Africa. The bigger picture on the same page shows the other side of the coin. Some masked protesters stand between barricades and smoke and the title reads 'The road to anarchy'.[39]

In the majority of the photographs published on these days, the policemen are not visible. Neither are the thousands of protesters who were in Genoa and demonstrated peacefully. This is indicative of the ideology pervading the media today, which prioritises commerciality. Any 'serious' analysis of the anti-globalisation movement is really far from commercial, not to say quite 'dangerous', while what bleeds, 'runs the venerable guideline of tabloids and twenty-four headline news shows'.[40] That is why the image of Carlo Giuliani's dead body made front pages all over the world on 21 July 2001.

While one of the reasons for publishing this photograph is that it fits well into the narrative about protest violence, it seems the image contains some iconic power, which can easily be recognised by newspaper editors. This may be due to association with other iconic images of dead bodies of people who had participated in earlier social struggles and political protests. The best-known is that of Che Guevara's corspe laid out on a concrete slab in Bolivia, produced for the world as evidence of his death, hours after his murder. The fallen Che Guevara was depicted surrounded by the Bolivian military officers who had captured and killed him. Che Guevara, who was shown with his eyes open, was compared to images of Christ in Western art.[41] Another is John Paul Filo's 'Kent State – Girl Screaming over Dead Body' taken on 4 May 1970. The picture is of the dead body of a student protester and of a girl screaming above him. The popularity that these pictures have obtained becomes obvious in their continuous reproductions in newspapers, on posters, T-shirts, record album covers. Filo's picture not only became the symbol of the American anti-war movement, but contributed to the revival of the movement with a new wave of demonstrations across the United States and Europe.[42] They both inspired protesters all over the world, not only in the 1960s and in the 1970s, but also in the following decades.

The fact that these images were easily recognisable in different contexts, provoked sentimental responses of millions of people and were effortlessly associated with a specific period of time reveals their unquestionable power.[43] The photograph of Giuliani was immediately used by activists on posters and flags as well as on the organisations' websites. Within the movement there are continual references to him: a flourishing body of literature and filmmaking has arisen around his image.[44] His death not only shocked the participants in the demonstrations of Genoa but also raised a movement of solidarity, provoking demonstrations all over Europe. Photographs of Carlo Giuliani acquired a symbolic impact on the protesters, creating an effortless connection to the protests of Genoa. In the European Social Forum that took place in Florence in November of 2002, huge numbers of trades unionists, peace campaigners, socialists, environmentalists, anti-racists and many more from all over the world travelled to Florence to take part in the conferences, to discuss and debate and participate in the anti-war demonstration. The Forum with its slogan 'Another World is Possible'[45] dealt with issues such as neoliberalism, imperialism, war, racism, social and political rights and the environment.[46] In the central entrance of the Forum, there was a huge photographic portrait of Carlo Giuliani. The photograph was not accompanied by any caption. Inside the building an exhibition of photographs of Genoa was held. A section was devoted to photographs of Carlo Guiliani. The majority of them were images of his dead body taken from different angles.

The activists attempt was to offer an alternative visual story from the one reproduced in the mass media, where spectacular images of violent confrontation between protesters and the police or images of destroyed property are valued as newsworthy and as such are favoured in the press coverage of the Genoa events. Photojournalism failed to represent the diversity that the movement experienced in Genoa, through a combination of diverse groups, direct action, small events, demonstrations and independent media. A cluster of different ideological groups and traditions from Europe and the United States addressing a great variety of issues have been reduced to images of violence. The majority of the protesters who decided on non-violent action were neglected and mostly out of sight. In the same way, images of carnival and giant puppets that were dominant both in the events in Genoa did not find their way into the mass media. Moments of peaceful demonstrations and debate have been left out of sight. Their visual representation was never considered, since debate is certainly less photographic than violence and it did not fit the dominant ideology of the contemporary mass media. Therefore, the readers of the mainstream press could not be informed about the movement's demands and goals. Even fewer people have read any writings about the organisations that took part in the events and their ideology. However, a great number of people may have encountered the photograph of the protester who was shot dead by the police in the demonstrations.

The question that is raised next is whether shock, fear or even sympathy for the young protester's death can be transmitted into thought, critique and understanding not only of the events in Genoa and the anti-capitalist movement but of contemporary politics as well. The picture itself cannot teach us anything, cannot carry any information about the movement itself. Neither can the picture alone act as motivation for reacting against the status quo or for participating in subsequent protests. As the viewers become more and more familiar with the image, the picture does not have an impact on them any more. In Susan Sontag's words:

> The vast photographic catalogue of misery and injustice throughout the world has given us a certain familiarity with atrocity. Making the horrible seem even more ordinary, making it appear familiar, remote ('it's only a photo'), inevitable.[47]

This picture is not anything more than a picture of a dead person whose death is presented as a rational result of the protesters' violence during the events. Other readings of his death, as a result of the excessive violence by the Italian police force, that were presented in the alternative media were never presented, excluding the other readings of his death from the mainstream accounts.

Notes

1 D. della Porta, M. Andretta, L. Mosca and H. Reiter (eds), *Globalization from Below: Transnational Activists and Protest Networks* (Minneapolis, MN: University of Minnesota Press, London, 2006), p. 3.

2 The photographs have been reproduced broadly and in different contexts. Martinez's and Karpukhin's, Banchero's and Bruno's photographs were mostly distributed in the mass and online media. Jess Hurd's photograph of dead Carlo Giuliani was selected for the John Kobal photographic awards at the National Gallery in London and was exhibited in

many exhibitions including Jess Hurd's *Rebel Flower* exhibition at the Foundry, Shoreditch London, August 2005. See: www.jesshurd.com/.

3 S. Sontag, *On Photography* (Harmondsworth: Penguin, 1979), p. 11.

4 Most of the accounts refer to the object that Giuliani was holding as a fire extinguisher. See: R. Carroll, 'The Wild Boy who Became a Martyr', *The Observer* (22 July 2001), www.guardian.co.uk/world/2001/jul/22/globalisation.businessandmedia (accessed 19/03/2012). Internet discussions have characterised the object otherwise, and it is unclear how Giuliani obtained it. D. Perlmutter and G. Wagner, 'The Anatomy of a Photojournalistic Icon: Marginalization of Dissent in the Selection and Framing of "a Death in Genoa"', *Visual Communication*, 3: 1 (2004), p. 104.

5 Ibid., p. 102.

6 Ibid.

7 Ibid., p. 100.

8 *The Guardian* (21 July 2001), *The Times* (21 July 2001), *Daily Telegraph* (21 July 2001), *El País* (21 July 2001); *El Mundo* (21 July 2001); *Libération* (21 July 2001); *Η Καθημερινή* (21 July 2001) and *La Stampa* (21 July 2001).

9 Just to state some of the newspapers that reproduced the image in their cover stories: *The Guardian* (21 July 2001), p. 5, *El País* (21 July 2001), p. 3, *La Corriere della Sera* (21 July 2001), p. 23, *La Corriere della Sera* (23 July 2001), pp. 2–3, *La Republicca* (22 July 2001), pp. 7–8, *La Stampa* (21 July 2001), p. 3, *La Stampa* (22 July 2001), p. 7, *Η Καθημερινή* (21 July 2001), p. 3, *Le Figaro* (21 July 2001), p. 2, *L' Humanité* (23 July 2001), p. 5.

10 For a discussion of the censorship of the photographs of 11 September, see both S. Sontag, *Regarding the Pain of the Others* (London: Penguin Books, 2003), pp. 61–5; A. Solomon-Godeau, 'Remote Control', *Art Forum* (2004), pp. 61–4.

11 Sontag, *Regarding the Pain of the Others*, p. 63.

12 Solomon-Godeau, 'Remote Control', p. 61.

13 Sontag, *Regarding the Pain of the Others*, p. 63.

14 For a relevant discussion, see: J. Stallabrass, 'Not in Our Name', *Art Monthly*, 293 (2006), pp. 1–4; Solomon-Godeau, 'Remote Control', pp. 61–4.

15 S. Gay Stolberg, 'Senate Backs Ban Photos of G.I. Coffins', *New York Times* (22 June 2004), www.nytimes.com/2004/06/22/us/senate-backs-ban-on-photos-of-gi-coffins.html (accessed 19/03/2012).

16 For more on war, photography and trauma, see: H. Bresheeth, 'Projecting Trauma: War Photography and the Public Sphere', *Third Text*, 20 (2006), pp. 57–71.

17 *La Corriere della Sera* (21 July 2001), p. 1.

18 Ibid.

19 *La Corriere della Sera* (21 July 2001), pp. 2–3.

20 The titles in Italian read: 'I Black Bloc', 'Come Se Muovono', 'La Formazione', 'La Storia', 'Dove Sono', *La Corriere della Sera* (21 July 2001), p. 5.

21 *Il Corriera della Sera* (21 July 2001), p. 6.

22 Black Block, *International Genoa Offensive*, July 2001, at www.nadir.org/nadir/aktuell/2001/07/18/5040.html (accessed 20/05/2007).

23 J. S. Juris, 'Violence Represented and Imagined: Young Activists, the Black Block, and the Mass Media in Genoa', Imaging Social Movements, Second International Conference,

The Social and Cultural Movements Group, Edge Hill College, UK, 1–3 July 2004, www.edgehill.ac.uk/Research/smg/Conferences2004/info/agenda.htm (accessed 30/05/2006).

24 della Porta *et al.* (eds), *Globalisation from Below*, p. 133.
25 Ibid.
26 Ibid.
27 Ibid., pp. 138–41.
28 Ibid., p. 120.
29 Ibid., p. 137.
30 Ibid.
31 D. della Porta, A. Peterson and H. Reiter (eds), *The Policing of Transnational Protest* (Albershot: Ashgate, 2006), p. 22.
32 N. Davies, 'The Bloody Battle of Genoa', *The Guardian* (17 July 2008).
33 Ibid.
34 Ibid.
35 J. Sternfeld, *Treading on Kings: Protesting the G8 in Genoa* (Göttingen: Steidl Publishers, 2002).
36 *Daily Telegraph* (21 July 2001), p. 1.
37 Ibid., p. 4.
38 Ibid., p. 5.
39 Ibid., p. 4.
40 Sontag, *Regarding the Pain of Others*, p. 16.
41 J. Berger, 'Che Guevara Dead', *Aperture*, 13: 4 (1968).
42 S. Kasher, *The Civil Rights Movement: A Photographic History, 1954–68* (New York, London, Paris: Abbeville Press, 1996).
43 On the iconic power of the images, see indicatively: V. Goldberg, *The Power of Photography: How Photographs Changed Our Lives* (New York, London, Paris: Abbeville Press, 1991); R. Hariman and J. L. Lucaites, *No Caption Needed: Iconic Photographs, Public Culture and Liberal Democracy* (Chicago and London: The University of Chicago Press, 2007).
44 A growing literature in Italian about the events in Genoa and their aftermath can be found in the website of 'The Piazza Carlo Guilliani O.N.L. U.S. Committee: www.piazzacarlogiuliani.org/ (accessed 19/03/2012). Most of the books about the events in Genoa refer to Carlo Giuliani and his violent death. We could mention here just a few of them that have as their subject Carlo Giuliani such as: N. Vendola, *Lamento in Morte di Carlo Giuliani* (Agosto: Fratelli Frilli, 2001); G. Farinelli, *Il Caso Carlo Giuliani* (Antinebbia, 2002); 'Snur Cgil Universita degli Studi di Salemo', *Per non DimentiCarlo* (Gutenberg Edizioni, 2003); S. Bonsignori, *Il Caso Genova* (Manifestolibri, 2002); A. Marrone, *Un Anno Senza Carlo* (Baldini & Castoldi, 2002); and the videos: *Genova in Tre Atti*, by Regia Argomento, 2001; *Genova Libera*, by Regia Argomento, 2001; *Carlo Giuliani Ragazzo*, by Regia Argomento, 2002.
45 The slogan 'Another Way Is Possible' has been identified with the anti-globalisation movement.
46 The European Social Forum (ESF), held in Florence, Italy 7–10 November 2002, was the first Europe-wide gathering of the growing movements against neoliberalism, racism and war. The ESF was called after the success of the second World Social Forum (WSF) in

Porto Alegre, Brazil, January–February 2002 and was attended by 70,000 people. The aim of the WSF was to build a global movement that can stop militarism and the drive to war and point the way towards a world in which people come before profit, to demonstrate that 'Another World Is Possible'. The ESF's aim was to mobilise the European Community around these same principles.

47 Sontag, *On Photography*, p 21.

Part II

4

The student movement of May 1968: activist photography, self-reflection and antinomies

M AY 1968 in Paris conjures up black-and-white photographs of students demonstrating, occupying universities, constructing barricades; setting fires on street corners, throwing flaming Molotov cocktails and fighting with the police. During the events, all these photographs became available to the public through the mainstream press and the communication systems that served the movement. Nevertheless, as the events accelerated the public showed a growing mistrust towards mainstream mass media, as discussed in Part I. The student newspapers not only became then a source of information within the ranks of the movement, but were also disseminated in the occupied Sorbonne and the surroundings, reaching out to a wider public.

The student newspapers, which were published during the events namely *Action, Barricades, L' Avant Garde Jeunesse, Servir Le Peuple, Le Monde Libertaire* and *Lutte Socialiste* were, to a great extent, ephemeral publications.[1] For the period of the events, they formed the platform for the dissemination of the movement's demands. The photographs published within this context are important not least because they were chosen by the participants themselves, reflecting on their own view of the events. In this instance, photography was employed to promote the movement's vision as well as to fight back to either the absence of images in the public domain or the ambiguous imagery published in the different mainstream newspapers. It is significant to note that the majority of these photographs were not attributed to a photographer, with the exception of few instances, which urges us to focus on the decisions made about which photographs were published and the juxtaposition of these photographs with texts and headlines.

This chapter provides an analysis of the photographs published in student newspapers during May and June 1968, considering these photographs not simply as an 'exercise in nostalgia',[2] but as a path to re-explore, rethink and discuss the French May '68. The photographs chosen to be discussed are not the only pertinent examples, but they are indicative of the main recurrent themes. The discussion sheds light on the emphasis given to particular themes and the lack of emphasis given to some others, opening up the discussion about the contradictory character of the May movement and the failure of the student movement to connect with the workers' movement in an effective way.

The student movement and its publications

The events of May '68 started as a large-scale student protest. The movement was born at the Nanterre campus in March 1968 and expanded to the Sorbonne and other branches of the university on the 3 May, when a general meeting had been called to discuss the closure of Nanterre by the administration. As is well known, the government's tactics and the increasing brutality of the police contributed to the explosion of public meetings, organised action committees, vigorous demonstrations along the boulevards and the narrow streets of the Latin Quarter, widespread occupations that culminated in the highly symbolic 'night of the barricades' on the 10 May.[3]

The movement was organised by various groups and Committees and was lacking formal leadership, hierarchy and centralised structure. After the war in Algeria, the *Union des Étudiants Communistes* (UEC), the student organisation of the orthodox *Parti Communiste Français* (PCF), and the main component of the *Union Nationale des Étudiants de France* (UNEF) had gradually lost its strength and failed to attract a great number of the activist student youth.[4] Various revolutionary and sometimes conflicting groups, affiliated with Maoism, Trotskyism, anarchism and looser forms of revolutionary socialism, the *enragés*, filled the void.[5] At the dawn of the student mobilisation in May '68, the main groups were the two Trotskyist groups, *Jeunesse Communiste Révolutionnaire* (JCR) and *Fédération des Étudiants Révolutionnaires* (FER), the Maoist group *Union des Jeunesses Communistes Marxistes-Leninistes* (UJCML), the *Fédération Anarchiste* (FAF) and the small socialist group *Étudiants Socialistes Unifiés* (ESU). The newspapers run by all these groups and by *comités d'action* became the mouthpieces of the movement and circulated information about its evolution, political ideas, goals and strategies.

The movement's main paper, which became very popular and was widely disseminated during May, was *Action*. *Action* represented the *comités d'action*, which consisted of the UNEF, the *Syndicat National de l' Enseignemen Supérieur* (National Union of Higher Education, SNEsup) and the 22 March movement.[6] It often had a detachable front page that could be used as a street poster, and was notable for the absurdity, eccentricity and humour of its slogans and cartoons, frequently by Siné.[7] Siné was a French political cartoonist, well-known for his anti-colonialism and anti-capitalism, whose numerous sarcastic cartoons appeared in *Action* and *L' Enragé* during the events. *L' Enragé*, published by Siné and the French publisher Jean-Jacques Pauvert, was the 'official bulletin' of the movement.[8] *Action*'s popularity grew rapidly during May and June and provided daily information about the evolution of the events. After the decline of the movement, in the second half of 1968, *Action* 'was one of the outlawed publications particularly pursued by the government, in part because of its rapid growth from 100,000 printings of each issue to 550,000'.[9]

Barricades was published by the high-school student organisation, *Comité d' Action* Lycéens (CAL) and was circulated during May. CAL was created shortly before the May crisis as a combination of Comité Viêtnam de Base (CVB) and Comité Viêtnam National (CVN), both organisations opposing the Vietnam War.[10] Most of the members of the CAL were 'militants of far Left youth movements who had broken with young Communists because of the soft attitude of PCF towards the Vietnam War'.[11] The Trotskyist part of the movement was represented by the monthly circulated journal *L' Avant Garde Jeunesse*, which was the mouthpiece of the JCR, one of the two Trotskyist groups. The JCR exercised the greater influence on the movement, as it 'proved more open in its theoretical approach, more flexible in its tactics, more aware of the specific problems of the student movement, and as such was to exercise a greater influence during the crisis'.[12] It was among the initiators of the 22 March movement in Nanterre and without doubt played an important role in the student movement.[13] *L' Avant Garde Jeunesse* stopped being circulated in June 1968, when the group was declared illegal by the government. Smaller minorities within the movement were the Maoist, anarchist and 'socialist' groups. The Maoist group's (UJCML) journal was published by both students and workers and was called *Servir Le Peuple*.[14] The anarchist part FAF, published a newspaper called the *Le Monde Libertaire*, while the ESU, a small socialist party, and their equivalent workers' groups, published *Lutte Socialiste*.

Whereas before May these groups numbered only a hundred or so members, their numbers swelled during the events.[15] Although their initial membership might have been small, their dynamism not only significantly influenced the majority of the students, but also contributed decisively to the movement's momentum and finally to the explosion of events. Acknowledging their political divergences and ideological nuances, this part draws on the predominant student iconography and examines how the movement was self-reflected in this iconography.

Photography and self-reflection

The students' demands were not restricted to the democratisation and decentralisation of the French educational system and the subsequent ending of class bias, the modernisation of an outdated curriculum and the decrease in unemployment. Their critique moved from a critique of the university to a critique of society.[16] Their demands for radical reconstruction and democratisation touched upon every sphere of life. The students critiqued capitalism, the culture of consumption and the mass media, and questioned the oppression of women, discrimination against minorities and segregation of youth. Although their demands covered a broad range, it is this chapter's main argument that they all derived from a common basis, that is 'destructive critique'.[17] By 'destructive critique' is meant a critique that operates outside the rules, norms and limitations of liberal parliamentary democracy and seeks to demolish the status quo and all its structures of inequality, subordination and power. The student movement was ignited by the explosive power of 'destructive critique' and its characteristics, namely doubt, negation, irony and destruction. Indeed, the motto 'De omnibus dubitandum' (doubt everything) was omnipresent within the movement. The movement doubted the existing 'system of order' and therefore demanded its destruction. Nevertheless, this critique was not accompanied by a developed model for a new society. The movement's future vision was abstract as described by George Katsiaficas: 'a vision for the future where nations, hierarchies of domination, boredom, toil, and human fragmentation no longer would exist'.[18]

The target of the students was any form of power and repression as exercised and experienced in factories, schools, universities and the whole of society. Within this range of repressive forces, the police had a predominant position, personifying the oppressive and authoritarian nature of the existing government. The images of the police that were repeatedly reproduced in student publications portray them in a disapproving light. As an example from the *L' Avant Garde Jeunesse*, the two series of photographs on the edges of the two pages show policemen in aggressive positions, being violent and using tear gas. The atmosphere in most of the pictures is chaotic and the policemen are depicted either in groups ready to confront the demonstrators or individually in aggressive attitudes. In most of the photographs, the demonstrators are not seen, although their presence is implied. In the only pictures where a demonstrator is present – the first photograph of both series – the demonstrator is shown as having fallen on the street, a victim of the police's violence.

In a similar way, *Action* made the police the target of its criticism. In the first issue of the newspaper, published on the 7 May, the front page was covered by a photograph that depicted policemen blocking the entrance of the Faculté de Lettres (figure 8). The headline 'Repression: Faire Face!' (Repression: Stand up!) equates police with repression. The following article entitled 'Pourqoui nous nous battons' (This is why we fight) explains the reasons for the uprising, arguing against the misrepresentation of their mobilisation by television and radio. In

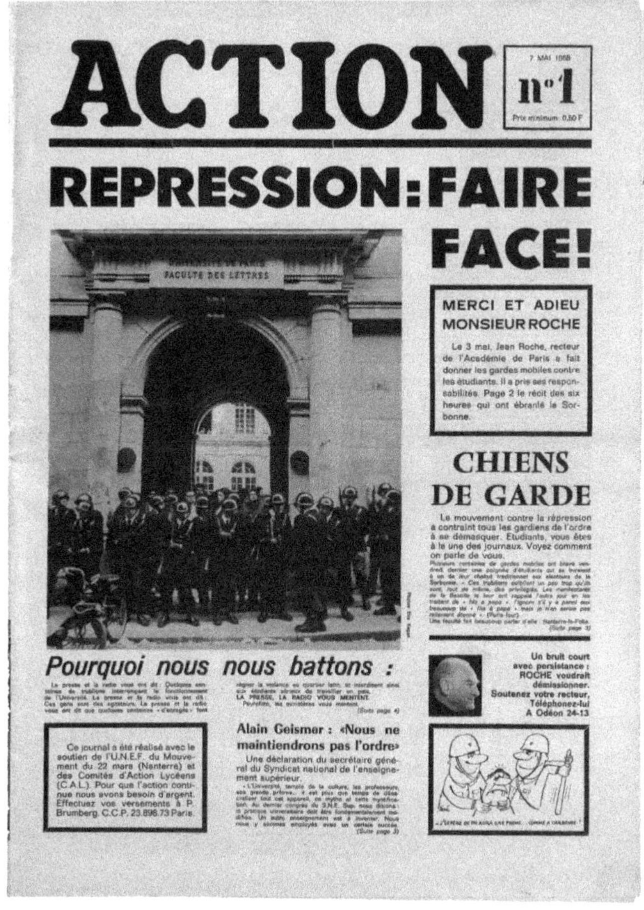

8 *Action*, No. 1, 7 May 1968, p. 1

the issues that followed, the police became the personification of an authoritarian and repressive state. Photographs of policemen brutally beating protesters with truncheons appeared in almost all the issues of *Action*.

In many cases, photographs were seen together with cartoons, most of which were explicitly ironic towards the police. Indicative is the photograph published in *Barricades* that shows a group of armed policemen beating a demonstrator. The headline 'Les Voyous' (the hooligans) creates an ironic inversion. Although the article that follows refers to the protesters who performed acts of violence during the events, the immediate connection that can be made is to relate the headline to the policemen's thuggish behaviour. This irony becomes even crueller if one takes into account the coverage by the mainstream press both of the Right and Left that accused the students for their insults, violence and irresponsible acts.[19] In contrast to these accusations, the article that accompanies the photograph in *Barricades* gives reasons for the insulting behaviour of a section of the students, presenting it as an unavoidable outcome of the social and economic inequalities of capitalist society. The cartoon underneath extends the sarcastic character of the page.

In fact, there were many examples of photographs of police being juxtaposed with cartoons that commented on their brutality. An interesting example is a photograph that was published in the first issue of *Action* (figure 9). The photograph shows policemen lined up and is taken from the back so that their faces are not visible. One cannot see any violence or conflict depicted, but only some smoke on the right of the photograph. Nevertheless, the cartoon by Siné, just above the photograph, depicts the arrest of an injured student. The drawing of one policeman with a moustache like Hitler's and the ironic dialogue 'Il était armé? Oui, chef … d'un diplôme' (Was he armed? Yes, sir … with a degree) are caustic comments on the police's extreme brutality against the students.

While negation and irony as characteristics of the students' destructive critique are depicted in many photographs, as shown in the examples from *Action*, *Barricades* and *L' Avant Garde Jeunesse*, photographs depicting violence are very rare. While there are many photographs taken by photojournalists, that show students in violent and destructive gestures, similar images are absent from student publications. An exception is a photograph published in the newspaper *Le Monde Libertaire*, where an open air meeting of high school students is depicted. The meeting numbers only a few participants and looks like a spontaneous gathering of students rather than a well-organised meeting. Although the young people seem to look in different directions, there is a speaker among them. Nevertheless, neither the gazes of the students depicted

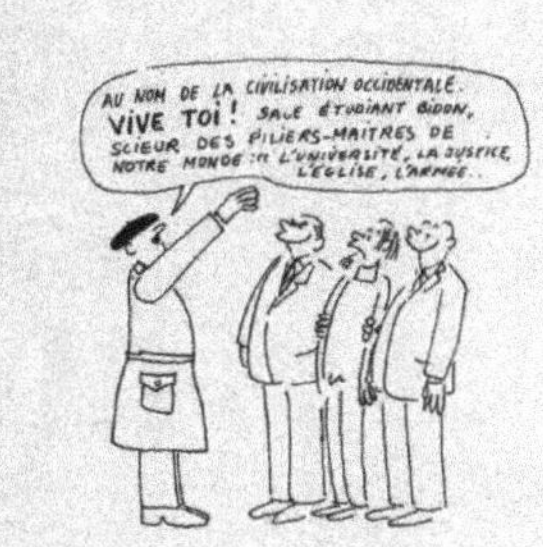

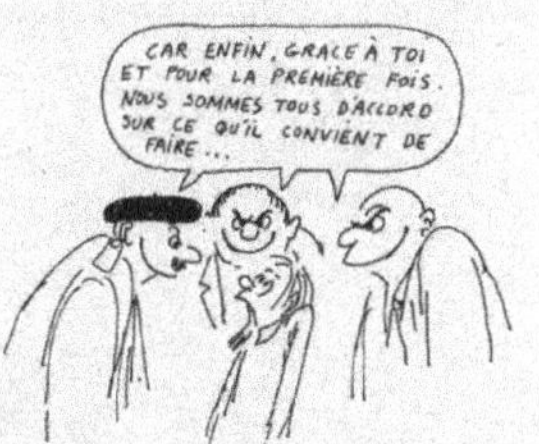

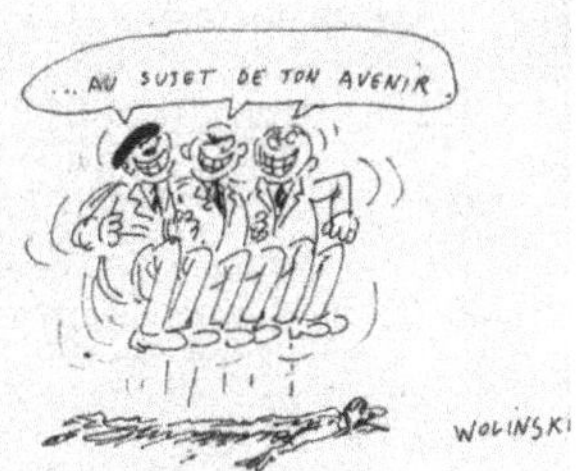

Alain Geismar "nous ne maintiendrons pas l'ordre"

Mais l'Université dans son ensemble continue d'apparaître aux étudiants les plus conscients comme une institution périmée. Ceux qu'elle forme seront, pour une part importante, des chômeurs s'ils obtiennent un diplôme ou des ratés s'ils n'en obtiennent pas. L'Université reste une institution intégrée à l'ordre social établi ; de surcroît, son fonctionnement a lieu dans les plus mauvaises conditions, étant donné les restrictions budgétaires prévues par la dernière loi de finances.

Institution qui diffuse une idéologie liée à la classe dominante et dont les produits, dans leur grande majorité, s'intègrent naturellement à l'ordre bourgeois, l'Université apparaît donc dans une large mesure comme un élément de répression. Quand elle ne parvient plus à jouer ce rôle, le pouvoir lui substitue les gardes mobiles et les mousquetons. Si les universitaires ne peuvent partager les modes d'action des étudiants — en particulier des éléments les plus avancés — ils deviennent pourtant conscients de la crise générale de l'institution. Quand la police entre à l'Université, leur solidarité apparaît nettement : face à la répression, la solidarité ne se divise pas. La place des professeurs se trouve à côté des étudiants. Assurément ils ne partagent pas toujours toutes leurs analyses et, en majorité, s'inquiètent des formes parfois prises par leur action. Mais il leur semble indécent et inimaginable de renvoyer dos à dos étudiants et policiers ou d'émettre à ce moment-là des réserves sur la solidarité. Les problèmes posés sont des problèmes de fond. La police ne les résoudra pas. La répression élargira le mouvement.

Les étudiants mettent en cause l'Université et, à travers elle, l'ordre social. Qu'une large partie de la presse tente de les discréditer, cela est banal. Que le ministre de l'Education Nationale du régime reprenne les arguments de Springer, cela est dans la logique du système. Qu'il fasse venir la police à l'Université, cela est de sa part une faute politique.

En ce qui concerne l'attitude du recteur Roche, nous rappellerons seulement qu'après avoir recouru à la police, le vice-recteur de l'Université de Madrid a démissionné sous la pression des enseignants au mois de février dernier. De son côté, le professeur Tejero, doyen de la faculté de droit, démissionnait pour protester contre la présence des forces de l'ordre dans sa faculté.

Le syndicat appelle à la Grève. Sa direction a pris ses responsabilités. Il n'était pas concevable pour des syndicalistes que l'Université accepte la situation faite aux étudiants. »

Chiens de garde

Savez-vous comment y vivent les étudiants ? au milieu de bidonvilles où croupit un sous-prolétariat, la bourgeoisie a installé toutes les commodités dues à ces fils. « Lorsqu'ils sont fatigués, les résidents de Nanterre vont se reposer dans leurs chambres. Bien modestes à leur avis. Vous savez le genre de chambre qui coûte trois mille cinq cent anciens francs la nuit dans un hôtel : grandes baies vitrées, panneaux de liège pour afficher ce qu'on veut, cabinet de toilette séparé par une cloison, eau chaude, eau froide, prise pour le rasoir électrique. Sur le palier salle de douche. Téléphone et petite cuisine avec réfrigérateur et cuisinière, et ascenseur bien sûr. Comme se sont des intellectuels, des femmes de charge s'occupent de nettoyer chaque jour chaque chambre... Le confort cinq étoiles ». (Paris-Jour) Mais aux dires du doyen Grappin, cette expérience reste un échec :

« Le mariage d'une résidence et d'une faculté s'est révélé malheureux à l'expérience. Le campus est devenu, je n'ose pas dire un chaudron de sorcière, mais un espace clos replié sur lui-même où toutes les rumeurs se sont développées ». (L'Aurore).

Les « fils à papa » méconnaissent le problème, ils insultent à la mémoire de leurs aînés qui ont tant fait de sacrifices pour leur assurer ces conditions de vie paradisiaques.

« J'ai été étudiant, moi aussi, il me semble qu'aujourd'hui les étudiants ont la vie facile. Nous n'avions pas nous — sauf quelques privilégiés de résidence universitaires — nous vivions le plus souvent dans des chambres sans feu. Nous n'avions pas de ces restaurants corporatifs où l'on peut aujourd'hui faire un repas convenable pour 1,50 F. Vos cités, pour nous, ç'aurait été le paradis. Alors travaillez et tenez-vous tranquilles. (Camille Leduc - Paris-Jour).

Mais parfois les chahuts peuvent dégénérer en drames. Les trublions s'en moquent. Ce ne sont pas eux qui payent les vitrines cassées. Le peuple est profondément désorienté, mais les bons Français veillent : ils dénoncent avec force les provocateurs qui prennent leurs directives à l'étranger.

« Certains groupuscules (anarchistes, trotskystes, maoïstes) composés en général de fils de grand bourgeois et dirigés par l'anarchiste allemand Cohn Bendit, pren-

(Suite page 4)

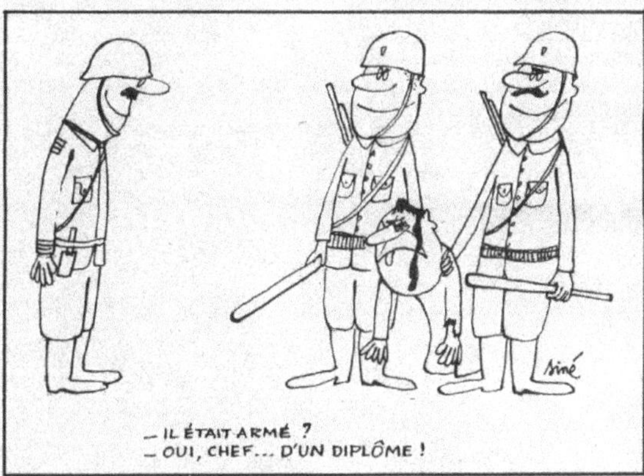

**Un autre bruit :
ROCHE avant
de démissionner
ferait appel aux C.R.S.
pour corriger
les examens.**

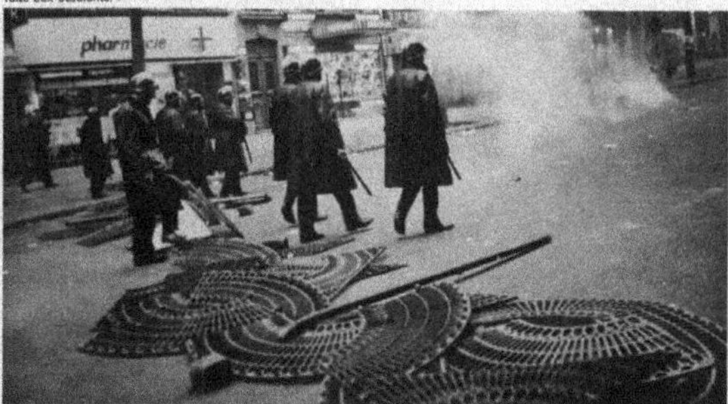

9 *Action*, No. 1, 7 May 1968, p. 3

nor the focus of the photograph directs our attention to the speaker. Instead, the picture focuses on another student who is lifting an object into the air. The student looks profoundly irritated and his gesture implies that the he is under inordinate stress. There is nothing in the picture that indicates what the student is pointing at. Nor does he seem to be confronting the police or any other material forces. Instead, he seems to be performing an act of violence without an immediate recipient. What caused this compulsive behaviour is not indicated. The photograph shows only the externalisation of repressed anger. The focus is on the violent gesture, which, compulsive, dramatic and aggressive as it is, functions as a signifier of violence.

While one can without difficulty assume that this violent gesture is the result of the repression of living with capitalist injustices and exploitation, destruction as such did not seem to be valued in the May movement. Violence was seen only as a response to police repression in street fighting and barricades. In a very well-known text entitled 'Aminstie des Yeux Crevés' ('The Amnesty of Blinded Minds') written on the 13 May by a student committee called 'Nous Sommes en Marche' ('We are on the way'), posted on the walls of the Sorbonne and later distributed as a leaflet, it was written: 'If our situation leads us to violence, it is because the whole society does violence to us.'[20] Feenberg and Freedman cite text from other leaflets that were distributed in the movement justifying protesters' violence. One, written by students to workers, states:

> Workers ... You know that violence is in the nature of the existing social order. You know that it strikes down those who dare to challenge it: the batons of the CRS answered our demands, just as the rifle butts of the Mobile Guards answered the workers of Caen, Redon and Mans.[21]

Nevertheless, while violence may have been justified verbally, there were no visual representations of the protesters' violence as opposed to numerous photographs that depicted police violence.

What is also significant about the *Le Monde Libertaire* picture is the depiction of the meeting. As in many other pictures that showed student meetings, such as the photograph published in *Action* that depicts a meeting at the occupied Sorbonne (figure 10), the meeting is not hierarchically structured. The student speaking is just one of the participants and he does not seem to have a leading role within the movement. It is true that the movement was fiercely resistant to any kind of leadership and hierarchies within the university, society and in mainstream party politics. In the student meetings, anyone could have the floor and no order or

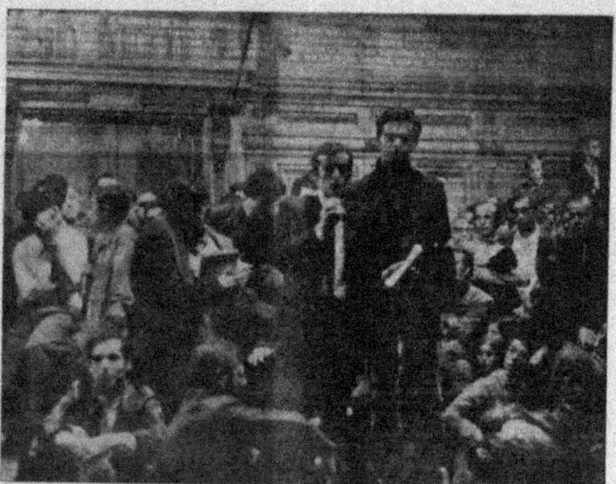

S'ORGANISER

(Suite de la première page)

organisé, deux fois par jour, dans divers salles d'une commune de banlieue des séances de cinéma révolutionnaire, etc.

De façon générale, les comités d'action visent à renforcer l'union étudiants-ouvriers, à organiser partout — dans la rue — le mouvement d'opposition au régime, à battre, dans les facultés, les tenants du réformisme universitaire et à éliminer de la scène ceux qui veulent dévoyer dans un folklore apolitique le combat engagé le 3 mai et si magnifiquement exprimé par les barricades du 10 et les occupations d'usines.

L'assemblée de dimanche, outre la désignation d'une coordination générale comportant notamment une commission organisation, une commission agitation-propagande, et une commission information, a pris une décision capitale : elle a lancé un appel à tous les comités d'action, fondé sur une base politique de lutte contre le régime qui ne sont pas encore coordonnés avec elle, ainsi qu'aux comités d'action du mouvement du 22 mars, ou à ceux coordonnés par d'autres instances pour qu'ils se réunissent JEUDI 23 MAI en une vaste assemblée constituante du mouvement des comités d'action. A cette assemblée, qui réunirait en un mouvement unique tous ceux qui étaient le vendredi 10 sur les barricades, pourraient être déterminées les bases de l'action commune à entreprendre et mis en place des formes de coordination de cette action.

CULTURE SUR LE TAS

L'action directe, remettant pratiquement en cause le système, a touché à son tour le milieu culturel. Cela a commencé par le coup de semonce de l'Odéon occupé dans la nuit du 16 au 17 mai. Puis, comme une traînée de poudre, théâtres, radios, musées, cinémas voient fleurir des comités d'action occupant des locaux parfois illustres, balayant la poussière d'une société apparemment saine, mais profondément décomposée.

Au Théâtre de France, symbole de l'avant-garde culturelle officielle du régime, le débat quoique confus, a très vite touché à la racine des choses : au ballet anodin de ceux qui veulent démocratiser l'ordre existant est venu s'opposer une contestation de tout ce que « la Culture » elle-même signifie dans une société de consommation dans l'exploitation. La culture, produit de consommation pour meubler les loisirs, est la triste rançon d'une soumission au travail exploité, au régime du travail. Elle participe donc elle-même de la soumission.

De ce débat confus, une ligne générale ressort : chaque homme doit pouvoir créer sa propre culture. A la culture de l'Université, à ces fêtes mortes de l'esprit, il faut opposer une culture vivante qui prend racine dans la vie quotidienne.

SABOTER LE SPECTACLE

Les événements qui se sont déroulés depuis le 3 mai donnent un exemple spectaculaire des bouleversements idéologiques et scientifiques qui secouent la vie quotidienne. Assailli par ces bouleversements et leurs contradictions, l'homme d'aujourd'hui veut changer le monde et se changer lui-même. Projeté en quelques jours dans son futur, l'homme qui vient de se créer, se veut responsable de son devenir. Il est insurgé, violent, il veut construire un homme meilleur que celui que la société lui impose. Le révolté issu des barricades (même quand il n'y a pas participé) exprime son idée sur la culture à travers l'une des pièces d'Armand Gatti : Les Treize Soleils de la rue Saint-Blaise » (« balbutiante, coléreuse, généreuse... avec la parcelle de vérité transitoire à trouver chaque jour pour reconquérir un peu de chaleur dans l'indifférence et la froideur d'un monde qu'on ne connaît pas. »

C'est dans cette optique que les étudiants, les travailleurs du spectacle ont travaillé au théâtre de l'Odéon. Malgré les critiques qui ont été portées à cette occupation (faible participation d'acteurs, etc.), il est intéressant de noter que le Comité d'Action Révolutionnaire qui maintenant dirige le théâtre, a précisé dans un tract que ses buts étaient « le sabotage systématique de l'industrie culturelle et en particulier de l'industrie du spectacle afin de laisser place à une véritable création collective ». C'est aussi dans cette optique que les comités d'action du théâtre se sont créés chez les étudiants, chez les jeunes travailleurs, chez les artistes afin de promouvoir un art révolutionnaire représentant les véritables aspirations du prolétariat. Ces camarades ont déjà prévu des actions concrètes telles que présenter des spectacles sur les événements des

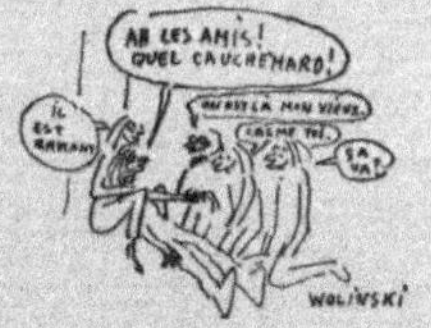

quinze derniers jours aux ouvriers en grève de chez Renault. Soulignons aussi que dans certains théâtres, les acteurs, techniciens et personnel administratif se sont regroupés pour créer des comités de gestion révolutionnaires, afin de mettre l'activité théâtrale au service du peuple.

Dans le domaine du cinéma, la réaction, la prise de conscience a été tout aussi vive. D'un seul coup, des réalisateurs, des acteurs, des techniciens du film ont pris leurs destinées en main en créant partout où cela était possible, des comités. Ces groupes s'organisent, réfléchissent sur la fonction du cinéaste dans une société révolutionnaire. Ils ont déjà accompli un gros travail d'information dans tout le milieu cinématographique. Mille professionnels du cinéma ont décidé dans la nuit de vendredi à samedi le boycott du festival de Cannes. Cette manifestation représentait « le type même d'une manifestation culture de consommation. »

MAQUIS DE PEINTURE

Sans vouloir décrire l'ensemble des comités d'action existants dans le secteur culturel, il faut indiquer ici le travail particulièrement intéressant qu'un certain nombre de jeunes peintres ont entrepris à l'intérieur du comité d'action des Arts plastiques. Dans ce secteur jusque là complètement désorganisé (aucun mouvement, aucun syndicat), ils ont réussi grâce à leur comité, à regrouper un grand nombre de gens intéressés par des réformes fondamentales de l'art dans une optique révolutionnaire de leur participation dans la société future. Vingt-quatre heures sur vingt-quatre ils tiennent un forum permanent dans un amphi de l'Ecole des Beaux-Arts. Dès maintenant ils envisagent pour participer concrètement au mouvement, d'aider ainsi la coordination des comités d'action : tout d'abord, en vendant leurs œuvres au profit du mouvement, d'autre part en mettant leur art au service de cette révolution naissante (pour faire des affiches, etc.). Certains d'entre eux ont aussi décidé de retirer leurs œuvres de tous les musées et galeries.

Maintenant que ces groupes existent, maintenant qu'une position commune commence à se dessiner, ces comités doivent opposer à la notion de loisirs culturel, celle d'agitation culturelle. C'est-à-dire créer une culture sur le tas quasi autodidacte, sorte de maquis de la connaissance et de la discussion qui brasse les idées au niveau de l'action quotidienne et s'empare de toutes les manifestations du monde moderne. A partir de maintenant, l'homme doit créer une culture qui lui corresponde sans aliénation ni trahison, celle qui doit l'armer pour le libérer de ses prisons.

Nuit et jour, la démocratie directe dans la Sorbonne occupée.

O.R.T.F. LOCK-OUTÉ ?

Le pouvoir ne peut laisser s'engager à l'O.R.T.F. un mouvement de contestation comparable à celui de l'Université. Pourtant une bataille est commencée. Voici les obstacles auxquels elle se heurte.

Le mouvement qui agite l'ensemble du personnel de l'O.R.T.F. n'a abouti ni à une grève totale ni à une occupation des lieux de travail. A l'origine ce mouvement, est parti de journalistes, de producteurs et de réalisateurs d'émissions d'information (Zoom, Caméra 3 et Cinq colonnes). Ils ont recouru à une sorte d'action directe : menace d'empêcher le passage de plusieurs émissions à l'antenne si le numéro de Zoom consacré à la lutte étudiante était interdit. Le mouvement s'est fondu aux journalistes de France-Inter qui ont refusé toute autorité du Service de Liaison de l'Information, organisme par lequel s'exerce la tutelle des ministères de l'Intérieur, des Finances et des Affaires Etrangères.

A ce moment-là, les directions syndicales sont intervenues. Une assemblée générale du personnel de l'O.R.T.F. a été réunie. Ceux qui avaient lancé le mouvement essayaient de concrétiser radicalement l'organisation et le contenu de la radio et de la télévision. L'assemblée générale, quant à elle, s'est bornée à proposer une bataille pour l'objectivité de l'information.

La division du travail et la division syndicale rendent très difficile toute entreprise de contestation à l'O.R.T.F. Le personnel est divisé artificiellement en trois grandes catégories : les artistiques, les techniciens et les administratifs. Pour prendre un exemple simple, une équipe de reportage comprend trois hommes dont le statut chevauche sur plusieurs catégories : le réalisateur peut être journaliste; le cameraman peut être réalisateur, tandis que le preneur de son est considéré comme un simple technicien. Tout empiètement donne lieu à des frictions entre syndicats. De plus, alors que dans le travail les réalisateurs sont les patrons, ils ont, sur le plan syndical, des positions plus avancées que les techniciens.

A la complexité de la division du travail correspond une invraisemblable division syndicale : syndicats autonomes de journalistes, de réalisateurs, des producteurs; syndicat unifié des techniciens regroupant tout le personnel qui contrôle l'appareillage électronique; syndicats C.G.T., F.O., C.F.D.T. et C.F.T.C. des scripts, assistants, maquilleuses, ouvriers de plateau, monteurs, chauffeurs, administratifs; syndicat artisanal des journalistes de radio et de réalisateurs affilié à la C.G.T.; syndicat de cadres, etc.

Les membres de l'assemblée générale se sont réunis dans deux studios reliés en duplex. Les débats se sont déroulés dans la plus grande confusion. Pour étouffer toute tentative de remise en cause radicale de l'O.R.T.F. les techniciens chargés du duplex sont allés jusqu'à menacer de couper la liaison entre les deux studios.

Ce mouvement de contestation s'est heurté à deux obstacles :

Les syndicats d'administratifs et de techniciens ont montré leur désintérêt habituel pour ce qui concerne le contenu de la radio-télévision, y compris le problème de l'objectivité.

L'argument selon lequel les circonstances présentes (grèves et négociations entre Hanoï et Washington) exigeaient que la mission de l'information soit remplie a fait pression sur la conscience professionnelle des journalistes.

D'où la résolution prise : grève de la production artistique et des employés de l'administration : maintien d'un journal parlé et télévisé et d'un magazine hebdomadaire : commission de garantie de l'objectivité de cette information : menace de grève totale en vue d'assurer cette objectivité.

Ainsi les grandes formations traditionnelles de l'opposition et de la majorité restent devant l'opinion publique les seuls participants du débat politique. Waldeck Rochet et de Gaulle nous parlent.

Nous n'avons pas encore commencé la lutte pour le droit d'expression de la minorité contestatrice extra-parlementaire sur l'antenne. Le mouvement pour une radio et une télévision critiques et populaires n'est pas amorcé. Déjà à l'O.R.T.F. un « comité républicain » sort des tracts. On y retrouve les mêmes hommes que ceux du comité de salut public du 13 mai 1958.

---

niveau 3

Revue éditée par le Syndicat National de l'Enseignement Supérieur (F.E.N.)

28, rue Monsieur-Le-Prince, Paris-6^e
Tél. 633-37-33.

A quoi sert l'Université ?

L'enseignement supérieur. — Les étudiants. — La recherche et la formation professionnelle.
Un enseignement sans enseignant.
Le travail scientifique, travail exploité.
La réforme de l'université ne se fera pas contre les étudiants ou sans eux.

En vente dans les librairies et les kiosques spécialisés, au siège du S.N.E. Sup. et auprès de ses militants.

Pour les envois par poste, joindre 2 F. C.C.P. : Paris 7544-66.

opinion was imposed. This practice was also a negation of traditional politics as understood within the participatory organisational structures of the old labour and Communist movement. The students' originality was the break with the old world and especially with the habits of the political establishment. The photographs reproduce exactly this refusal of any kind of leadership, hierarchy or traditional political organisation.

This lack of visually represented hierarchy is obvious when contrasted with photographs of workers' meetings which were published in trade union publications such as *La Vie Ouvrière*, the weekly newspaper of the Confédération Générale du Travail (CGT) the largest French trade union grouping, which took the largest part in controlling the workers' strikes during May '68. The photograph published here is the same photograph that was published in *L'Humanité* (figure 2). The photograph reproduces a specific stereotype about the hierarchy of workers' organisations and their structured meetings.

Another novelty of the student movement that is also evident in the photographs is the focus on the youthfulness of the participants. Contrary to the old labour movement's beliefs that the working class was the only agent of social change, the pictures in student publications demonstrate the young challenging the status quo and attempting to change the world. In many photographs, the students are depicted as passionate, full of revolutionary ardour, and often seem to be acting on a sudden irresistible impulse. This impulse is possibly directly linked to the youthfulness of the protesters. In fact, there were hardly any photographs of older people and specifically of workers in these publications. A careful examination of student publications during the events show that photographs of workers occupying factories or marching along with the students did not appear in the student publications, even when the students had made an alliance with the workers.

The movement's antinomies

The movement soon went far beyond its university origins to unite students, workers and professionals in a common struggle against de Gaulle's regime. On 13 May, the students took a decision of decisive importance, to allow the workers to enter the Sorbonne.[22] On the same day, the two main unions, the CGT and the CFDT, following the student mobilisation decided on a general workers' strike.[23] Although the strike was initially small in scale, it provoked a chain of reactions and within a few days seven-and-a-half to nine million workers went on strike.[24] By this time, almost all universities and schools were occupied. The workers entered the struggle in great sympathy with the student movement. On the 13th, students and workers demonstrated together in Paris, in a march led by both student leaders and trade unions. The following weeks saw extended occupations in schools and universities and strikes in factories, department stores, banks, public transportation, gas stations and even those working in newspapers and television all over the country.[25] The majority of the intellectual and literary world also expressed their support for and solidarity with the movement.[26] By the 24 May, France was paralysed by the biggest strike that France and probably any other European country had ever known up to that time.[27] This student–worker juncture was exceptional, as in no other major Western country did the student and worker movements intersect as they did in France.

It seemed then that the slogan of the demonstration 'Students–Workers–Solidarity' was taken seriously for the first time. Soon student leaflets began to draw a parallel between student and labour demands. 'Between your problems and ours there are certain similarities: jobs and opportunities, standards and work pace, union rights, self-management' read one of the student leaflets.[28] As soon as the strike was announced, silkscreen posters by the Atelier Populaire promoted student–worker solidarity. On 14 May, the first posters that supported the student–worker alliance appeared with the slogans: 'Usines, Universités, Union' (Factories, Universities, Union), 'Ensemble: Etudiants, Travailleurs' (All together: Students, Workers), 'Le Même Problème, La Même Lutte' (The same problem, the same struggle). The slogans became more concrete particularly at the Renault Factory at Flins, such as 'Ouvriers, Etudiants, Population, Liaison Effective Flins' (Workers, Students, The People in Effective Liaison at Flins), 'Solidarité Effective, Étudiants, Travailleurs' (Students, Workers, Effective Solidarity).[29]

Although the alliance between students and workers was verbally articulated in student posters and publications, there was no photographic equivalent of these statements. An indicative example is the photograph on the cover of *Action* of the 21 May, which depicts a student demonstration (figure 11). The caption underneath gives us the time and the place: 'Le vendredi 17 mai, pour la première fois en France, une manifestation etudiante a pris le chemin d'une usine occupée par les travailleurs: Renault' (Friday, 17 May. For the first time in France, a student demonstration went to a factory occupied by the workers: Renault).[30] The students are presented in a frontal view, demonstrating outside Renault. What is worth noting, however, is that although the presence of the workers is implied, there are no actual photographs of the workers in the publication. The

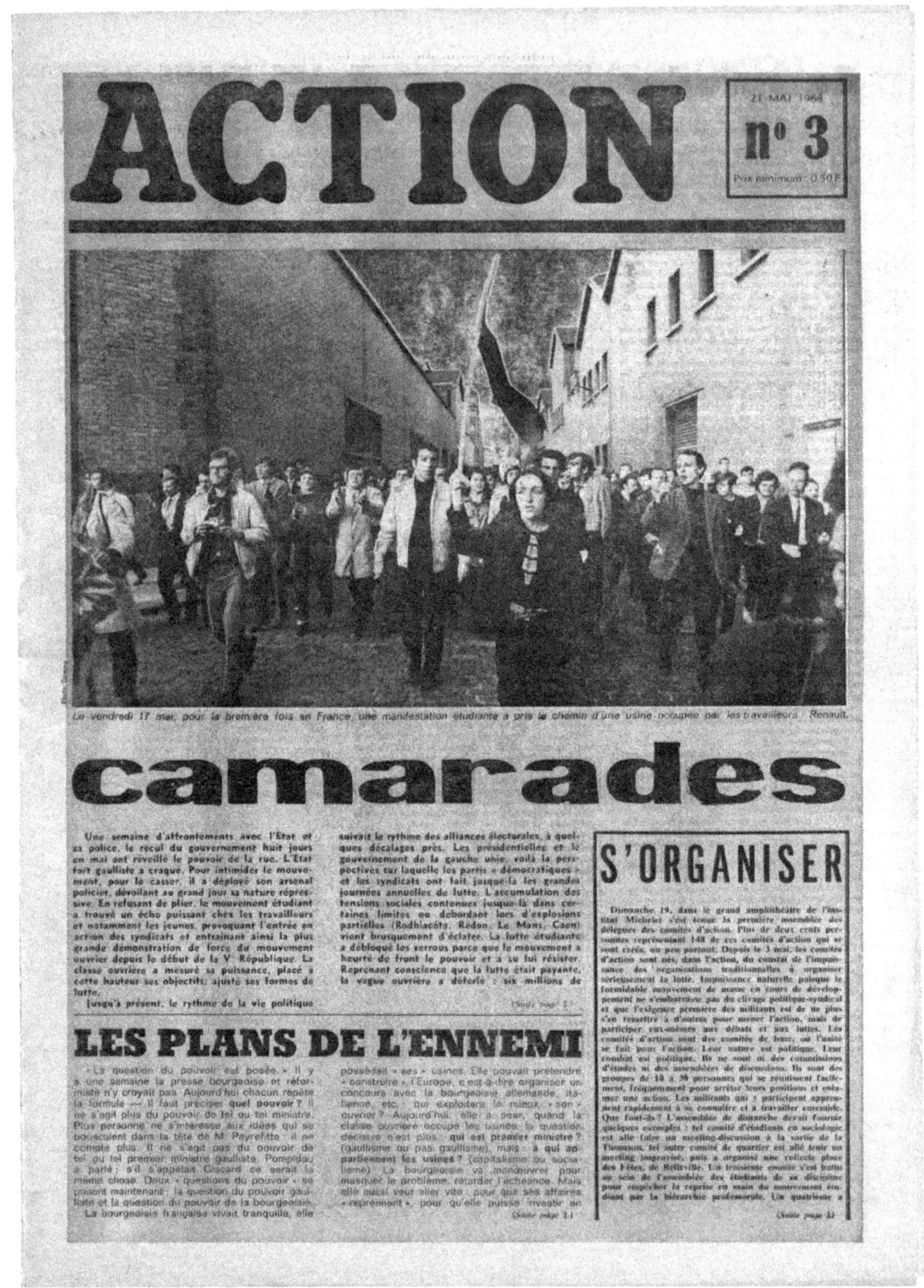

Le vendredi 17 mai, pour la première fois en France, une manifestation étudiante a pris le chemin d'une usine occupée par les travailleurs : Renault.

camarades

Une semaine d'affrontements avec l'Etat et sa police, le recul du gouvernement huit jours en mai ont réveillé le pouvoir de la rue. L'Etat fort gaulliste a craqué. Pour intimider le mouvement, pour le casser, il a déployé son arsenal policier, dévoilant au grand jour sa nature répressive. En refusant de plier, le mouvement étudiant a trouvé un écho puissant chez les travailleurs et notamment les jeunes, provoquant l'entrée en action des syndicats et entraînant ainsi la plus grande démonstration de force du mouvement ouvrier depuis le début de la V° République. La classe ouvrière a mesuré sa puissance, placé à cette hauteur ses objectifs, ajusté ses formes de lutte.

Jusqu'à présent, le rythme de la vie politique suivait le rythme des alliances électorales, à quelques décalages près. Les présidentielles et le gouvernement de la gauche unie, voilà la perspectives sur laquelle les partis « démocratiques » et les syndicats ont fait jusque-là les grandes journées annuelles de lutte. L'accumulation des tensions sociales contenues jusque-là dans certaines limites ou débordant lors d'explosions partielles (Rhodiacéta, Redon, Le Mans, Caen) vient brusquement d'éclater. La lutte étudiante a débloqué les verrous parce que le mouvement a heurté de front le pouvoir et a su lui résister. Reprenant conscience que la lutte était payante, la vague ouvrière a déferlé : six millions de

(Suite page 2.)

LES PLANS DE L'ENNEMI

« La question du pouvoir est posée. » Il y a une semaine la presse bourgeoise et réformiste n'y croyait pas. Aujourd'hui chacun répète la formule — il faut préciser **quel pouvoir ?** Il ne s'agit plus du pouvoir de tel ou tel ministre. Plus personne ne s'intéresse aux idées qui se bousculent dans la tête de M. Peyrefitte : il ne compte plus. Il ne s'agit pas du pouvoir de tel ou tel premier ministre gaulliste. Pompidou à part, s'il s'appelait Giscard ce serait la même chose. Deux « questions du pouvoir » se posent maintenant : la question du pouvoir gaulliste et la question du pouvoir de la bourgeoisie. La bourgeoisie française vivait tranquille, elle possédait « ses » usines. Elle pouvait prétendre « construire » l'Europe, c'est-à-dire organiser un concours avec la bourgeoisie allemande, italienne, etc., qui exploitera le mieux « son » ouvrier ? Aujourd'hui, elle a peur, quand la classe ouvrière occupe les usines, la question décisive n'est plus : qui est premier ministre ? (gaullisme ou pas gaullisme), mais : à qui appartiennent les usines ? (capitalisme ou socialisme). La bourgeoisie va manœuvrer pour masquer le problème, retarder l'échéance. Mais elle aussi veut aller vite : pour que ses affaires « reprennent » pour qu'elle puisse investir en

(Suite page 2.)

S'ORGANISER

Dimanche 19, dans le grand amphithéâtre de l'Institut Michelet s'est tenue la première assemblée des délégués des comités d'action. Plus de deux cents personnes représentant 148 de ces comités d'action qui se sont créés, un peu partout. Depuis le 3 mai, les comités d'action sont nés, dans l'action, du constat de l'impuissance des organisations traditionnelles à organiser sérieusement la lutte. Impuissance naturelle puisque le formidable mouvement de masse en cours de développement ne s'embarrasse pas du clivage politique-syndical et que l'exigence première des militants est de ne plus s'en remettre à d'autres pour mener l'action, mais de participer eux-mêmes aux débats et aux luttes. Les comités d'action sont des comités de base, où l'unité se fait pour l'action. Leur nature est politique. Leur combat est politique. Ils ne sont ni des commissions d'études ni des assemblées de discussions. Ils sont des groupes de 10 à 30 personnes qui se réunissent facilement, fréquemment pour arrêter leurs positions et entamer une action. Les militants qui y participent apprennent rapidement à se connaître et à travailler ensemble. Que font-ils ? L'assemblée de dimanche devait fournir quelques exemples : tel comité d'étudiants en sociologie est allé faire un meeting-discussion à la sortie de la Thomson, tel autre comité de quartier est allé tenir un meeting improvisé, puis a organisé une collecte place des Fêtes, de Belleville. Un troisième comité s'est battu au sein de l'assemblée des étudiants de sa discipline pour empêcher la reprise en main du mouvement étudiant par la hiérarchie professorale. Un quatrième a

(Suite page 3.)

11 *Action*, No. 3, 21 May 1968, p. 1

only reference to the workers is the industrial background, against which the spontaneity and the impulsiveness of the students appear as a visual disruption. The background seems theatrical and overly contrived, and the sky and the banner are retouched heavily, so that the scene, although it may not be, seems constructed.

One of the very few, if not the only photograph of workers that appeared in *Action* on 11 June 1968 depicted the workers standing on the balcony of their factory. The workers do not face the camera and it is not known where they look. There is no action shown in the picture or any visual reference to their factories' occupation or their strike. The photograph could have been taken on a normal working day. Only the caption reminds us that the photograph was taken at Sud-Aviation in Nantes, the first factory that was occupied by the workers on 14 May. This photograph is similar to photographs of workers published in *La Vie Ouvrière*, the only trade union publication circulated during the events. These photographs that showed workers posing in front of the occupied factory are symptomatic of the different all-embracing iconography that excluded photographs of workers demonstrating. In two photographs from *La Vie Ouvrière*, it is clear that the workers are not unaware of the camera's presence. The workers seem to have posed in total control of the factory. Nevertheless, they seem static, in contrast to the students, who appear militant.

The gap between the students as bearers of new ideas and demands and the working class persisting in the old form of struggle is omnipresent in the photographic representations of the period. The absence of photographs portraying students and workers together was expected due to the spatial separation of the groups, a separation that was favoured by both the trade unions and the government, as discussed in part I. In the few images of workers, they were depicted as either static, posing in front of their occupied factories, or participating in a hierarchically structured meeting that resembled mainstream politics. In contrast, photographs of students reproduced a specific idea about the movement, being a spontaneous, impulsive youth movement. Therefore, student publications only represented one face of the movement. The other face was that of the workers and their unions. According to Feenberg and Freedman this alliance was at odds. In their words:

A movement built on this alliance inevitably had two contrary faces. The one embodied the energy of student leaders, diffused and avowedly immoderate; this student energy had driven the police to commit brutalities that inspired a popular demonstration unequaled in the history of the Fifth

Republic. The other aspect, that of the Communist Party and France's major union, the General Confederation of Workers (CGT), presented a reformist, almost moderate face.[31]

The students rejected the old ideas and organisational structures of the labour movement, and challenged the existing hierarchies in their political praxis, and especially in the student sit-ins and open meetings.[32] These anti-hierarchical and anti-authoritarian demands did not ever gain the support of the communist-oriented CGT. The workers' initial demands, which prior to the May events were not fundamentally different from those of their unions, were soon re-articulated, to include not only wage increases and a reduction of working hours, but also structural changes in industry, such as a reduction in hierarchies, worker self-administration and reorganisation of decision making.[33] But that applied only to a minority of workers. The major workers' organisations, and consequently the majority of the workers, were not actually influenced by the goals of the student movement, continuing for the most part to restrict their demands to improvements in wages and working conditions and to the forging of electoral alliances.

The main trade union CGT not only attempted to prevent the alliance between students and workers, it discouraged the student demonstration at Renault, refused to support the students in public and declined to meet with representatives of the UNEF.[34] In reality, the CGT struggled to keep students out of the factories on strike, calling them the 'children of the big bourgeoisie' and tried to isolate the student movement.[35] The CGT also aimed to direct 'the protest into the orderly channel of a mediated settlement'.[36] Therefore, in the middle of June after a gradual decay of the movement, the workers' unions decided on a general return to work and agreed to resolve the conflict in reformist ways. The students were promised a democratisation of the educational system, and although occupations, demonstrations and barricades continued for a while, the movement lost its strength and vitality, was isolated and easily suppressed by force. De Gaulle's electoral victory at the end of the month came as no surprise to most people.

It is true that when the students allied with the workers they 'had accomplished what the major unions had considered practically impossible, what the Communist Party had declared theoretically absurd, and what the government had never imagined'.[37] When the student mobilisation was extended to the working population, student leaflets drew parallels between the student and worker demands. While student texts celebrated this alliance, the photographs failed to represent it. An examination of the student movement's self-reflection reveals an iconography of impulsive and young students demonstrating, participating in anti-hierarchical meetings and expressing their 'destructive' critique against the state. Photographs depicting police violence were omnipresent, while images of the striking workers were absent.

The problematic nature of the alliance, which was proclaimed in student texts was reflected in this iconography. As Feenberg and Freedman correctly pointed out, the student activists 'could not overcome in a few weeks the effects of the years of mutual ignorance'.[38] The fact that the trade unions did not fully support the student movement and their difficulty in embracing the students' demands for the transformation of every day life and culture kept the workers enclosed in their occupied factories. It is where photographs of posed and static workers were taken, but were not published in student publications. Their resemblance to photographs of old labour movements and mainstream politics was at odds with the students' rejection of conventional Leftist perceptions of revolutionary practice and denunciation of the political status quo. This is not to ague that workers did not join the students in the barricades, committees and demonstrations, but that the photographs in student publications failed to represent the student–worker alliance with its strong points and weaknesses.

Notes

1 The chapter draws upon unpublished material extracted from *The Bibliotheque d'Histoire Sociale Du XXe Siècle* (Université Paris I, Pantheon Sorbonne) and the May Events Archive at Simon Fraser University.

2 F. Ritchin, '1968: Unbearable Relevance of Photography', *Aperture*, 171 (Summer 2003), pp. 62–73.

3 For accounts of the events, see particularly: K. A. Reader, *The May 1968 Events in France: Reproductions and Interpretations* (New York: St Martin's Press, 1993), pp. 1–19; D. Singer, *Prelude to Revolution: France in May 1968* (Cambridge: South End Press, 2002), pp. 37–206.

4 M. Seidman, *The Imaginary Revolution: Parisian Students and Workers in 1968* (New York and Oxford: Berghahn Books, 2004), p. 24.

5 As Daniel Singer explains, the UNEF was in the hands of various radical Leftist groups after the mid-fifties. Although in its heyday during the Algerian war, after the war UNEF gradually lost its strength. The Gaullist government contributed to its decay, since it deprived it of its subsidy and sponsored a non-political union, which definitely weakened the UNEF. Singer, *Prelude to Revolution*, p. 55. For a similar discussion, see also: P. Seale and M. McConville, *French Revolution 1968* (London: Penguin Books, 1968). Also, Robert Daniels argues that the UNEF moved towards the radical Left, under the militant president Jaques Sauvageot. In March 1968, UNEF joined the anti-Vietnam campaign proving its radical orientation. See: R. V. Daniels, *1968: The Year of the Heroic Guerrilla* (Cambridge,

MA: Harvard University Press, 1989), p. 155.

6 A. Feenberg and J. Freedman, *When Poetry Ruled the Streets: The French May Events of 1968* (Albany: State University of New York Press, 2001), p. 43. Also for more details on the 22 March movement, see: D. Cohn-Bendit, *Obsolete Communism: The Left-Wing Alternative* (Edinburgh, London, San Francisco: AK Press, 2000), pp. 46–53.

7 K. Ross, *May '68 and Its Afterlives* (Chicago and London: The University of Chicago Press, 2002), pp. 114–15, footnote 123. Examples of Siné's slogans include: 'Debout les damnés de Nanterre!' (Arise, wretched of Nanterre!), 'Les Chiens de Garde Aboient Toujours de la Même Façon' (The Guard Dogs Bark Always in the Same Way), 'La rue vaincra!' (The Street Will Win!)

8 Since *L'Enragé* never published photographs, it is not directly studied in this chapter, although examination of its twelve issues was crucial for my understanding of the movement.

9 Ross, *May '68 and Its Afterlives*, pp. 114–15, footnote 123.

10 Ibid., Abbreviations, p. 217.

11 Ibid., p. 217.

12 Singer, *Prelude to Revolution*, p. 58.

13 The JCR, which was later renamed *Ligue Communiste Révolutionnaire* (LCR), a Trotskyist group that was formed in 1966 as a splinter from the orthodox *Union de Étudiants Communistes* (UEC), was among the initiators of the 22 March movement in Nanterre and without doubt played a decisive role in the student movement in May 1968. See: Reader, *The May 1968 Events in France*, pp. ix, 6, 22; Singer, *Prelude to Revolution*, p. 57.

14 The *Union des Jeunesses Communistes Marxistes-Leninistes* (UJCML) along with the JCR (see footnote above) split from the orthodox *Union des Étudiants Communistes* (UEC, Union of Communist Students). Singer argues that the UJCML was quite successful among the younger generation. In his words: 'Quotations from the little red book and the cult of Mao were not the ideal means of attracting critical students, but they were attracted by China's cultural revolution, with its anti-bureaucratic message and its appeal to youth. Their ideological enthusiasm and personal abnegation enabled the young Maoists to make substantial gains among the university and high school students.' Singer, *Prelude to Revolution*, pp. 56–7.

15 As Michael Seidman stresses 'During the 1967–1968 academic year, a handful of *groupuscules* gathered between thirteen and 140 students or a little over 1 percent of the student population, who were mostly in the humanities and social sciences. At the height in 1968, the activists never exceeded 12 percent of the student body.' See: Seidman, *The Imaginary Revolution*, p. 23.

16 'De la Critique de l' Université a la Critique de la Sociéte' was one of the slogans of the movement.

17 I owe the term to Johannes Agnoli, who provides us with a very interesting analysis of both the role of intellectuals in the contemporary age, and the terms 'constructive' and 'destructive' critique. See: J. Agnoli, 'Destruction as the Determination of the Scholar in Miserable Times', in W. Bonefeld (ed.), *Revolutionary Writing* (New York: Autonomedia, 2003), pp. 25–38.

18 G. Katsiaficas, *The Imagination of the New Left: A Global Analysis of 1968* (Boston: South End Press, 1987), p. 102.

19 Singer, *Prelude to Revolution*, pp. 122–3.

20 Feenberg and Freedman, *When Poetry Ruled the Streets*, pp. 77, 83.

21 Ibid., p. 124.

22 R. Viénet, *Enrages and Situationists in the Occupation Movement: France, May 1968* (New York and London: Autonomedia and Rebel Press, 1992), p. 44.

23 Reader, *The May 1968 Events in France*, p. 117.

24 I. Gilcher-Hotley, 'May 1968 in France', in C. Fink, F. Gassert and D. Junker (eds), *1968: The World Transformed* (Cambridge: Cambridge University Press, 1998), p. 263.

25 For a detailed overview of the various sectors' strikes, see: Seidman, *The Imaginary Revolution*, chapter 4, pp. 161–214.

26 Singer, *Prelude to Revolution*, p. 159.

27 Ibid., p. 156.

28 Feenberg and Freedman, *When Poetry Ruled the Streets*, p. 124.

29 Atelier Populaire, *Posters from the Revolution, Paris, May 1968* (Usine Université Union, 1969), p. 39.

30 *Action* (21 May 1968), p. 1.

31 Feenberg and Freedman, *When Poetry Ruled the Streets*, p. 28.

32 C. Castoriadis, *World in Fragments: Writings on Politics, Society, Psychoanalysis and the Imagination* (Stanford, CA: Stanford University Press, 1997), p. 49.

33 I. Gilcher-Hotley analyses how the workers' demands evolved from requests for increase of wages and reduction of working hours to more complicated demands. The new term *autogestion* coined mainly by the CFDT embraced demands of an anti-hierarchical and anti-authoritarian nature. See: Gilcher-Hotley, 'May 1968 in France', p. 263.

34 Feenberg and Freedman, *When Poetry Ruled the Streets*, pp. 49–50.

35 Katsiaficas, *The Imagination of the New Left*, p. 110.

36 Ibid., p. 265.

37 Feenberg and Freedman, *When Poetry Ruled the Streets*, p. 36.

38 Ibid., p. 126.

5

Zapatistas, photography and the internet or winning the game of visibility

T H E EZLN movement has placed great importance on visual imagery for their struggle, with direct references to easily recognisable portraits of Zapata and Che Guevara in an attempt to re-appropriate them from mainstream discourse. Photographs can also be weapons, to paraphrase Marcos, in the struggle for social justice and equality, as illustrated by Marcos's self-conscious construction of an image for the media spectacle, discussed in part I. Marcos seems to be fully aware of this subversive role of photographs, when he writes:

> Question the images. Take them by the hand and don't let the sweet distancing they offer you vanquish you; do away with the distance's comfort or the soft indifference you derive from concentrating on the quality of framing, the use of light and shadows, the successful composition. Force these images to bring you to the Mexican Southeast, to history, to the struggle, to this taking sides, to choose a faction.[1]

In his call to think about photography beyond aesthetics, Marcos not only puts emphasis on photography's close relationship with history and politics, but also points to photography's ability to raise public awareness about the struggle, which can potentially be transformed to solidarity and support.

The numerous photographs on the EZLN website can then be seen within this context: they are weapons for the visibility and sustainability of their struggle. Although the indigenous people may not be in control of the photographic means of production, this online photographic archive can be seen as representative of the way they visualised their movement and of the image promoted to the rest of the world. This chapter takes as a case study the photographic archive available on the official website of the EZLN and discusses the role of photography in contributing to the visibility of the Zapatista struggle and in promoting the struggle to the rest of the world.

Breaking with years of silence

The impoverished conditions within which the uprising occurred, including the lack of housing and basic services, such as electricity, drinking water and transportation, render any association between the uprising and the concomitantly expanding communication technologies rather absurd. Nevertheless, the internet played a crucial role in the Zapatista struggle, as it provided the platform for what Harry Cleaver termed 'contro-informazione (counter-information)', for information that 'is opposed to the official reports of governments and commercial mass media'.[2] This 'counter-information' consisted of communiqués, articles, reports, letters, personal accounts, poems and photographs, uploaded initially by Zapatista supporters and later by the Zapatistas themselves.

The internet allowed the Zapatistas and their supporters, activists around the globe, to organise themselves, to form 'cyber-communities' and coordinate 'action in dispersed, non-hierarchical networks'.[3] In this way, an 'electronic fabric of the struggle' – a net of non-governmental organisations, international, local groups and individuals – was created.[4] All these supporters and the non-governmental organisations (NGOs) acted as mediators of the movement, sometimes translating the Spanish documents into other languages. Lists of various networks were collected, reproduced and republished by other interested parties on the internet, while local NGOs and university-based websites forwarded large sets of lists and related information to other networks, and provided links to other related websites. This international electronic network consisted of mailing lists, conferences for the dissemination of information and websites for archiving the history of the struggle, all making the Zapatistas pioneers in the successful use of the electronic media for activist purposes.[5]

The significance of the use of the internet was not only limited to organisational and networking opportunities. It directly challenged the mainstream media's generally limited coverage of the Zapatistas, which tended to either present their writings in a fragmented way or not to include any serious analysis of their political ideology. More importantly, the internet helped the Zapatistas to draw international attention to the government's corruption and lack of concern about the miserable conditions in the state of Chiapas. The solidarity took the form of written statements and of physical actions, including demonstrations in Mexico, and on a smaller scale in the United States and Canada. In more imaginative cases, virtual sit-ins by the Electronic Disturbance Theatre (EDT) drew attention to the Zapatistas' case. The twenty-four hour virtual sit-in against the websites of the Pentagon, Mexican President Zedillo and the Frankfurt Stock Exchange organised by the EDT in September 1998 introduced a new activist tactic that was termed 'electronic civil disobedience'.[6] Activating the FloodNet software, which was directed towards a target-website and sending thousands of hits at the same moment so that the website was blockaded, EDT drew conflicting responses from the general public, but managed to attract the attention of both the mainstream media and the Mexican government to the Zapatista uprising. Overall, all these actions of solidarity contributed decisively to preventing any organised military counter-offensive of the Mexican state, forcing the government to negotiate with the rebels, not an obvious choice if it had been able to do otherwise.[7]

By 2001, there were an estimated 45,000 Zapatista-related websites over twenty-six countries. Along with these websites, the Zapatistas created their own, with a twofold character: a means of fighting back against the dominance of mass media and an archive of maintaining the uprising's history, providing an antidote to the monolithic appropriation of the uprising's memory by the state and its official institutions.[8] The website is today a locus that consists of a great number of personal reports, eyewitness accounts, oral testimony, communiqués, documents, tales, anecdotes, poems, photographs, graphic images and videos.

The online photographic archive numbers approximately five thousand photographs, with a range of photographs dating back to the appearance of the movement as well as very recent ones. The visitor to the website is most likely to access an assortment of information about the movement from the time of its formation up to now in their effort to access the photographic material. As with all archives, unity of the archive is imposed by ownership, but openness and inclusivity are also its characteristics. Photographs are accepted without regard to iconic status, aesthetic value or any reference to a recognised author; quite the contrary, there is no reference to professional photographers or any selection of representative photographs. What seems to be the unifying characteristic of the collection is a deliberate effort to create an alternative representation from the one offered by the official media and the apparatus of the state. An alternative archival strategy is therefore based on an anti-hierarchical mode: the photographs are not attributed to the photographers whether they are recognised photojournalists or anonymous amateurs. As a result, various different practices are in symbiosis. Photographs by well-known photojournalists, Mexican in particular, initially destined to appear in the press, co-exist with digital photographs taken by amateurs on digital cameras and mobile phones. The images, whether derived from an analogue or digital camera, are accompanied only with basic information about time and place and are not supplemented by captions.

This anti-hierarchical mode of organising the online archive is also reflected in the subject matter omnipresent in the individual photographs. While one has to acknowledge the difficulty of dealing with such a vast and diverse collection, it is exactly this assortment of photographs that bears the message: the multiplicity of images as a means of contestation of the single image promoted by the official discourse. Instead of the image of Marcos promoted as symbolic of the struggle, the website promotes an image of democratic indigenous community insurrection. This image is created through the proliferation of certain recurring themes throughout the website, which can be summed up as follows: the predominance of masked citizens, the outstanding absence of armed Zapatistas, the plethora of open meetings and peaceful assemblies and the prominent role of women in the movement.

A democratic image from the jungle

The most predominant feature of the images available online is the omnipresence of masked Zapatistas. The indigenous people appear wearing masks in most photographs, in particular the posed ones (plate 5). Although the Zapatistas may not wear their balaclavas in their everyday life, they consider them necessary in the presence of the camera. A rare exception to the use of the balaclava is the children, who may be presented with their faces uncovered on some occasions. The use of the balaclava has undeniably symbolic overtones, which transcend the obvious practical function of protection.

The extensive use of balaclavas in the majority of photographs available on the website comes as no surprise given the fascination with the mask in Mexican culture since pre-Columbian times. A means of protecting oneself or as a barrier between the self and the world, the mask is omnipresent in Mexico: on the Day of the Dead, among popular heroes such as El Zorro and Super Barrio, in 'lucha libre', the popular Latin American equivalent of wrestling.[9] Even more importantly, the use of the mask links the Zapatistas with other Latin American revolutionary movements of the twentieth century, in which covered faces became the emblem of the revolution. One of the most recent examples is the Sandinistas' revolt in Nicaragua, which was photographed by the prominent American photographer Susan Meiselas.

Meiselas travelled to Nicaragua during the rebellion as a commissioned photojournalist. Although Meiselas may have been sympathetic towards the movement – for which she has been heavily criticised – when her photographs were published in the mass media, they attained other interpretive meanings, sometimes opposite to Meiselas's intentions. 'Getting a story out to a particular market may lead to the diminishing and distortion of their intended meanings', Meiselas stressed, as she became increasingly dissatisfied with the incomprehensibility and decontextualisation of her photographs and at the same time more conscious of the process of distributing them.[10] These concerns led her to create a photographic book entitled *Nicaragua June 1978–July 1979*, which features seventy-one full-page uncaptioned colour photographs.[11] Towards the end of the book, a final section provides a smaller reproduction of each photograph in black and white, accompanied by, and explicated through, a detailed caption. There is also supplementary material of historical texts, testimonial accounts, literature and poetry, which offer the viewer a contextualised reading of the visual imagery.

In Meiselas's book, the Sandinistas initially used traditional Indian dance masks, which as the rebellion spread were replaced with bandanas and ski-masks (plate 6).[12] What is striking in the book is that the mask acts as a distinguishing feature between those who were involved in the struggle, and therefore masked, and those who are not actively engaged in it, and therefore unmasked. There are a few photographs in the collection that depict masked guerrillas engaged in conflict, while unmasked citizens watch the unfolding action. This dichotomy, when not presented in a single photograph, is noticeable in the separation between photographs that depict strong masked rebels and photographs of impotent ordinary citizens, who suffer the consequences of the turmoil. In total contrast to the photographs of the Sandinistas, in the majority of the web-photos of the Chiapas all members of the Zapatista army and ordinary citizens in the villages of Chiapas, regardless of age and gender, appear masked (plate 5). All the citizens are masked, all the masked citizens participate in the movement and, therefore, the mask not only becomes a symbol, but also a signifier of the widespread acceptance of the movement. It is the whole community in insurrection, in opposition to Mexican politics, and in command of a new Mexican society. This differs from earlier revolutionary movements both in its starting point and its aspiration.

Another distinctive difference between the photographs of Sandinistas and the web-photographs lies in the representation of the armed conflict. In the Nicaraguan revolt, it is not only the mask that functions as an emblem of the guerrilla warfare, but even more importantly the gun. The masked rebels are also bearers of guns, while the unmasked citizens are represented unarmed. The omnipresence of guns, tanks and armed forces in the book reflects the indisputably military character of the movement. Seen in an urban environment the armed guerrillas appear as a visual inversion of the women and terrified citizens who watch their struggle. Strong images of violence, direct confrontation and death are also present in the book, giving us the sense of warfare. In contrast, on the EZLN website there are relatively few photographs of armed Zapatistas, while there are almost no photographs that show armed guerrillas involved in a conflict. Besides the short duration of the armed conflict in Chiapas, it seems that the remarkable lack of representation of latent violence and brutality on the Zapatista website is deliberate. There are no photographs which show the battles of the Zapatista Liberation Army with the Mexican army or even Zapatistas holding guns.

This deliberate choice can be directly related to the EZLN's denunciation of armed struggle. In its embryonic stages, EZLN appeared to be an armed *foco* movement merging Leninism, Maoism and Guevarism. It understood itself as a 'revolutionary vanguard', which would lead the 'prolonged popular war', in a similar way to other Latin American Leftist movements.[13] EZLN denounced the tactics of guerrilla warfare and words replaced weapons in the communiqués and poetic letters of Subcomandante Marcos, for whom 'Ideas are also weapons'.[14] The relationship with previous Latin American guerrilla movements is more of a rupture, rather than continuation, as Subcomandante Marcos once noted:

Nosotros nos estábamos planteando la posibilidad de no ser guerrilla, por eso los ejemplos militares nos servían como conocimiento, pero no como ejemplo. Ahora, en términos politicos no había ninguna cercanía porque para entonces esta generación está muy celosa de su mexicanidad, de su originalidad, y se plantea mantener distancia respecto de todos los demás movimientos'.[15]

(We suggested the possibility of not being guerrilla and that's why the military examples serve as knowledge but not as an example. Now, in political terms there is not nearness because, contrary to that time, this generation is more keen on its Mexican identity (Mexinidad), on its originality and intends to keep a distance with regard to the other movements.)

The distance that Zapatistas keep from the model of the *foco* guerrilla movement is the same distance that exists between the EZLN and Che Guevara's thought and revolutionary praxis. For Zapatistas, 'the reference is Che who leaves Cuba and goes to Bolivia, is Che who goes on fighting'.[16] It is the unity between thought and action, the human elements of his praxis and his continual resistance that continue to inspire the Zapatistas, more than his political message, his attachment to *foco* guerrilla fighting and his manual for taking power. In other words, 'the Zapatistas are not a "guerrilla force", not an "armed party" with a particular social base, but rather they are the social base itself – the communities – in insurrection; this runs counter to both reformist and Leninist practices'.[17]

Within this social base, the use of the mask functions as a unifying element between the citizens and not as a mode of separation between the guerrillas and the social base, as discussed in the example of the Sandinistas. The mask renders everyone equal in front of the camera, since the individual characteristics of each Zapatista can hardly be distinguished. Individuality is, therefore, subsumed into a faceless anonymous collective body. This becomes even more interesting in photographs of open assemblies, in which all Zapatistas are aligned wearing their masks (plate 7). The participants' individuality, facelessness and anonymity make them equal members of the movement, who enjoy equal privileges within Chiapas. The intended anonymity can be seen here as an ironic comment on the non-existence that the Mexican state imposes on the Zapatistas by not providing them with a birth or death certificate.[18] In contrast to the confiscation of their existence imposed by official politics, it is anonymity of equality that each Zapatista enjoys within the community. In the open meetings, the whole community attends and makes decisions on both warfare and politics. The multiple masked faces add to their numerical power, and contribute to their communal strength stemming from a democratic life without inequality, racism or sexism.

This democratic collective power is enforced by the lack of leadership and the omnipresence of women, which find their visual equivalent in the web-photographs, while Marcos may be one of the few subcomanders, who is easily recognisable due to the endless reproductions of his photographs, as argued in part I. In the majority of the web-photographs, he is represented as an inseparable member of the community (plate 1). The anti-hierachical structure of the movement disassociates the EZLN from older Latin American guerrilla movements. Democratic meetings and assemblies of the communities have come to the centre of the movement. In these meetings, decisions are taken collectively, while leadership functions on a rotating basis.[19] The photographs of open assemblies indicate an iconographical rupture with older images of Latin American uprisings, in which the depiction of the meetings is not customary. This rupture seems to be only part of a break with the politics of the older movements in the continent. In most of the *foco* movements, such as the Sandinistas, the power is with the party elite, who make decisions and then seek to persuade their followers, while in Chiapas the community itself decides by vote after long debates about the movement (this in fact happened with the ceasefire.) The Zapatistas put emphasis on their markedly democratic character, opening up the invitation for communication and cooperation with international struggles.[20] A number of gatherings, which they called *'Encuentros'*, became a free political space for dialogue, analysis and direct action. In 1996, in order to show this universal character, Zapatistas called journalists, activists and citizens from all over the world to an International Encuentro (Encounter) Against Neoliberalism and For Humanity in Chiapas, attempting to build a 'collective network of all our particular struggles and resistances, an intercontinental network of resistance against neoliberalism, an intercontinental network of resistance for humanity'.[21] The anti-hierarchical fashion of these meetings resembled the assemblies of the local communities, and their emphasis on collective decision making.

An inseparable part of this collective body is the women, distinguishable because of specific characteristics of the body and details of clothing regardless of their masks. Women are depicted as having an active role within the movement, either taking part in the decision-making processes, or speaking in the open meetings. The women occupy both prominent political and military positions within the movement, as commandants, officers and political leaders (plate 8). This outstanding position can be seen as a result of the democratic processes in the communities. While in older struggles, such as the Sandinistas, women were restricted to the passive role of the spectator and the guerrilla fighter tended to be associated with male figures, women occupy a predominant role in Zapatista iconography.

The political message is strongly tied to the movement's struggle for the abolition of sexual inequalities, against the traditional position of women in indigenous society. The indigenous traditions and customs had to be surpassed, so that women not only acquire equality, but can put forward gender demands:

> democratic relations within the family, the community and the organisations themselves; their participation as women in decision making in communal and organisational bodies; the right to inherit land; the right to decide

when and whom they marry; the right to work and study and, when in position of authority, the right to be respected by men.[22]

These demands opened up a discussion about the contradictory issues of 'respect for tradition' and change, which were prevailing within the EZLN.[23] Making choices about whom they marry and when to become a mother were innovative elements for the indigenous communities in Chiapas and pointed towards change.[24] Photographs highlighting their active participation in the movement in parallel to their role as mothers are also omnipresent in the website (plate 9).

A last point that is worth bringing up is the lack of photographs of suffering and death, photographs that focus on the indigenous people's low quality of life and harsh living conditions. This is striking given that some thousands of indigenous people die of starvation and curable diseases in Chiapas. This omission brings the archive into direct contrast with Meiselas's photographs of pain and death, omnipresent in her collection on Nicaragua. It also shows the web-photographs in contradiction with the black-and-white documentary projects of famine and poverty in Latin America, such as Sebastião Salgado's controversial photographs of agrarian communities in Brazil.[25]

This omission cannot be accidental, chiming with the Zapatista struggle's calls for dignity. Dignity is only one of the new ideas that the EZLN focused on in their attempt to denounce the old revolutionary praxis, such as overthrowing the existing government, taking power and establishing socialism. Rethinking the relevance and connection of the Zapatistas to older ways of struggle, but also redefining the core of the revolutionary practice, constituted the theoretical and political basis of the movement that came to be known as Zapatismo. As Subcomandante Marcos has stressed, 'The old recipes or the old parameters should serve as a reference of what was done, but not as something that should be re-adopted to do something new.'[26] Zapatismo brought new radical ideas regarding social change. The communities are the base of the movement, and they decide on both military tactics and politics. They espouse the non-existence of any political party, and the negation of taking power. The idea of 'changing the world without taking power', to borrow from John Holloway's celebrated book title, is probably unique within the history of social movements, and contrasts with older Latin American movements' conception of political struggle.[27] Their demands ask 'for a recasting of democracy in ways which would break the power not only of the central government but of the political parties in Mexico'.[28] 'Changing the world without taking power' might be described at best as 'romantic' and at worst as naïve or impossible.

This demand for the impossible, for the creation of a new world of dignity and humanity, and for a direct participatory democracy, echoes the May '68 aspirations. Despite their distinct characteristics and chronological distance, in examining their self-representation common motifs arise. The most important one is the existence of photographs depicting anti-hierarchical assemblies, suppressed by the mainstream discourse and its fascination with spectacular images. Something hopeful and resistant arise in these depictions of the faceless Zapatistas making democratic decisions about their lives. Their struggle for 'faceless visibility' is a struggle for rejection of hierarchies and direct democracy. Through the innovative use of media and circulation of images the Zapatistas won the game of visibility.

Notes

1 Subcomandante Marcos, *La Jornada* (8 February 1996), as reprinted in A. D. Coleman, *Depth of Field: Essays on Photography, Mass Media and Lens Culture* (Albuquerque: University of New Mexico Press, 1998), p. 167.

2 H. Cleaver, 'The Zapatistas and the Electronic Fabric of Struggle', p. 84, https://webspace. utexas.edu/hcleaver/www/zaps.html (accessed 19/02/2012).

3 M. E. Martinez-Torres, 'Civil Society, the Internet, and the Zapatistas', *Peace Review*, 13: 3 (2001), pp. 347–55.

4 Cleaver, 'The Zapatistas and the Electronic Fabric of Struggle', pp. 81–103.

5 D. Halleck, 'Zapatistas Online', *NACLA Report on the Americas*, 28: 2 (1994), pp. 30–2; H. Cleaver, 'Computer-Linked Social Movements and the Global Threat to Capitalism', www.eco.utexas.edu/~hmcleave/anti-hellman.html (accessed 30/05/2012).

6 See: G. Meikle, *Future Active: Media Activism and the Internet* (London: Routledge, 2002), pp. 140–72.

7 H. Cleaver, 'Beyond the News: The Chiapas Uprising and the Future of Class Struggle', *Common Sense*, 15 (1994), p. 7.

8 The Zapatists website is to be found at: http://enlacezapatista.ezln.org.mx/.

9 I. Stavans, 'Unmasking Marcos', in T. Hayden (ed.), *The Zapatista Reader* (New York: Thunder's Mouth Press/Nation Books, 2002), p. 188.

10 S. Meiselas, 'Some Thoughts on Appropriation and the Use of Documentary Photographs', *Exposure*, 21: 1 (1989), p. 12.

11 S. Meiselas and C. Rosenberg (eds), *Nicaragua June 1978–July 1979* (London: Writers and Readers Publishing Cooperative, 1981).

12 J. Breckenridge, 'Narrative Imag(in)ing, Susan Meiselas Documents the Sandinista Revolution in Nicaragua', in M. E. Schwartz and M. B. Tierney-Tello (eds), *Photography and Writing in Latin America* (Albuquerque: University of New Mexico Press, 2006), p. 75.

13 As Luis Lorenzano has argued, the mixture of these characteristics is not surprising. As he stressed: 'In its various modalities, it was characteristic of almost all the Latin American radical Left in the years between the Cuban Revolution and the Sandinista triumph in

Nicaragua. It was to be found, with its own particular characteristics, in the Ejército Revolutionario del Pueblo (Argentina), the Movimiento de la Izquierda Revolucionaria (Chile), the Fuerzas de la Liberación Nacional (Venezuela), the Ejército de Liberación Nacional (Colombia) and the MLN-Tupamaros (Uruguay).' L. Lorenzano, 'Zapatismo: Recomposition of Labour, Radical Democracy and Revolutionary Project', in J. Holloway and E. Peláez (eds), *Zapatista!: Reinventing Revolution in Mexico* (London: Pluto Press, 1998), p. 127.

14 Subcomandante Marcos, 'Do not Forget: Ideas Are Also Weapons', in Hayden (ed.), *The Zapatista Reader*, pp. 311–15.

15 Y. LeBot, *Subcomandante Marcos: El Sueño Zapatista* (Barcelona: Plaza & Janés, 1997), p. 135.

16 Ibid.

17 Lorenzano, 'Zapatismo', p. 130.

18 R. Debray, 'A Guerrilla with a Difference', *New Left Review*, 218 (1996), pp. 128–37.

19 M. Mentinis, *Zapatistas: The Chiapas Revolt and What It Means for Radical Politics* (London: Pluto Press, 2006), p. 101.

20 Ibid., p. 138.

21 Subcomandante Marcos, *Our World Is Our Weapon: Selected Writings* (New York: Seven Stories Press, 2002), p. 125.

22 M. Millán, 'Zapatista Indigenous Women', in Holloway and Peláez (eds), *Zapatista!: Reinventing Revolution in Mexico*, p. 67.

23 Ibid., p. 70.

24 Ibid., p. 77.

25 S. Salgado, *An Uncertain Grace* (New York: Aperture, 1990).

26 Subcomandante Marcos and the Zapatistas, *The Other Campaign* (San Francisco: Open Media Series, City Lights, 2006), p. 155.

27 J. Holloway, *Change the World without Taking Power* (London: Pluto Press, 2002).

28 H. Cleaver, 'The Zapatista Effect: The Internet and the Rise of an Alternative Political Fabric', www.eco.utexas.edu/~hmcleave/zapeffect.html (accessed 30/05/2012).

6

Carnival Against Capitalism: global days of action and photographs of resistance

C ARNIVALS AGAINST CAPITAL were mounted on numerous Global Days of Action in the late 1990s, signalling the emergence of a movement against neoliberal globalisation and for global justice. The first global street party was called on 16 May (M16) 1998 by London Reclaim the Streets (RTS) and the newly founded People's Global Action (PGA) to coincide with the G8 summit in Birmingham and the following week's WTO ministerial meeting in Geneva. Over thirty street parties happened around the world from Bogotá, Columbia to Melbourne, Australia and from Stockholm, Sweden to Tel Aviv, Israel. On 18 June 1999, the Carnival Against Capital (J18) took place in the city of London and simultaneously in over seventy-five cities around the globe, an immediate precursor of the global actions in Seattle in 1999 and in Genoa in 2001. This chapter examines the photographic documents of the J18 party available on the website of Reclaim the Streets, offering an analysis of the recurrent themes and examining photography's role in the production of an alternative narrative of protest to the one constructed by the mainstream mass media.

Resistance is the secret of joy

The Global Street Parties, held in financial districts or outside superstores, banks and multinational headquarters and aimed at corporate power, were organised by a grassroots counterglobalisation network, People's Global Action (PGA), along with other activist groups, such as Reclaim the Streets (RTS) and Earth First. The PGA was an offshoot of the ideas of the Zapatistas that first emerged in

1997. Nevertheless, the actions owed a great deal in terms of their inspiration to RTS, a network of direct action. RTS grew out of the anti-roads movement in Britain in the early 1990s, when the building of new roads inaugurated a period often identified with changes in the character of British environmentalism.[1] It emerged as part of the 'DiY culture', of the 1990s counterculture, which included 'a youth-centred and -directed cluster of interests and practices around green radicalism, direct-action politics, new musical sounds and experiences'.[2] The protesters used direct-action techniques such as locking themselves to machinery, street blockades and various other small-scale actions.

The year 1994 was a turning point for the anti-road movement, since it mounted two big campaigns. During the summer, the long campaign against the M11 highway link took place and along with the squatting in the residential district of Claremont Road, where the protesters inhabited the streets, and built scaffolding and aerial netting. This was also the year of the Criminal Justice and Public Order Act (CJA), which enabled the authorities to ban open techno parties.[3] In the next few years, RTS staged direct actions which were not only preoccupied with environmental issues and the 'car culture', but with a more prominent political agenda. Environmental concerns merged with an attack on consumerism, the political and economic forces behind the 'car culture' and capitalism. The M41 party in July 1996 is a typical example of a street party combining direct action, fun, humour and rave and it was one of the largest parties, attracting some thousands of protesters. It also signalled the political and theoretical opening of the group, proclaiming support for the tube workers in slogans such as 'Support the Tube Workers' and extracts from the Situationists such as 'the society that abolished every adventure makes its own abolition the only possible adventure'.

RTS actions were a cluster of innovative practices and elements found in earlier collective attempts at social transformation. There are several close affinities between RTS street actions and art groups' activities, which have used the language of propaganda and activism. The roots of these actions can be traced to the long tradition of events that began with Dadaism and Futurism, furthered by happenings, art performances or performance-based activities that arose at the end of the 1960s and during the 1970s. The creativity and festivity of the street parties can be linked with the 'constructed situations' and the street theatre actions in the Parisian uprising of 1968. The continuities are also to be found in the RTS slogan 'Above the tarmac the Beach', which resembles 'The Beach Beneath the Paving Stones' dominant in the French May '68 protests. In both cases, 'the Beach' stands for notions of festivity, freedom, creativity and self-determination, which can be found underneath the 'stones' of repression, bureaucracy, a lack of democracy and of freedom, which characterise capitalist society. The theoretical lineage between the two moments can be seen in RTS drawing directly upon Raoul Vaneigem's *The Revolution of Everyday Life* and Guy Debord's *The Society of Spectacle*, as becomes clearly apparent on the RTS website and in the group's writings.[4] Other theoretical references include Bakhtin's writings on carnival and Hakim Bey's thinking about a 'temporary autonomous zone'.[5] The RTS slogan asks for creativity and festivity, which can be seen as a prolongation of the 'constructed situations' and the street theatre actions in the Parisian uprising of 1968. Similar festive elements can also be found in many past protest movements and countercultures of the 1960s, 1970s and 1980s, namely: the Guerrilla Theater of the Youth International Party (Yippies), the theatrical anti-Vietnam war demonstrations with 'Bread and Puppet Theatre' leading the way and the squatter battles in Germany or Italy in the 1970s and 1980s.

The RTS introduced innovative tactics, mainly the imaginative action of the street party, which was based on the idea of taking over major roads in London and transforming them into communal creative spaces. The direct action of a street party was not simply the product of anti-road and ecological principles, but of a wider critique on consumerism and capitalism and of a continuous struggle to reclaim the commons, an element that RTS shared with many social networks, activist groups and radical movements that emerged in the 1990s, such as the Brazilian landless peasants (MST) in their efforts to squat on huge tracts of empty land and build cooperative farms and communities, the Argentinean workers and their taking over of factories abandoned by their owners, the indigenous people in Mexico and their claiming of their land rights and the Bolivian people and their struggle against the privatisation of the water supply in their country.[6] This opening of RTS to an anti-capitalist political language and agenda was realised in the alliance of the group with other social groups, such as the Liverpool Dockers, the Hillingdon hospital and Magnet strikers, which brought together RTS activists, environmentalists, dockers and trade unionists.[7] This widening became more obvious when the RTS became part of the People's Global Action (PGA), a global network in support of the Zapatista movement.[8] Then, the 'global street party' as a tactic became part of the 'global days of action' against neoliberalism.

The RTS enthusiastically embraced the technological innovations of the 1990s, including the internet and computer generated sounds and images. In particular, the networking, campaigning and mobilising capacities of the internet were used by the RTS as early as 1997, when their website was first constructed. The website acted as a platform for information and political ideas, where updated information could be found about the group's actions as well as political analyses of the group's political agenda. Nevertheless, it is necessary to bear in mind that the web was in its embryonic stage and it may not have been accessible to all RTS members or to a large number of the general public. Therefore, RTS relied on more traditional means of communication, such as spoof newspapers and leaflets to mobilise activists and communicate their political messages. For example, the group used to publish their own newspaper the *Evading Standard*, a parody of the London newspaper the *Evening Standard*.[9] The newspaper, as well as various leaflets, was distributed during RTS actions and highlighted direct action as the only alternative to conventional politics and representative democracy.

Photographs of Carnival/photographs of resistance

The Carnival Against Capital, called by London Reclaim the Streets, was organised as an international day of carnival, action and protest to take place in the financial district of London on the 18 June 1999 (J18). The J18 Global Street Party took place simultaneously in over seventy-five cities around the globe from the United Kingdom, Spain and the Czech Republic to the United States, Nigeria and Australia. In London, some thousands of people flooded the City of London wearing masks, and carrying flags of black, green, red and gold. The activists, who came from different directions, filled the Square Mile in a 'Carnival Against Capital'. As *Maybe*, a newspaper attached to RTS, proclaimed 'for a few hours the world's prime profit zone became a revolutionary pleasure zone'.[10] The 'Square Mile' of London's prestigious financial district was blocked with protesters dancing to the rhythm of the music, hoisting puppets and waving the RTS flags in the air. Their slogans 'Our Resistance is as global as capital', 'The earth is a common treasury for all' and 'Revolution is the only option' appeared on posters, stickers and banners, while many copies of a spoof newspaper were handed out en masse on the day of the protest under the title 'global market melt-down'. At the same time, 50,000 metallic gold flyers with a quote from the Situationist Raoul Vaneigem saying 'to work for delight and authentic festivity is barely distinguishable from preparing for general insurrection' were distributed internationally.[11] In this way, protesters invited passers-by, traders, bankers and all kinds of City workers to join the party.

The significance of the event lies not only in the embodiment of the attractive principles of creativity, horizontality and direct action, but also in the 'volatile mixture of carnival and revolution, creativity and conflict, using rhythm and music to reclaim space, transform the streets and inject pleasure into politics'.[12]

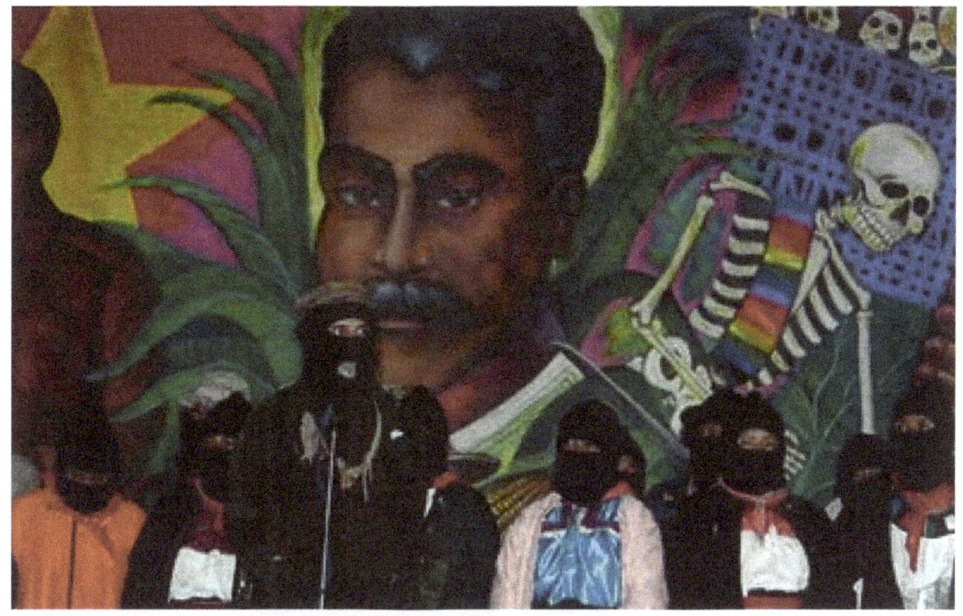

1 Photographer Unknown, EZLN website

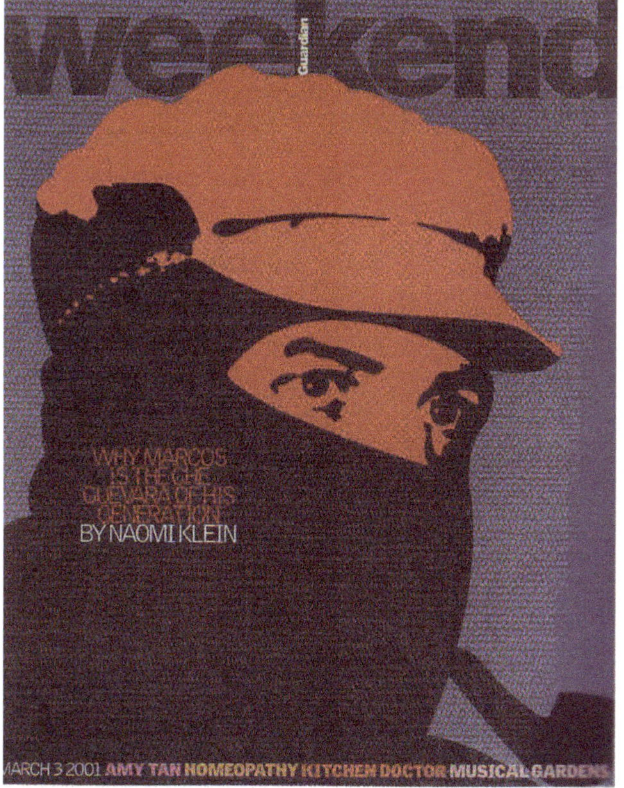

2 *Guardian Weekend*, Cover, 3 March 2001. (© Guardian News & Media Ltd 2001)

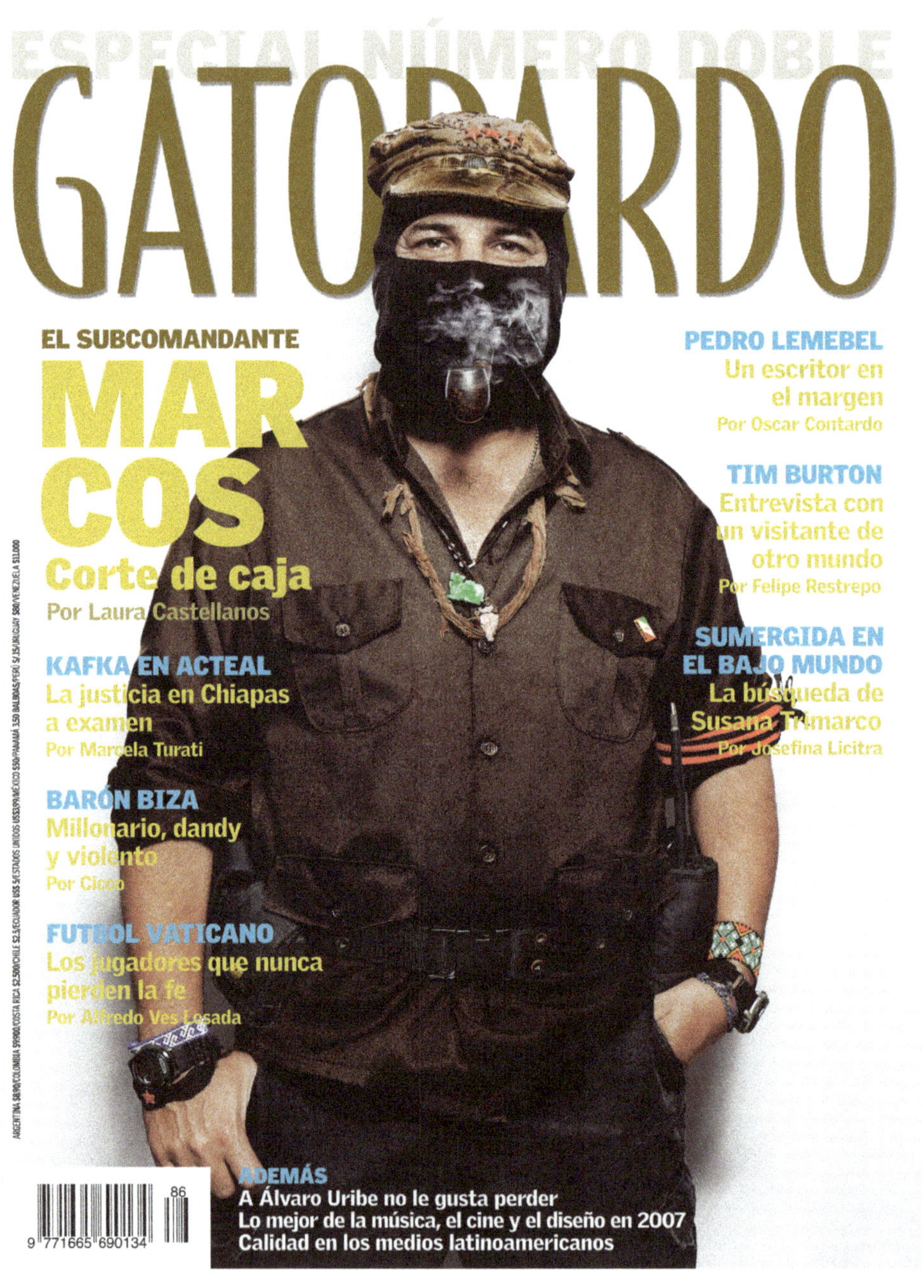

3 Ricardo Trabulsi, Subcomandante Marcos, *Gatopardo*, Cover, December 2007.
(© Gatopardo)

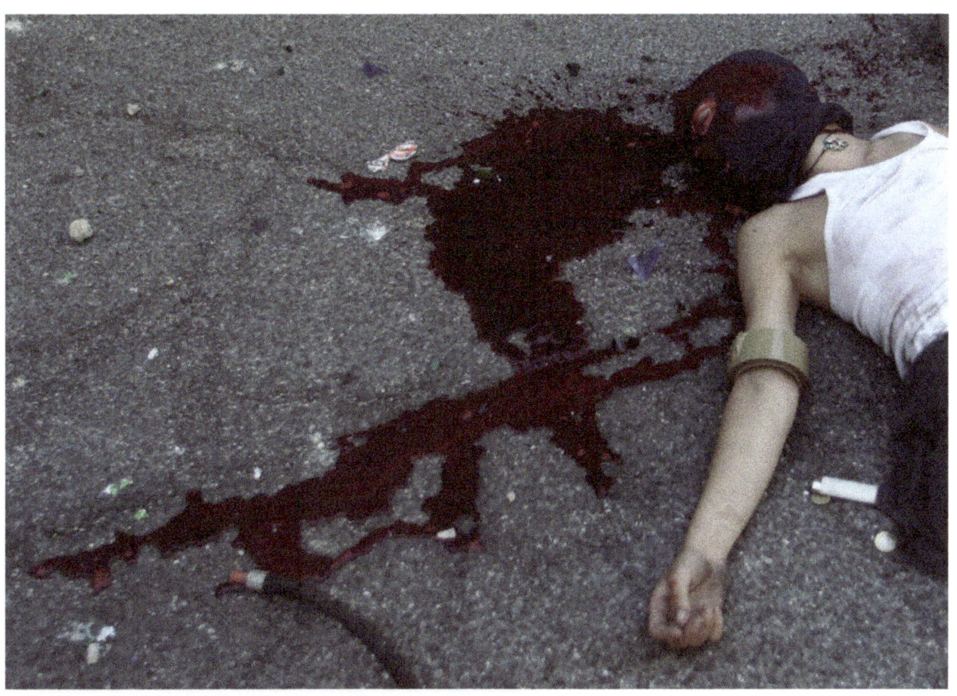

4 Dylan Martinez, Carlo Giuliani Dead, July 2001. (© Reuters)

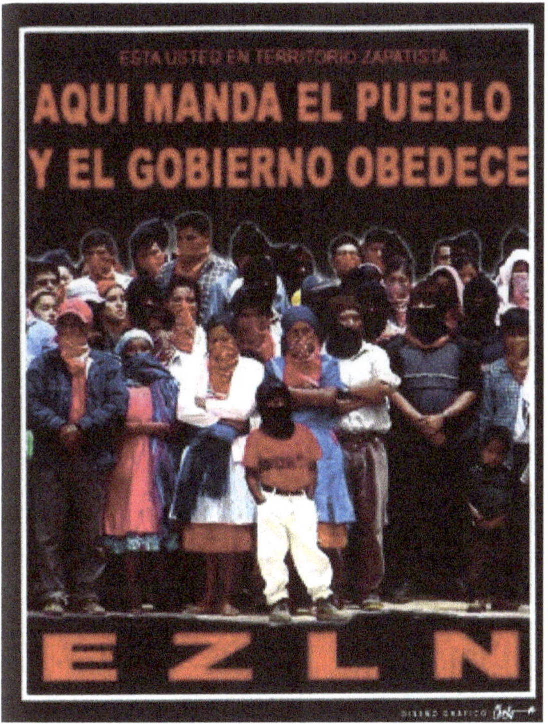

5 Poster, EZLN website

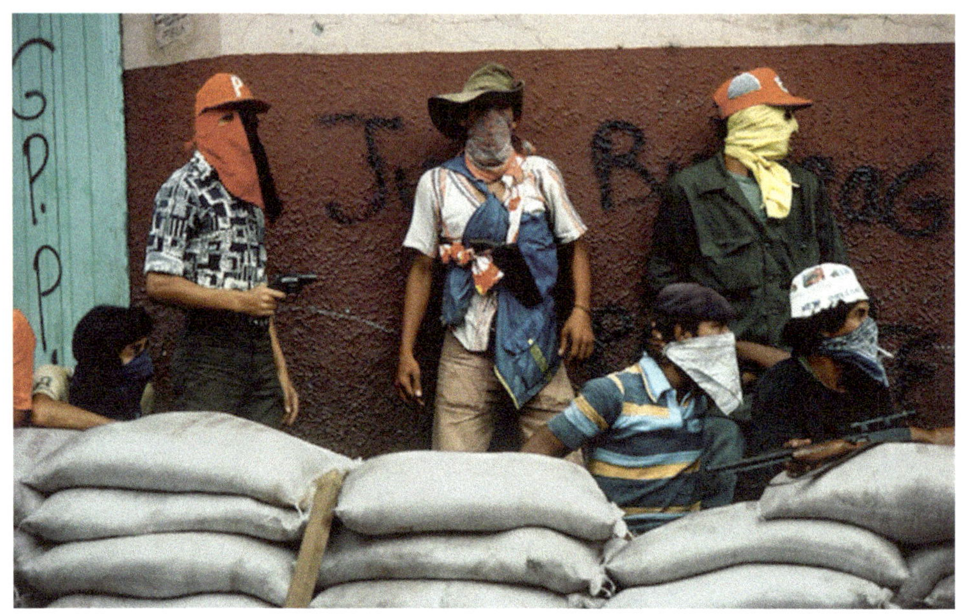

6 Susan Meiselas, *Matagalpa. Muchachos await the Counterattack by the National Guard*. Nicaragua. Book. June 1978–July 1979. (© Magnum Photos)

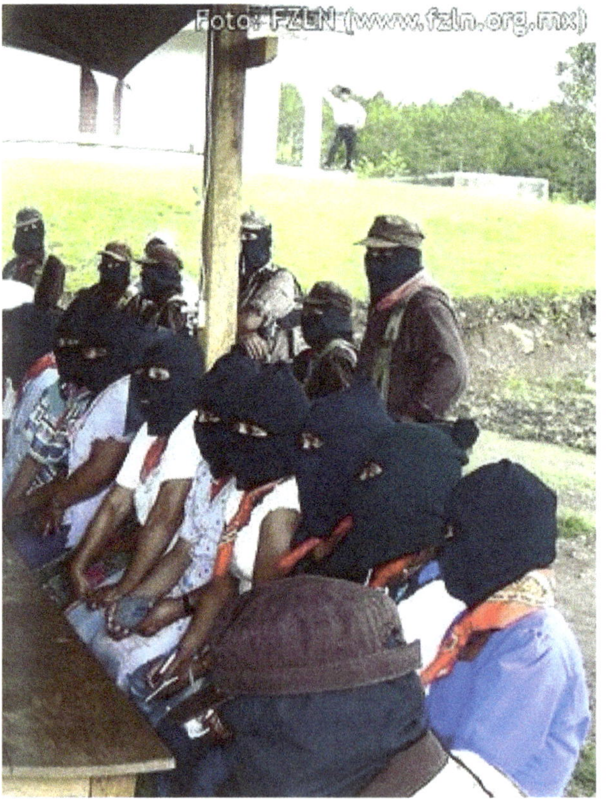

7 Photographer, EZLN website

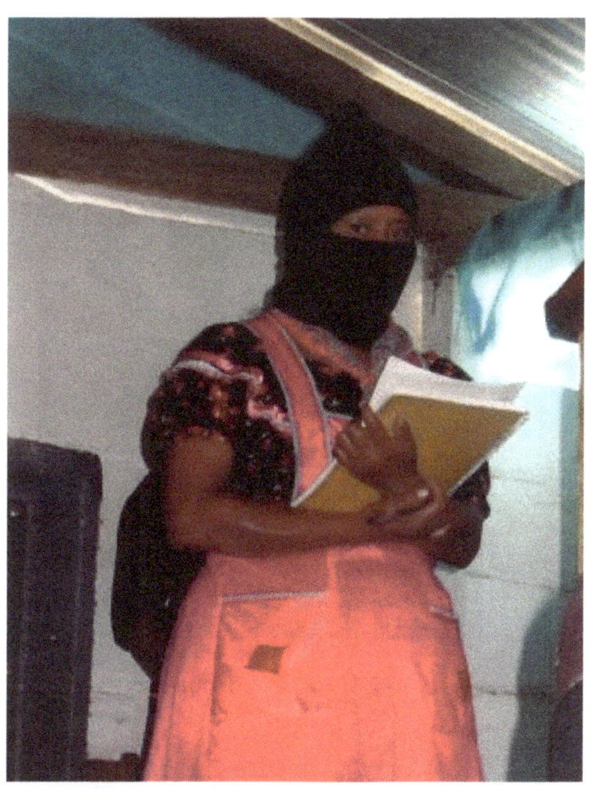

8 Photographer, EZLN website

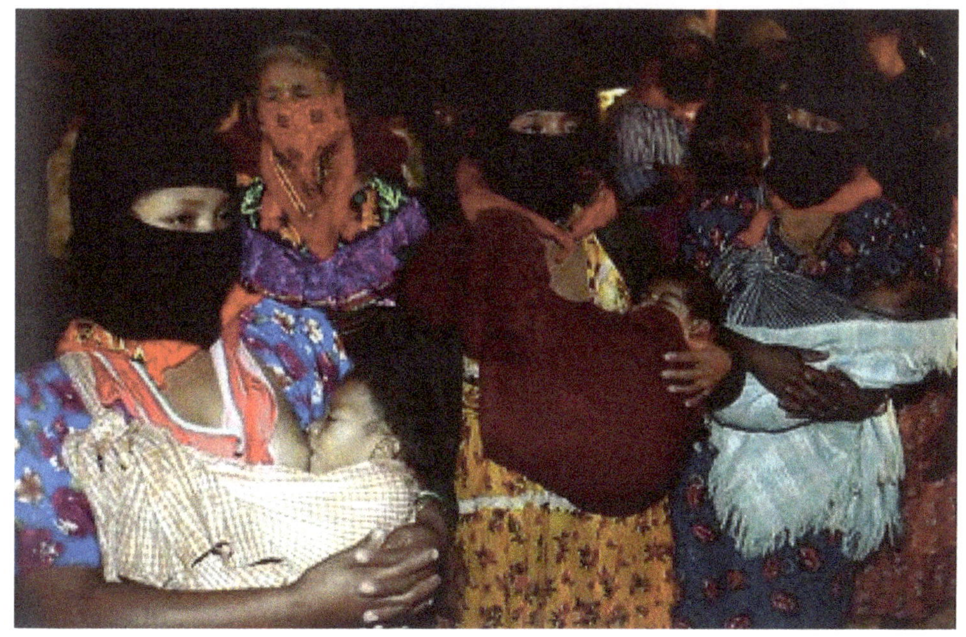

9 Photographer, EZLN website

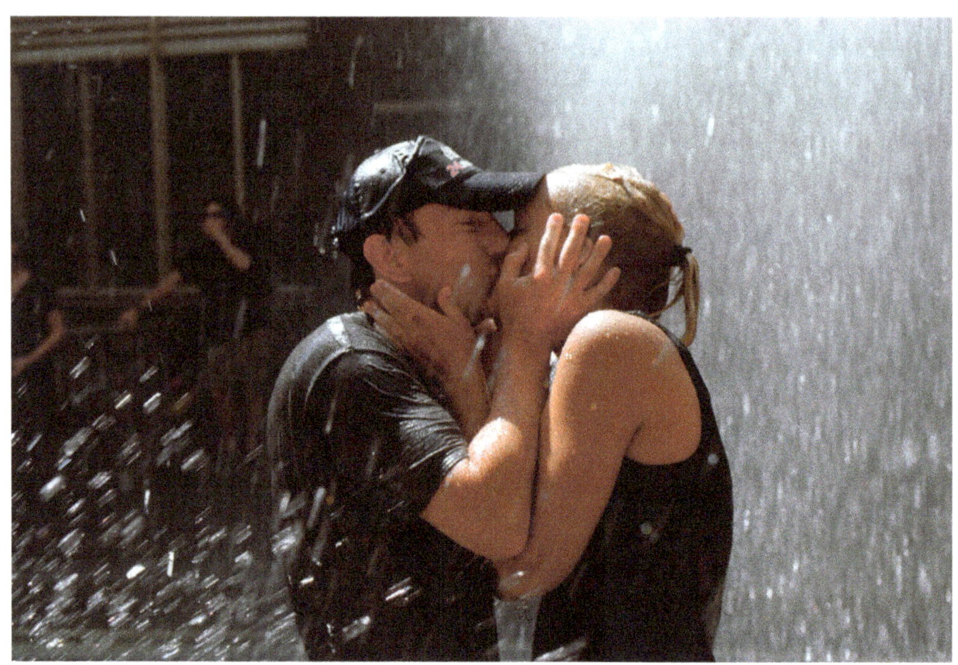

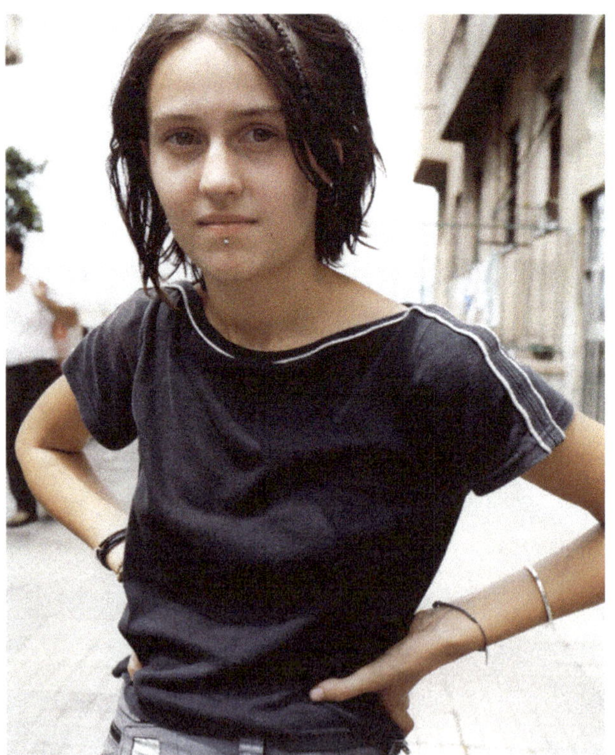

10 Nick Cobbing, Protesters gather in the heart of the City of London's financial district in the J18 Carnival Against Capitalism. A lot of water from an opened water main helps cool the crowds as the protest develops into a party atmosphere, 1999. (© Nick Cobbing)

11 Joel Sternfeld, '*Because it's right*', A protester, Genoa, 2001. (C-print, Courtesy of the artist and Luhring Augustine, New York)

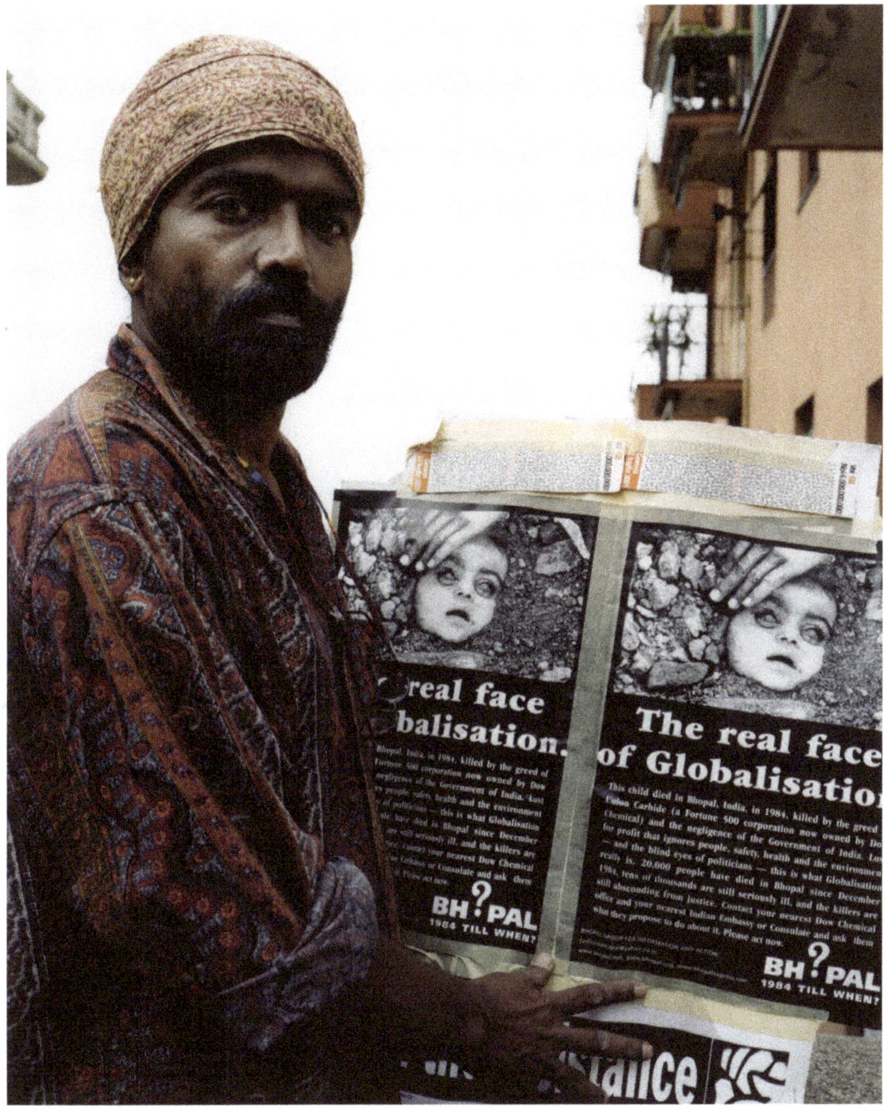

12 Joel Sternfeld, A protester from Bhopal, Genoa, 2001. (C-print, Courtesy of the artist and Luhring Augustine, New York). People are still dying in Bhopal. Over twenty thousand have died, and those born after the disaster have growth and menstrual problems. Over one hundred twenty thousand are still suffering from chronic diseases of the eye, the brain and reproductive and immune systems. Five thousand metric tons of chemicals were dumped into the ground and inside and outside the factory – it's gone into the drinking water, the only source of drinking water for ten communities. Union Carbide evades justice, and now it has sold itself to Dow Chemical.

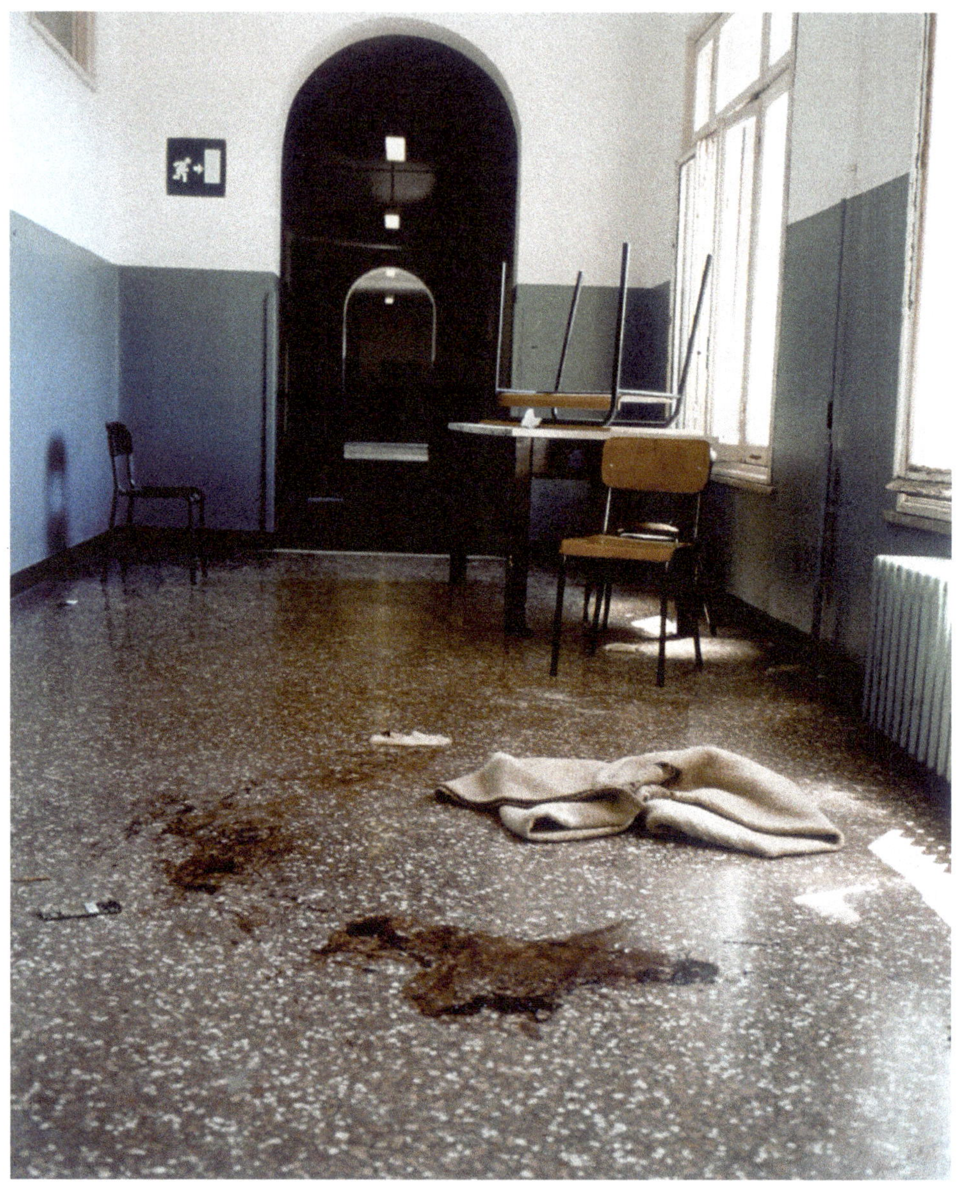

13 Joel Sternfeld, The Fifth Floor of the Armando Diaz School after a Police Raid, Genoa, 21 July 2001. (C-print, Courtesy of the artist and Luhring Augustine, New York)

This insertion of pleasure into political action, the fusion of carnival and protest challenged more conventional forms of mobilisation, such as the demonstration. In a parallel way, photographic documents of these actions break with a long tradition of protest iconography in terms of their subject matter, presentation and dissemination.

To start with the latter, photographs of these actions were and are available to contemporary viewers via the RTS website. The website was constructed in 1997 and was extensively used by the group to organise actions, mobilise, build coalitions, communicate and campaign. This early use of the new technology's possibilities by the RTS activists enabled the creation of an online photographic archive consisting of a large amount of visual documentation, posters and leaflets as well as accounts of the group and its actions.[13] The online archive was 'owned' by the activists themselves, resisting the unity imposed by ownership in private and state archives and challenging the limited nature of the circulation of these photographs. Most importantly, the online photographic archive resists the conventions of photographic reportage, attempting to accommodate diverse practices that would 'preserve' the memory of the RTS actions.

The archive is organised in diachronic order, starting with photographs of the first party, held in Camden High Street on the 14 May 1995 and containing photographs of all the street parties held in the United Kingdom, Europe, Australia and the United States. The archive is a peculiar assortment of photographs, diverse in style and technique, taken by different practitioners, including activists, amateur photographers and professional photojournalists, including Alex Macnaughton, Nick Cobbing, Alan Lodge (better known as Tash) and Gideon Mendel.[14] These photographers' involvement in the activities and their understanding of the group's aims and political ideas varied. Macnaughton, whose photographs were also published in *The Guardian*, was always treated with great suspicion by the group.[15] On the other hand, photographs by amateur photographers, most of them activists themselves, whose photographs were taken for personal use, as memorabilia of their activism, were probably intended to end up in personal files or be part of their correspondence with other members of the group. These different practices were purposefully put together by the activists, in a similar way that the Zapatista website assembled a great variety of practices in order to create a visual narrative that contrasts with the stereotypical narratives constructed by the commercial mass media. This alternative narrative concentrated on the festive character and pleasurable moments of the actions, aspects that to a great extent were underplayed or ignored in the mainstream media.

In the case of J18 in the financial centre of London, twelve amateur colourful snapshots with joyful subject matter are presented in exactly the same manner: there is no reference to the name of the photographer, while each photograph is accompanied by a very brief comment. The still images accumulated here are homogenised under the general principle that 'joy is revolutionary'– to paraphrase the SI's motto that boredom is counter-revolutionary. They are all colourful photographs of a happy crowd, highlighting the celebratory nature of the party. In a rather amateurish snapshot of the crowd – the fourth in the series – the red and green flags contrast with the building with the glass façade in the background, adding to the joyous effect of the image. The red, green and black flags symbolised the different ideological tendencies, namely communism, environmentalism and anarchism, replacing the traditional placards and posters with political slogans. The celebratory nature of the event is highlighted both with the depiction of coloured masks and the short caption reading 'Party-time in the sunshine' which accompanies the photograph. In a similar manner and without reference to the photographer, the next photograph is captioned: 'Party goes on and on'. The photograph taken from a high viewpoint is presented in low resolution, seemingly taken by an amateur photographer. The photograph focuses on musicians surrounded by the crowd. The whole surface of the image is in focus, so each person does not stand as a unit but as part of a whole.

Another photograph of the series depicts three protesters in white costumes and colourful masks and lying in the middle of the street. The photograph depicts bodies escaping for a while from their isolation and alienation, being fused with other bodies, feeling the excitement and the joy of the carnival and refusing the static images of the perfect bodies on television, billboards and magazines developed by Western capitalism. In other photographs, the bodies of the protesters contrast with the monotonous grey buildings of London's financial district. It is the pleasure taken in being part of a collective that is captured in the last four photographs in the series. These photographs depict protesters in ecstatic moments, enjoying the waterfall (plate 10).[16] Captions such as 'water rains down' and 'water, water, everywhere' do not provide us with any information about the actions, but rather add to the festive atmosphere of the photographs.

These photographs can be seen as a continuation of the emphasis on the festive elements of the street parties, evident in the photographic documentation of the other parties on the website. The ten photographs documenting the M41 party in July 1996, one of the largest RTS parties, repeat exactly the same iconographical themes. Accompanied by short, descriptive captions that emphasise the pleasurable nature of the party and look amateurish, these photographs insist on joyful subject matter. What is distinct about both cases is the striking lack of further contextual information about the activities depicted. The focus on joyful subject matter maximised by the use of colour and descriptive captions, lacks any direct reference to political context. While the street parties were conceived as a fusion of politics and festival, these photographs lack explicit reference to the political, reducing these photographs to documents of festivities.

This overemphasis on the festivity of the actions, characteristic of the representations of both these events, fails to acknowledge the striking differences between the two street parties. M41 was a typical example of a street party, which signalled an opening up to other social groups in the following years, including solidarity actions with the Liverpool Dockers, and the Hillingdon hospital and Magnet strikers.[17] This gradual opening up of the RTS to new groups meant a widening of their political language and agenda. As the activists themselves declared in the alternative publication *Do or Die*:

> We are saying that the power that attacks those who work, through union legislation and casualisation, is the same power that is attacking the planet with over-production and consumption of resources; the power that produces cars by four million a year is the same power that decides to attack workers through the disempowerment of the unions, reducing work to slavery.[18]

Nevertheless, this opening became more explicit during the J18, the first event, within four years of RTS actions and sixty-five recorded parties, with an explicitly anti-corporate and anti-capitalist agenda. The 'Carnival Against Capitalism' took place in the world's prime profit zone and its name, as well as its dominant slogans, was clearly against capitalism and neoliberal politics.

It becomes, therefore, clear that the activists deliberately insisted on the joyful photographs, resisting the conventions of photographic reportage which present the protester as a violent subject. There was a common feeling among RTS activists that the mainstream media underplayed or ignored their actions, or at times totally misrepresented them. An RTS protester claimed about the J18:

> Predictably over the following days, self-styled journalists from so-called newspapers went to town, misrepresenting us all. None of the pictures showed people dancing, peaceful or happy – the only moments deemed sufficiently photogenic for the tabloids and broadsheets are fighting and

bleeding and smashed windows. Of course, they'd all missed the real story.[19]

The 'real visual story' was an alternative to the mainstream newspapers' stereotypical visual story of violent protesters and clashes with the police. In fact, the J18 was widely covered in the British mainstream press – in contrast with the limited coverage of the M41 – making the front pages in broadsheets and tabloids alike. The mainstream representation of the J18 focused on images of damage, fires, violence and injury, accompanying them with texts that underlined the violence shown by protesters. For most of the newspapers, 18 June became synonymous with protest violence, a metonym evoking visual images of protesters clashing with the police. The headlines read 'Anarchists in fistfights with City traders', 'Day the City Turned into a Battleground', 'Evil Savages', 'The day the mob brought violence and destruction to the square mile'; the editorial commentary, often a detailed description of the public disorder and destruction, provided the contextual interpretative frameworks within which photographs of violence, injured protesters and battles acquired their meaning. The predilection to seizing on the violent moments of J18 was absolute in the British press, excluding any photographs of the big crowd gathered outside the Warburg Dillion Read building in Liverpool Street or any photographs of protesters partying. This fitted in with the dominant dramatisation of news imagery in the mainstream mass media, reproducing the predominant discourse that protesters cannot be peaceful.

It is exactly this rhetoric that the online archive refuses to acknowledge, constructing an 'oppositional visual story' which emphasised the non-violent character of the actions. It is significant that any photographs of violence are left out, reflecting RTS's attempts to defend one of the basic principles of the group, namely non-violent action. For the RTS, as well as for many other contemporary environmental organisations, non-violence was seen as a principle rather than just a tactic. Many other contemporary environmental organisations, such as the radical group Earth First! and groups which participated in the anti-roads protests such as the so-called Dongas highlight the nature of their non-violent actions.

Joy is revolutionary

All these elements of laughter, street theatre, carnival and non-violence, which constituted a 'new language of civil disobedience',[20] persisted in subsequent

Global Days of Actions. By the turn of the millennium, these activities became embodied in actions of Tute Bianche and Ya Basta in Global Days of Actions, including the 'Battle of Seattle' on 30 November 1999 (N30) and J20 in Genoa, 19–21 July (J20) 2001. The 'Pink and Silver Bloc', consisting of women dressed in pink and wearing wigs, emerged at the Global Day of action in Prague on 26 September (S26) 2000, activists wearing cooking pots on their heads and calling themselves the 'Medieval Bloc' appeared in Quebec City in 2001 and there was the Revolutionary Anarchist Clown Bloc in Philadelphia in 2000. In 2003, the Clandestine Insurgent Rebel Clown Army was founded, followed by the Laboratory of Insurrectionary Imagination in 2004 combining rebel clowning with direct-action tactics and participating in various days of action.[21] These groups brought to these events the 'culture of laughter' and the 'laguague of the carnival' creating 'autonomous convergence sites' and experimenting with alternatives.[22]

In Genoa, the confrontational tactic was direct action implemented by Ya Basta and Tute Bianche, the strongest presence in the demonstrations numbering more than 100,000 activists.[23] Tute Bianche/White Overalls emerged in September 1994, when activists dressed in ghosty white overalls took to the streets of Milan against the Mayor's comments on the eviction of the social centre. Tute Bianche were a mock army of activists wearing elaborate padding made of cardboard, foam, old mattresses, inner tubes, chemical-proof white jumpsuits and helmets, protecting the most exposed parts of their bodies. In Genoa, Tute Bianche attempted to push through the police lines non-violently, using shields made of junk, carrying coloured ballons and banners with writing 'El Pueblo Unido, Jamas Sera Vencido' (People United, Never Defeated), 'Genoa Libera' (Free Genova), 'E-Z-L-N'.[24]

Despite the omnipresence of these groups in the Global Days of Actions that followed the J18, the photographic documentation that dominated the mainstream and alternative media alike did not focus on the non-violent actions. The photographs of the Genoa demonstrations were not altogether different between the mainstream press and the alternative media, as it had been in J18. A representation of violence became the focal theme of all photographs and the central point of all public debates. In terms of the mass media, from whom such a coverage was to be accepted, this iconography was not any different from the coverage of the J18. It is the omnipresence of violence in the activist archives that is of interest here.

The Archive of Global Protest (AGP) put together by the People's Global Action is characteristic in this respect.[25] The AGP provides the most complete online archive of all the global actions from 1994 to 2009, bringing together photographs with activist reports and testimonies, among other things. The photographic archive of the Genoa protests is arranged chronolologically, starting with the preparations for the anti-summit under the title 'at the borders of Italy', which features photographs depicting the deportation of Greek activists and closing with photographs of the police raid on Diaz School.[26] Only the photographs collated to represent the first day of action, the 19 July, under the title 'migrants march', show protesters demonstrating peacefully.

The photographs of the 20 and 21 July are photographs of police violence, clashes between protesters and the police, chaos and gas. Under the section 'police shoot demonstrator' Dylan Martinez's eleven photographs of the shooting of Carlo Giuliani – discussed in part I – are presented on the website along with detailed comments that direct the viewer to follow all the stages that preceded the shooting of Giuliani shooting and point out details within the photographs, such as a provocateur. Martinez's photographs are perceived here as proof of the police's explicit violence and as an accurate record of the scene of the crime, reaffirming photography's evidential status. Likewise, photographs of the demonstrations focus on the policemen's use of tear gas and overt violence, as in the case of Diaz School. Genoa's photographic representation revolves around the same central themes that dominate the public debate: the legitimisation of violence. Protest is not presented as an alternative space for creativity, or joy that breaks with capitalist discourse, but rather an indispensable part of the dominant discourse constructed by the hegemony of the mass media. Photography seems to play a central role in this discourse.

In contrast, the RTS website contributes to the collective struggles against capitalism by preserving the memories of protest as a joyful collective process. These photographic images can therefore be regarded as the documents of the collective refusal to accept contemporary consumer capitalism, its subsequent dissolution of human communities, the triumph of mechanisation, mercantilisation and reification. They also invite the viewers to rethink the pleasure taken from participating in a collective, the joy stemming from non-violent resistance. These photographic documents also break with the dominant representations of official politics in the mainstream press and on the internet.

These memories of joyful protest have been erased by the official narratives of protest, as well as, at times, from the Left's collective memory. Photographic documents of earlier moments of popular insurrection, such as photographs of people gathered to listen to the sound of a violin and an accordion and dance, coming from the strikes of 1936, which greeted the first Popular Front government in France, are buried in official archives.[27] The similarities between these documents of the strikers' effort to escape from the very harshness of life in the factories, the prevalent atmosphere of joy, music and dance, and the J18 documents available on the RTS archive are striking. Joy and laughter as vital components of revolutionary carnival, in which the low mock the high, seemed to be present in the photographic documents of May '68 in Paris and the theatrical anti-Vietnam war demonstrations, with 'Bread and Puppet Theatre' leading the way. The iconographical lineage can be extended to include Allan Sekula's photographs of the human body that asserts itself in the streets of Seattle against the abstraction of global capital and the photographic documents of the various instances of the anti-capitalist movement, including images of Tutte Bianche in Italy and the Rebel Clown Army in anti-G8 actions. The RTS archive attempts to retrieve this fundamental element: pleasure not pursued as an end in itself, but taken from simply overcoming social boundaries, isolation and marginalisation and forming a collective insurrectionary identity.

Evidently, this documentation cannot be without problems and limitations, raising questions about the website's contribution to the memory of RTS actions. A still photograph cannot depict the actual experience of a street party, nor can it document the sounds, the duration and excitement of the event. This becomes more complicated when the event stands on the edge where dance, music and festival meet political protest. Therefore, the photograph can only offer a partial image of a complex event, which offered the time and space for the effectuation of latent possibilities for another world. The participatory nature of the street party is inevitably lost in the photographic document. During the RTS street parties, the road became a stage for a participatory festival, in which no division between the performer and the audience existed. The experience is based on the spirit of face-to-face comradeship, avoiding any mediation. The medium of photography brings back the collapsed division between the performers and the viewers, but it keeps alive the pleasure emerging from collectivism, from the disappearance of social and professional divisions, from the creation of an alternative space and time to the one imposed on us by capitalism.

Notes

1 For a discussion on how the anti-roads movement of the early 1990s signalled changes in British environmentalism, see: B. Doherty, 'Paving the Way: The Rise of Direct Action Against Road-Building and the Changing Character of British Environmentalism', *International Conference on Alternative Futures and Popular Protest*, 1 (Manchester: Manchester

Metropolitan University, 1996).

2 G. McKay, *DiY Culture: Party and Protest in Nineties Britain* (London & New York: Verso, 1998), p. 2.

3 The CJA was passed by the British government in November 1994. It created a number of offences and gave the police additional powers to deal with these offences and with crowd situations. Protesters involved in the road movement believed that the law was repressive, and was aimed at banning any kind of protest.

4 Among the texts archived on the RTS website under the title RTS ideology, there are extracts from Guy Debord's *The Society of the Spectacle*, as well as a *Situationist Theory for Beginners*. See: http://rts.gn.apc.org/ (accessed 20/05/2012). Moreover, the words of Situationist Raoul Vaneigem, 'to work for delight and authentic festivity is barely distinguishable from preparing for general insurrection', were printed on the group's flyers and were distributed on the 18 June 1999. For other references to the SI, see: McKay, *DiY Culture* and *Do or Die*, issues 5 and 6.

5 G. Grindon, 'Carnival Against Capital: a Comparison of Bakhtin, Vaneigem and Bey', *Anarchist Studies*, 12: 2 (2004), p. 148.

6 For more information on 'Movimento dos Trabalhadores Rurais Sem Terra' (MST, Brazil's Landless Workers' Movement), see: www.mstbrazil.org/; for 'El Manifesto de La Coordinadora de Defensa del Agua y la Vida' (The Manifesto of Co-Ordinator for the Defense of Water and Life), see: www.constituyentesoberana.org/organizacioneseinstituciones/lospronunciamientos/manifiesto%20del%20agua.pdf; for the Argentinean workers' takeover of abandoned factories, see: www.thetake.org/index.cfm, http://cuc.labase.org/ (accessed 20/01/2006).

7 John Jordan, 'The Art of Necessity: The Subversive Imagination of Anti-Road Protest and Reclaim the Streets', in McKay, *DiY Culture*, pp. 129–51.

8 People's Global Action (PGA) is a grassroots network, which first emerged in 1997. PGA was part of the new anti-capitalist movement and calls for Global Days of Actions (GDA), local actions all over the world, which propose daily resistance to the existing economic order and local alternatives. PGA organised a variety of different activities, always in collaboration with other regional groups, organisations and activists from all over the world.

9 I have seen this document in the personal archive of John Jordan, an artist, activist and key member of the RTS.

10 *Maybe* (1 May 2000).

11 http://rts.gn.apc.org/ (accessed 10/05/2012).

12 W. Tyler, 'Dancing at the Edge of Chaos: A Spanner in the Works of Global Capitalism', in Notes from Everywhere (ed.), *We Are Everywhere: The Irresistible Rise of Global Capitalism* (London: Verso, 2003), p. 174.

13 http://rts.gn.apc.org/ (accessed 10/05/2012).

14 For more details on these photographers' work, see: www.cobb-web.org/, http://tash.gn.apc.org.

15 In his words: 'Even though I had known some of the people in the anti road movement for a long time they were always worried that I was a spy for the police so they were not always very helpful.' Email Correspodence with Alex Macnaughton, 29/01/2006.

16 This photograph was taken by Nick Cobbing, a photographer closely related to the RTS

and shows two activists kissing under the waterfall during the J18. The photograph was not reproduced on the website but its subject matter captures the ecstatic moments of the carnival in a similar manner with the website photographs. Unfortunately, none of the website photographs could have been reproduced in the book due to their low resolution.

17 J. Jordan, 'The Art of Necessity: The Subversive Imagination of Anti-Road Protest and Reclaim the Streets', in McKay, *DiY Culture*, pp. 147–8.

18 *Do or Die*, 'Why Reclaim the Streets and the Liverpool Dockers?', No 6, online version, www.eco-action.org/dod/no6/rts.htm.

19 W. Tyler, 'Dancing at the Edge of Chaos: A Spanner in the Works of Global Capitalism', in Notes from Everywhere (ed.), *We Are Everywhere*, p. 194.

20 D. Graeber, 'The New Anarchists', *New Left Review*, 13 (2002), pp. 61–73.

21 G. St John, 'Protestival: Global Days of Action and Carnivalized Politics in the Present', *Social Movements Studies*, 7: 2 (2008), p. 181.

22 Ibid., p. 182.

23 W. Tyler, 'Dancing at the Edge of Chaos', p. 357.

24 Ibid.

25 www.nadir.org/nadir/initiativ/agp/index.html (accessed 20/05/2012).

26 www.nadir.org/nadir/initiativ/agp/free/genova/pics1.htm (accessed 20/05/2012).

27 S. J. Dell, 'Festival and Revolution: The Popular Front in France and the Press Coverage of the Strikes of 1936', *Art History*, 23: 4 (2000), pp. 599–621.

Part III

7

May '68 in the museum

'IF MAY lives on as image rather than narration, that is because its story is such an ambiguous and inconclusive one', wrote Keith Reader in his book on May '68.[1] In a similar tone, Kristin Ross, pointing out the lack of historical research on May '68, argued that 'it may be that a society finds it enormously difficult even to formulate a demand for historical knowledge when an event is so ambiguous'.[2] This ambiguity offered the ground for sociologists and reformed *gauchistes*, who, since the mid-1970s, systematically produced 'official narratives' which set the limits of how the events of May '68 in France are rethought, discussed, represented and remembered. These narratives, which dominated public discourse and were celebrated publicly in France and elsewhere ten, twenty, thirty and forty years after the events of May '68 – appropriating the memory of May '68, to paraphrase Walter Benjamin's famous thesis.[3] Benjamin elaborated the difficulties that the historical subject encounters in their efforts to save an image of a past endangered and under threat of becoming a tool of the ruling classes. He attributed to this moment of danger a twofold character: it threatens both the content of the tradition and those who inherit it at the same time.[4] The legacy of the events of May '68 in France has been threatened in just this fashion.

Exhibitions of photographic documents of the period – part of the commemorative events in London on the events' 40th anniversary – have also contributed decisively to such narratives; a process that has infected the possibility of 'remembering' with the fact of 'forgetting' these events. This chapter takes as its starting point an exhibition of photographs of May '68 by photojournalist Bruno Barbey at the Hayward Gallery in London in 2008, in order to examine the role that photography has played in shaping the memory *and* the forgetting of May '68, forty years on. The Hayward exhibition 'May '68: Street Posters from the Paris Rebellion' lasted for the whole month May 2008 and was the first ever such exhibition to be staged in the United Kingdom.[5]

It juxtaposed posters that were produced collectively in the occupied Atelier Populaire with Barbey's photographs. Barbey, who at the time had just become a member of the Magnum agency, was only one of many photojournalists who took to the streets of Paris to photograph the student uprising. Most of the resulting images appeared contemporaneously in the French mainstream press. Some were republished in photo-books and exhibitions, but only much later. Gilles Caron's photographs, for instance, appeared in a retrospective collection of his work on the tenth anniversary; Claude Dityvon's were re-published in a book entitled *Mai '68* on the twentieth; Serge Hambourg's were shown at the Hood Museum of Art under the title *Protest in Paris 1968: Photographs by Serge Hambourg*; Barbey's were collected in a small exhibition entitled 'Mai 68 ou l'Imagination au Pouvoir' at the Galerie Beaubourg that was organised to coincide with the thirtieth anniversary.[6]

The chapter discusses both the compositional decisions by Barbey and the subsequent institutional decisions in order to examine the problematic of documentation and display of protest photographs. It particularly highlights the subsequent institutional framing of these photographs, which have become slanted towards an overemphasis on individualism that ignores their intrinsically collective nature. This is achieved through the representational separation of a passive subject from the vigorous collective body, the depiction of women as subjects bereft of political agency and the reduction of the participants in the image to the figure of the leader or the young protester. These representational modes, reinforced by subsequent institutional decisions, support hegemonic narratives of the events and highlight questions regarding current difficulties of attending to the representation of collective political action.

Individualism vs. collectivism

At the Hayward, Barbey's black-and-white photographs were exhibited in a darkened room adjacent to the main gallery, which contained the posters of Atelier Populaire. The photographs were shown as a slide sequence without any supporting text and accompanied by nostalgic 1960s music. The lack of explanatory text is crucial here, as it suggests that the viewers would already be familiar with the movement's political demands and outcomes, its cultural aspects and its international impact. The photographs were positioned in a manner that made it clear they were supposed to act as a stand-in for this ambiguous historical event itself. It is this ability of photographs to filter the interpretive possibilities of such historical ambiguity that is of interest here and, more particularly, the way in which these photographs appear to stand in for an event that is repeatedly interpreted as a rupture within the history of post-war Europe.

The significance attributed to the events of May '68 could not have been foreseen from the point of view of the poorly attended general meeting held at the Sorbonne on the 3rd, at which students discussed the closure of Nanterre by the university administration. The arrest of 500 students after this meeting precipitated the occupation of the Sorbonne, provoked calls for the liberation of those arrested, led to the building of the first barricades and foreshadowed subsequent clashes between students and police.[7] What followed is quite well known: the government's tactics and the increasing brutality of the police contributed to an explosion of public meetings, organised action committees, vigorous demonstrations along the boulevards and the narrow streets of the Latin Quarter, and widespread occupations that culminated with the highly symbolic 'night of the barricades' on the 10th.[8] The movement soon went beyond its university origins to unite students, workers and professionals in a common struggle against de Gaulle's government. On the 13th, the students took the crucial decision to allow the workers' entry into the Sorbonne.[9] On the same day, the two main unions, the CGT – *Confédération Générale du Travail* (General Confederation of Labour) and the CFDT – *Confédération Française Démocratique du Travail* (French Democratic Workers Confederation), incited by the students' mobilisation, voted for a general workers strike.[10]

Although, initially, this action was small in scale, it provoked a chain reaction and within a few days seven-and-a-half to nine million workers were on strike.[11] By this time, almost all French universities and schools were occupied. The following weeks saw extended occupations in schools and universities, strikes in factories, department stores, banks, public transportation, gas stations and even in newspapers and television stations all over the country.[12] The majority of the intellectual and literary world also expressed support for and solidarity with the movement.[13] By the 24th, France was paralyzed by the biggest strike that this and probably any other European country had known to date.[14] The innovative forms of collective struggle that were undertaken – including sit-ins, teach-ins, consciousness-raising groups, marches within the factories and occupations of public and private spaces – indicate beyond doubt that the events were emphatically collective in form.[15] Nevertheless, these new forms of engagement and solidarity, which brought together groups of people previously separated, have tended to be elided with the stress laid on individualism that has come to characterise and inform both the dominant historical narratives and the subsequent institutional framing of this moment's photographic document.

Barbey's photographs are exemplary in this respect because they frame the relationship between individual and collective in ways that promote these narratives. There are at least two reasons for this that are inherent in the medium of photography. The first concerns the act of framing, that is the camera's ability to freeze an image into the frame, to focus on the individual, often privileging them over any group that is also present. The second relates to the photographer's own prejudices and his awareness of the political possibilities of the medium. In the case of Barbey, his tendency to focus on predominantly young and charismatic men, urged by his professional status as a photojournalist, favours the subsequent institutional framing.

In a substantial number of his photographs, the individual emerges as separate from the collective. This is evident in a photograph of a barricade erected on Saints-Pères street in front of the École de Médecine (figure 12). The subject, a fashionable young man, stands on a bench in the middle of the barricade above the crowd and his melancholic gaze is directed away from them. The camera is positioned quite low and the composition resembles an accidental snapshot; the subject, seemingly unaware of the photographer's presence, does not look into the lens. At the same time, a woman photographed from behind is included in the frame. The composition is also interesting for its emphasis on what is not included in the frame: the unknown space to which the gaze of the man is projected. The barricade divides the photograph in two and serves pictorially to emphasise a sense of physical separation. What, nevertheless, remains the most remarkable element of the composition is the fact that the crowd in the background seems constrained and inactive and the young man's body appears passive. He appears completely isolated. In the context, this heavily suggests that he is devoid of agency. This stands in dramatic contrast to the conventions of representation informing many other documents of the period, in particular the photographs published in student publications, depicting the collective body in demonstrations, occupations, sit-ins and teach-ins, as discussed in part II. Most of these documents, accompanied by rich textual material, visualise a political body that breaks the boundaries of egoism, isolation and individuality advanced by Western capitalism.

In another instance, the action is subsumed under the political message of the graffito 'la politique a tous' (politics to all) in an asymmetrical composition that also figures an encounter between a young man and woman. The man is depicted with his back turned to the camera, while the woman, here, is represented in stereotypical mode. Women – very much in the minority in these events – have tended to be represented according to one of two broad stereotypes. Either they

114

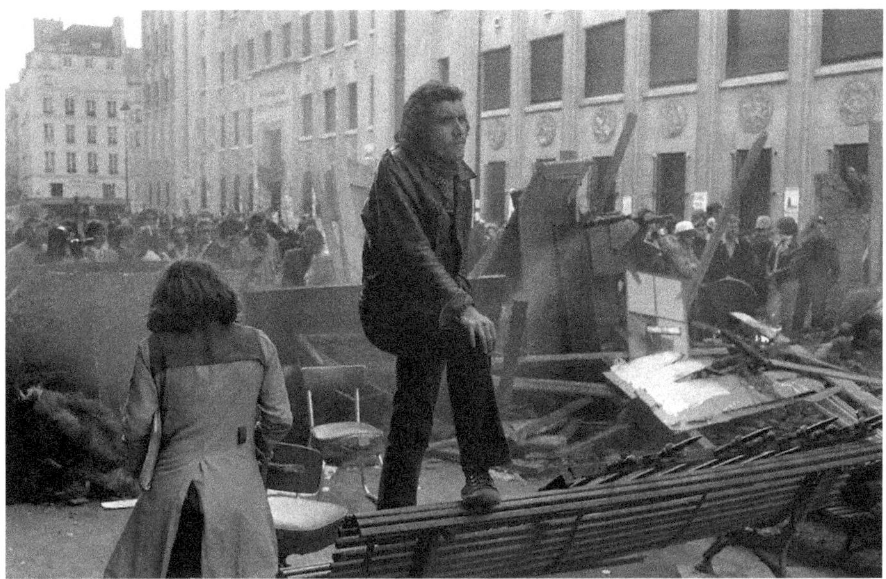

12 Bruno Barbey, France. Paris. May 68. France. Paris. Around 6 a.m. 6th arrondissement, Latin Quarter. Student standing on a barricade in front of the School of Medicine. This was the last barricade to be taken over by the police and only at 11 a.m. in the morning. 12 June 1968. (© Magnum Photos)

are pictured carrying flags at the head of demonstrations in the familiar and stylised mode of Eugène Delacroix's *Liberty Leading the People* (which is to render female participants as problematic emblems), or they are seen as passive, inactive and bereft of political agency. In this particular instance, the beautiful, smiling and inactive young woman is juxtaposed with the graffito to create an ironic antithesis. The feminine thus appears inimical to social and political action and as an exemplar of the tropes of individualism, which underpin Barbey's work. In this vein, one might also note Serge Hambourg's photograph of a couple talking on the base of the statue of Louis Pasteur at the Sorbonne and the way that it also emphasises the private through an exclusive opposition to the public.[16] Such tropes, one cannot help but think, serve to bring the subjects of collective action back onto the track of individualism.

Barbey's practice meshes neatly with photojournalism's general fondness for presenting an individual's experience as a 'standard lead-in for any feature news story', a set of conventions in which images of representative individuals serve as stand-in for social action.[17] Photojournalistic images are destined to be published along with detailed captions and more or less extended commentary but, as

Martha Rosler once observed, 'images without the verbal anchoring of what they show cannot rightly be termed journalism'.[18] The transition from photojournalism to art photography, from the form of reportage to art and from the institution of the newspaper to that of the museum entails the danger that specific historical information is elided and the particular is fatefully generalised.[19] The real danger here is that the assumed passivity of the reified figure of the individual comes to obscure the aliveness and uniqueness of this political uprising, a process in which historical knowledge about collective action falls by the wayside. Barbey's predilection for memorable individual figures is exacerbated by the curatorial decision not to include any textual information of the movement's political demands, collective endeavours and innovative forms of action.

The photographic translation of May '68 in the image of the individual chimes with recent individualistic readings of the movement as an isolated historical phenomenon. On the occasion of the twentieth anniversary, Gilles Lipovetsky, one of the then emergent 'new philosophers', interpreted the events as an anticipation of the individualistic spirit of the 1970s and 1980s and not as an attempt at socialist revolution.[20] In *L'Ère du Vide: Essaie sur l'Individualisme Contemporaine*, he argued that 'the 68 spirit' contributed decisively in precipitating narcissistic individualism's actualisation as the dominant form of contemporary subjectivity.[21] Likewise, Luc Ferry and Alain Renaut, in their pamphlet *La Pensée 68*, linked the writings of Derrida, Lacan, Foucault and Bourdieu with the 'thought' of '68 to argue that it was not only a premonition of the rise of contemporary individualism but, more importantly, that it was an inherently 'anti-humanist' tendency.[22]

Although from a different ideological viewpoint, Régis Debray's analysis of the events on their tenth anniversary arrived at similar conclusions, arguing that despite the actors' aspirations and aims, the result of the May movement heralded the emancipation of the individual and the concomitant triumph of advanced capitalist society. May '68 became, therefore, the 'cradle of a new bourgeois society'.[23] For Debray, individualism triumphed when 'the communion of egos on the barricades became generalized egocentrism, the gift of self, the cult of me, the exaltation of liberties, the enshrinement of inequalities, revolutionary romanticism, counter-revolutionary romanticism, challenge, submission, mad desire for justice and wide acceptance of injustices'.[24]

In his polemical intervention in these debates, Cornelius Castoriadis explained how such accounts drew on the failure of the movement, whilst ignoring its ephemeral successes and its direct and indirect effects. For Castoriadis, May '68 put into question precisely those reifying structures now labelled '"68 thought"';

thus, 'Ferry's and Renaut's misinterpretation is total. "Sixty-eight thought" is anti-'68 thought, the type of thinking that has built its mass success on the ruins of the '68 movement and as a function of its failure.'[25] Indeed, the thinkers chosen by Ferry and Renaut were all 'left speechless by '68', and beyond the obvious chronological coincidence their thought did not seek to relate directly to the events.[26] Such readings simplify the active solidarity among students, workers and professionals, which is perhaps best thought in terms of the opportunities given to everyone to talk in the large open assemblies held at the Sorbonne. Castoriadis alluded to these open spaces, which encouraged united action and active solidarity, when he argued that 'within the May movement and through it took place a tremendous process of resocialization, even if it proved fleeting'.[27]

Similarly, Ross has also denounced such interpretations.[28] Criticising Lipovetsky's focus on an abstract 'spirit of May '68', she wrote:

> to make something called the 'spirit of May' the protagonist of the narrative is to first attribute to May, without any clear justification, certain social 'effects' of the present, and then to make those effects into May's essence, effectively recuperating that essence.[29]

Asserting a reverse causality, Lipovetsky overlays characteristics of the 1980s onto 1968. Ross comments further on the lack of mass media coverage of twentieth anniversary: 'without visual or auditory evidence, the frontal political strivings of May, the ferocious anti-Gaullism, the general strike of nine million people, could very well have never occurred'.[30]

A collective body portrayed

These moments of resocialisation, in Castoriadis's sense, are enacted in numerous photographs published in student newspapers and kept nowadays in various French archives. The numerical proliferation of photographs representing the large majority of anonymous participants as politically active participants in open assemblies and anti-hierarchical meetings, stand in stark contrast to Barbey's emphasis on the minority of famous protagonists, as shown in part II. Some of his photographs, also included in the exhibition, depict these open assemblies, but once again the crowd is reduced in a few close ups on the faces of Daniel Cohn-Bendit, Jacques Sauvegeot and Jean-Paul Sartre. The reduction, here, does not only reside in the direct contrast between the single figure and the repressed crowd, but also takes place in a symbolic level at which the figure of the 'leader' stands-in for the popularity of the movement. The fact that Barbey's reportage was destined to be published in the French mainstream press is of great importance in this context, since the movement's leaders were seen as celebrities whose fame was exacerbated by media hype, as discussed in part I. Barbey's focus on this distinguished individual was driven by his determination to capture a highly important image, indulgent of mass media's lust for spectacle. In Barbey's photographs, the plurality of participants was reduced not only to the image of the single figure of the 'leader' but also to the 'young' protester, two subjects repeated throughout Barbey's exhibition, excluding photographs of workers, farmers and older people.

Barbey's choices of famous subjects displaces the movement's markedly fierce resistance to hierarchy, as evidenced by slogans such as, 'Don't let the loudspeakers speak for you'.[31] Contrary to this slogan, these 'loudspeakers' (exemplars of which were presented in Barbey's exhibition) were among the few famous individuals to have been granted, on the basis of their activism, the status to 'represent', 'interpret', 'deny' and 'repudiate' the events.[32] Cohn-Bendit is only one of these individuals, whose personal estimations of the movement have come to be recognised as the basically correct interpretation of the events. The past tense in the title of his 1986 book, *Nous l' Avons Tant Aimée, La Revolution* (The Revolution – We Loved it so Much), attributes to the revolt the ephemeral and spontaneous qualities of the youth. This interpretation is consistent with analyses of May '68 as a 'youth revolt' and as a 'pure expression of socio-hormonal frustration, a biological convulsion'.[33] Alain Touraine has argued that this was a new type of conflict, 'a new social movement', which emerged from new values and forms of action created by 'postindustrial' society. His point being that new societal groups participating in this conflict (i.e. students) manifested the diminishing role of the working class as the central actor of a struggle against technocracy and not against capitalism.[34] This fails to acknowledge the extensive form of a movement that combined various societal groups in an alliance 'the major unions had considered practically impossible', that 'the Communist Party had declared theoretically absurd' and that 'the government had never imagined'.[35]

The alliance was articulated in the silkscreen posters made by the Atelier Populaire and, overall, the movement's leaflets, tracts and slogans promoted student–worker solidarity.[36] The photographic equivalent of this can be found in images circulated by the movement's communication institutions and in the work of some photojournalists. Serge Hambourg's photograph of the students, Alain Geismar, Daniel Cohn-Bendit and Jacques Sauvageot marching with workers' leaders is one such example.[37] The alliance is visualised explicitly in this image's depiction of a banner that is seen in its background and which reads: 'Étudiants, Enseignants, Travailleurs, Solidaires' (Students, Teachers, Workers, In Solidarity.) One might also note, here, the manner in which they march together despite the disparity between social attitudes signified by the students' casual outfits and the older workers more formal dress.

The generalised image of May '68 as youth turmoil is further blurred by homogenised and ideologically undifferentiated photographs of the collective body. Two close-up images of demonstrations share striking pictorial similarities of composition, despite the particularities of the subjects depicted. The easily recognisable figures of Jacques Sauvageot (vice-president of UNEF) and Alain Geismar (general secretary of SNEsup) in one, and an array of French national flags alongside an image of de Gaulle in the other depict demonstrations with different aims, one against and the other pro de Gaulle (figures 13 and 14). Considered together, and uncaptioned, they create a visual narrative in which ideological differences are blurred and ideals are forgotten: the political demands, ideologies and forms of action collapse into one another. Two more photographs, depicting the Pro-Gaullist demonstration of 30 May (which appeared in *Protest in Paris 1968: Photographs by Serge Hambourg*, Hood Museum of Art 2006) stand in stark contrast to these. The first depicts three old people holding small banners reading 'Paix en France' (Peace in France), their motionless poses contrasting to the representation of enthusiastic young protesters. In the second, some elderly people, a few in uniform, pose in front of the Arc de Triomphe in a solemn manner that calls to mind a remembrance-day parade rather than a political protest.

Barbey's exhibition at the Hayward tended to equate anti- and pro-Gaullist demonstrations, as is evidenced by the way in which images of collective entities exclude rigorous slogans and creative banners as part of the demonstrations. For instance, one photograph depicts a homogenous mass of people and a large number of banners, which are seen from the reverse side and from an elevated viewpoint. The protesters' individual characteristics and the slogans remain hidden. Standing out against this is the figure of a young man on top of a traffic light with his clenched fist raised. The contrast of the individual and the mass positions the young man to act as a synecdoche for the whole demonstration.

Barbey's pictorial emphasis remains either on isolated subjects or on a collective deprived of politics – which dovetails neatly with the most recent predominant historical narratives of the events – and has also had the effect of sidelining related questions, such as what it would actually mean to attempt to maintain the visibility of socially radical and collective action in the face of historical interests that seek to render its appearances obscure. Taking up its place in the spectacular arena of the museum, the radical subject of '68 is deprived of its politics. It is this 'museumified' and depoliticised subject, which was once again (even if temporarily) defeated on both a political and representational level during the student radicalisations in Britain in 2010. Contrary to public discourse's superficial references to the May '68 uprising, the proliferation of images of protesters in the public domain open up thorny questions that are pertinent to our understanding and use of May '68 imagery, that is questions regarding the role of photographs not only in the formation, sustainability, reception and outcome of social movements, but also in the shaping of the way these are subsequently remembered.

The photographs at 'May '68: Street Posters from the Paris Rebellion' contributed to our remembering of May '68 by, once again, romanticising it, oversimplifying it, eliminating its political meaning, erasing the memories of past alternatives, adding to its ambiguity and simply commemorating it. If

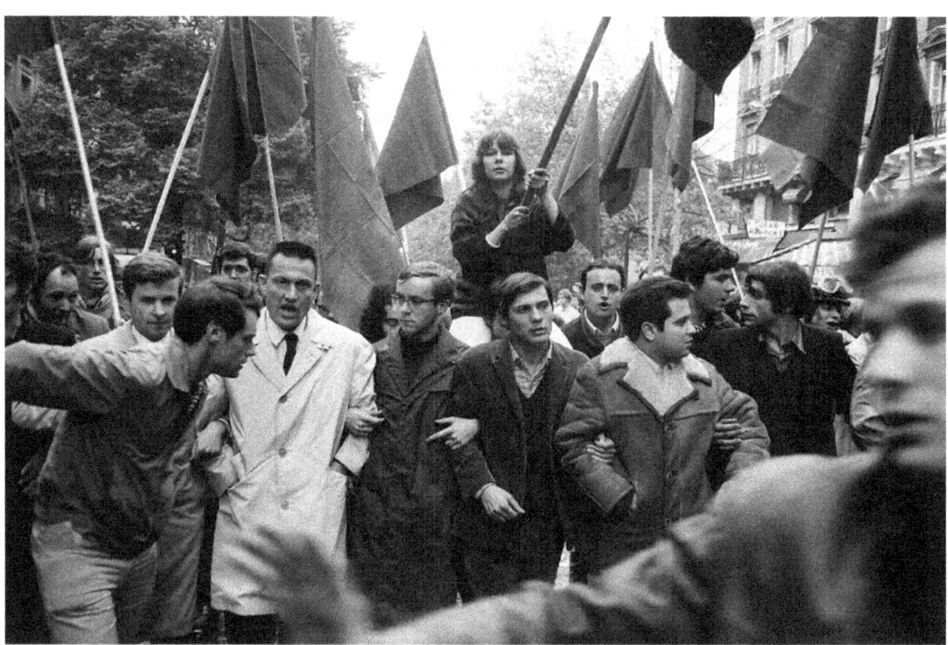

13 Bruno Barbey, France. Paris. May 68. France. Paris. Centre Jacques Sauvageot, on his left Alain Geismar, leader of the SNES, a student Union in a demonstration. Before a meeting at Charlety stadium. 27 May 1968. (© Magnum Photos)

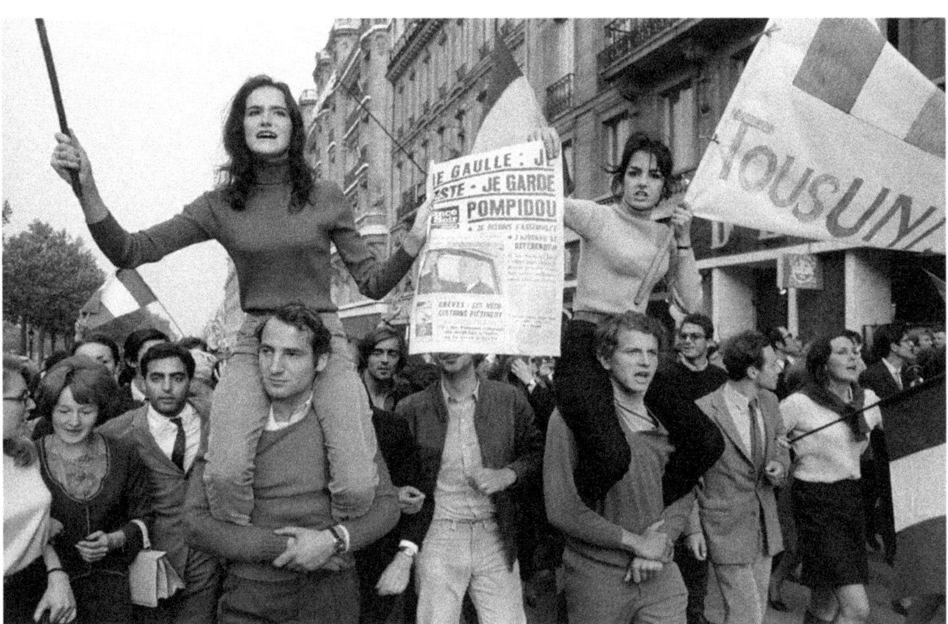

14 Bruno Barbey, France. Paris. May 68. France. Paris. Champs Elysees. During the pro-Gaullist demonstration, a girl is seen holding the last edition of the newspaper France-Soir. The headlines in bold letters read: 'I stay.' 'I keep Pompidou.' 30 May 1968. (© Magnum Photos)

May were to live on as an image in this commemoration, it seems it would be in the image of the individual, the leader or the amorphous crowd. If May were to be reduced to an image, this would be the photograph chosen by the organisers of the exhibition for the publicity of the commemorating events: Barbey's photograph of a pro-Gaullist demonstration (figure 14). This is only the most striking example of the historical forgetting of May '68's most radical and collective elements as imposed by this exhibition. Its antidote can be found in the underground press, the tracts, the posters, the documentary footage and the photographs published in the movement's journals, where one can rediscover the largest strike of French history, the unique alliance of students and workers, their anti-capitalist demands, their democratic anti-hierarchical assemblies, their innovative sit-ins, the numerous *committes d'action*, the extended political action outside the geographical limits of Paris, the Marxist and Utopian dimensions of the movement. Within these one may also find messages that are still relevant today, such as: 'La Lutte Continue' (The Struggle Continues).

Notes

1 K. A. Reader, *The May 1968 Events in France: Reproductions and Interpretations* (New York: St Martin's Press, 1993), p. 117.

2 K. Ross, *May '68 and Its Afterlives* (Chicago and London: The University of Chicago Press, 2002), p. 5.

3 W. Benjamin, 'On the Concept of History', in H. Eiland and M. W. Jennings (eds), *Walter Benjamin: Selected Writings, Vol. 4: 1938–1940* (Cambridge, MA: Harvard University Press, 2003), pp. 391.

4 Ibid.

5 Hayward Gallery (2008), 'May '68: Street Posters from the Paris Rebellion', London, 1 May–1 June 2008.

6 G. Caron, *Gilles Caron: Reporter 1967–1970* (Paris: Éditions de Chêne, 1978); C. Dityvon, *Mai 68, Camera Obscura* (Paris, 1988); Hood Museum of Art, Dartmouth College, *Protest in Paris 1968: Photographs by Serge Hambourg* (Hanover and University Press of New England, 2006); B. Barbey, *Mai 68 ou l'Imagination au Pouvoir* (Paris: Galerie Beaubourg, Editions de la Difference, 1998).

7 Reader, *The May 1968 Events in France*, pp. 5–15.

8 Ibid., pp. 1–19; D. Singer, *Prelude to Revolution: France in May 1968* (Cambridge: South End Press, 2002), pp. 37–206.

9 R. Viénet, *Enrages and Situationists in the Occupation Movement: France, May 1968* (New York and London: Autonomedia and Rebel Press, 1992), p. 44.

10 Reader, *The May 1968 Events in France*, p. 117.

11 I. Gilcher-Hotley, 'May 1968 in France', in C. Fink, F. Gassert and D. Junker (eds), *1968: The World Transformed* (Cambridge: Cambridge University Press, 1998), p. 263.

12 M. Seidman, *The Imaginary Revolution: Parisian Students and Workers in 1968* (New York and Oxford: Berghahn Books, 2004), pp. 161–214.

13 Singer, *Prelude to Revolution*, p. 159.

14 Ibid., p. 156.

15 Passerini L., '"Utopia" and Desire', *Thesis Eleven*, 68 (2002), p. 12.

16 Hood Museum of Art, 2006, Darmouth College, *Protest in Paris 1968*.

17 R. Hariman and J. L. Lucaites, *No Caption Needed: Iconic Photographs, Public Culture and Liberal Democracy* (Chicago and London: The University of Chicago Press, 2007), p. 90.

18 M. Rosler, *Decoys and Disruptions: Selected Writings, 1975–2001* (Cambridge, MA and London: The MIT Press, 2004), p. 253.

19 Ibid., p. 253.

20 G. Lipovetsky, *L'Ère du Vide: Essaie sur l'Individualisme Contemporaine* (Paris: Gallimard, 1983).

21 Ibid., pp. 244–5.

22 This argument is implied in the subtitle of the book, 'Essai sur l' anti-humanisme', L. Ferry and A. Renaut, *La Pensée '68* (Paris: Gallimard, 1985).

23 R. Debray, *Modeste Contribution aux Discours et Cérémonies Officiels du Dixième Anniversaire* (Paris: Maspero, 1978). For a translation of extracts of this book into English, see: R. Debray, 'A Modest Contribution to the Rites and Ceremonies of the Tenth Anniversary', *New Left Review*, 115 (1979), pp. 45–65.

24 Ibid., p. 64.
25 C. Castoriadis, *World in Fragments: Writings on Politics, Society, Psychoanalysis and the Imagination* (Stanford, CA: Stanford University Press, 1997), p. 54.
26 Ross, *May '68 and Its Afterlives*, p. 191.
27 C. Castoriadis, *World in Fragments*, p. 48.
28 Ross, *May '68 and Its Afterlives*, p. 191.
29 Ibid., p. 183.
30 Ibid., p. 84.
31 Ibid., p. 157.
32 Ibid.
33 Ibid., p. 206.
34 A. Touraine, *The May Movement: Revolt and Reform* (Random House, New York, 1971), pp. 27–8.
35 A. Feenberg and J. Freedman, *When Poetry Ruled the Streets: The French May Events of 1968* (Albany: State University of New York Press, 2001), p. 36.
36 Ibid., p. 124; Atelier Populaire, *Posters from the Revolution, Paris, May 1968* (Paris: Usine Université Union, 1969), p. 39.
37 Hood Museum of Art, 2006, Darmouth College, *Protest in Paris 1968*.

8

The End of Silence:
Antonio Turok's photographs
of the Zapatistas

T H E Chiapas rebellion in 1994 signalled a rupture with both the political and visual marginalisation of the indigenous peoples in Mexico. From its beginning, the struggle drew the attention of a new generation of photojournalists, whose practices, since the 1970s, included previously neglected subject matter, namely ordinary people, women and indigenous people. Antonio Turok's black-and-white photographs of the beginning of the uprising were among the photographs that were reproduced endlessly on various websites, including that of the Zapatistas. The photographs constitute the core of a photobook entitled *Chiapas: The End of Silence,* a collection of photographs taken in Chiapas, Mexico from 1973 to 1994. The photographs included in the book capture the indigenous people's everyday lives, their rituals, religious processions, fiestas and carnival dances. The format of the book, typical of many documentary photobooks, contains three parts: the introductory part consists of two essays by Francisco Álvarez Quiñones and Antonio Turok, the main body, which features sixty-four photographs without any captions or explanatory text and the last chapter, which offers a short explanatory text, consisting only of a title, place and year and a chronological index of Antonio Turok's life.

The significance of the photobook lies not only in the fact that this is the only photobook published after the beginning of the uprising that includes photographs of the struggle, but also in the fact that it produces a convincing narrative that locates the Zapatista struggle within the indigenous communities. Turok urges us to look at the communities' rituals, festivals, fiestas before we encounter the photographs of the uprising right at the end of the collection. This is significant since

No puede comprenderse el movimiento Zapatista, su especificidad, su originalidad, si en el centro del análisis no se pone a su actor central: el indígena'.[1]

(It is not possible to comprehend the Zapatista movement, its specificity and its originality, if we do not position in the centre of our analysis its central actor: the indigenous people.)

Bringing the indigenous people to the centre of this collection, Turok breaks with a long tradition of visual marginalisation of these communities, which had been concomitant with their political repression. This chapter examines the way the book informs us about the everyday life of the ethnic communities in Mexico and, most importantly, considers the ways in which the book enhances our understanding of the Zapatista struggle. This chapter compares the photobook with stereotypical photographic representations of Mexican twentieth-century photography and seeks to evaluate the contribution of Turok's book to the understanding of the indigenous people's struggle.

Photographing the indigenous people of Chiapas

Turok started taking photographs in the Highlands in Chiapas during his first visit there in 1973 at the age of eighteen. Born in Mexico City, the half-American Turok travelled in South and Central America documenting indigenous communities and local cultures. Turok worked as a freelance photographer for the Ministry of Education and the Mexican daily *Unomásuno* on the documentation of Indian cultures in Chiapas and as a war correspondent in Nicaragua. The photographs of Nicaragua constituted the main body of his first book *Imagénes de Nicaragua* (Images of Nicaragua) published in 1988.[2] In *Chiapas: The End of Silence*, Turok generally depicts the communities in Chiapas, indigenous people and mestizos living together. Within this emphasis, there is a preponderance of photographs of fiestas, carnivals and inexplicable scenes of everyday life. There is very little, if anything, about Western culture and its fascination with consumerism, mass-production and commerce in these photographs of this indigenous culture on the periphery of the globalised economic system.

After Turok moved to Chiapas in 1978, he became attracted by this local culture cut off from the technological developments of the Western world. Turok acknowledges in the introduction that he regards his photographs as documents for the preservation of a disappearing age. In his own words:

> Under the surface, under the skin, in the caves of the Earth Lord and in
> the caves of the heart, something was stirring. This world would not hold
> still, and my photographs were moving like the weather. Maybe the Mayan
> shamans knew which way the wind was blowing. Standing on the edge
> of joy and despair, I focused my lens at people, landscapes, fiestas and
> eventually produced abstractions of this extraordinary, ordinary, everyday
> reality in shades of black and white.[3]

The photographs in the book do not follow a chronological order, but are put
together by Turok constructing a narrative not always legible by potential
Western viewers.

The collection opens with a landscape photograph taken during a total eclipse
of the sun. There is a strong sense of mystery in the photograph exaggerated by
the wildness of the landscape and the birds flying. Turok briefly mentions the
event of him visiting Najá, the ceremonial centre of the traditional Lacandons
in his introduction, and explains the different approach to this rare astronomical
phenomenon between him and the descendants of Mayas. In the photographs that
follow, two female indigenous twins pose for the photographer; the indigenous
are photographed practising their religious duties; a man is caught asleep in
front of a church; two women in typical carnival costumes seated on the roof
of a car become the objects of the voyeuristic gaze of the young men present at
the scene as well as the viewers; bare-breasted indigenous women bathe in the
river. In these everyday activitities, religious rites and picturesque fiestas, Turok
is attracted to easily recognisable motifs – the culturally different and the exotic
– in a similar way to other foreign and native Latin American photographers
who photographed the indigenous Mexican population throughout the twentieth
century.

It is not an oversimplification to state that the relationship of the indigenous
people and visual representation had to face the Scylla of exoticism in Western
photographs and the Charybdis of their visual marginalisation in Mexico.
Mexican photographers rarely turned the lens towards the indigenous people.
In particular, Mexican photojournalists, at the peak of the illustrated magazines
from the late 1930s to the 1950s, focused on the president, the ruling class and
their everyday manifestations. This focus was deeply interrelated with the press's
financial and political interdependence with the government.[4] Therefore, the
press, as Roberto Blanco Moheno remarked, 'was always at the service of the
Señor Presidente, whoever and however the Señor Presidente was'.[5] Photographs
of the Mexican working class and the indigenous people, as well as photographs

of working conditions in factories, the mines and the fields were taboo in the Mexican commercial press.[6] On the rare occasions that these marginalised groups were represented, they were framed within stereotypical representations, as John Mraz explains:

> In relation to the working class, when not engaged in extended criticisms of the labour leaders, they followed the general tendency of 'industrialist photography', where machines and structures dominated the images and workers were generally absent. Campesinos and Indians were presented as picturesque, although images of bare-breasted *indígenas* often provided the publications with a form of soft-core pornography.[7]

There were only few exceptions of photographers who worked outside the restrictions of the official press and took photographs of indigenous people and members of lower classes. For example, one can mention the Casasola Archive's images of the Mexican revolution, Hermanos Mayo's photographs of the Spanish civil war, the labour struggles and the 1968 student movement, Nacho López's photo-essays of indigenous and working-class people and Héctor García's photographs of the 1958–59 strikes.[8] Although Héctor García was one of the first photojournalists who produced some critical photographs of the sharp class divisions in Mexico, he took many flattering photographs of president Luis Eschaverría during the 1970s and to a large extent his practices fit into the conventions of many other photojournalists of his generation. This is arguably one common characteristic of most of the aforementioned cases: most of the time, they shared the same ethnographic lens as their foreign contemporaries, mainly objectifying the people of the native communities.[9]

Their European and American counterparts, who travelled to Mexico after the beginning of the twentieth century, became fascinated by the rich cultures of the indigenous people and were attracted to the rich folk culture. They acted mostly as visual explorers, focusing on the extraordinary local fiestas and rituals.[10] Despite their motivations, most of these photographers showed a tendency to represent these communities in a picturesque and rather stereotypical way. A representative example of this tendency can be seen in the large collection of Mexican photography entitled *México Through Foreign Eyes, 1850–1990*.[11] The photographs in this collection reproduce the distance between photographer and subject, between ourselves and the Other. Most of these photographers explored these communities as outsiders since they were unable to speak Spanish or any of the local languages, and they therefore experienced difficulties in developing relationships with the native people and understanding their cultural diversity in depth.

One has to ask to what extent Turok's collection overcomes this dominant picture of the colonised Others 'portrayed as exotic creatures engaged in quaint rituals and inexplicable behaviour'.[12] In sharp contrast to the Western photographers, Turok is not a total outsider, but a Mexican citizen who lived with these communities and spent years taking these photographs. His middle-class and educated background differentiates him from the local community and was arguably one of the factors that allowed him to get funded for his project by *FONCA* – Fondo Nacional para la Cultura y les Artes (National Fund for Culture and the Arts), a state-funded organisation as well as by *Fundación Cultural Bancome* (Cultural Foundation Bancome), an organisation quite close to the government.[13] In a self-conscious statement, Turok admits 'I am a complete outsider, born in Mexico City, half-American, white, privileged, educated.'[14] Turok made the effort to enter this remote space of Chiapas, which 'despite television, tourists, and periodic upheavals', 'remains aloof from the outside world'.[15] Turok is praised by Quiñones in the book's introductory text for putting himself in danger to provide us with these extraordinary photographs and for his continuous commitment to his profession.[16] An example of this is the story that Quiñones narrates, according to which Turok would not stop taking photographs even when he was attacked by a gang.

Quiñones's account reminds us of the description of the typical documentarian in Martha Rosler's oft-cited critique of the documentary genre, according to which:

> documentary testifies, finally to the bravery or (dare we name it?) the manipulativeness and savvy of the photographer, who entered a situation of physical danger, social restrictedness, human decay, or combinations of these and saved us the trouble. Or who, like the astronauts, entertained us by showing us the places we never hope to go.[17]

To a certain extent, Turok acts as the mediator between the indigenous people and middle-class Mexican, American and European citizens, who constitute the potential audience of the book. Therefore, *Chiapas: The End of Silence* presents its readers, mostly Western buyers, with a reality absolutely different from their own experiences. The presentation of his photographs is of key importance: the collection lacks explanatory texts or more comprehensible captions that would contribute to the viewers' better understanding of the situation depicted. Based on the introductory essays and the visual narrative of the book, Western citizens who experience a globalised neoliberal system in their everyday realities are asked to read photographs of economies and cultures that stand outside of and even resist the universalisation of the Western capitalist system.

The lack of textual information in the collection reinforces the oft-repeated paradox that photography is 'a language in its own right', 'an independent and autonomous language system'.[18] As Turok states in his introduction, 'my photos of Tzotziles and Tzeltales convey cultural information without me trying'.[19] This is a rather problematic assumption on the basis that photographs alone without any explanatory text cannot bear information about the idiosyncrasy of this indigenous culture on the periphery of the globalised economic system. This becomes even more complicated, given the illegibility of this project for the potential Western viewers, and their ability, if any, to think critically about the political, social and economic conditions under which the indigenous communities live.

Photographing the Zapatista rebellion

The largest part of *Chiapas: The End of Silence* appears to conform to at least some of the conventions underpinning the photographic representations of the indigenous people in Mexico throughout the twentieth century. Yet, against these dominant representations, which would turn these people into objects, the last fifteen photographs of the collection bring out their active resistance. Turok was compelled by the circumstances to recognise that the seemingly harmonious symbiosis of the Maya and mestizos, conquerors and conquered for 500 years came to an end on the first day of 1994. Turok vividly describes the symbolic takeover of San Cristóbal on 1 January as a complete surprise to him. On the eve of the rebellion, Turok celebrated the opening of his exhibition, entitled *Eroticism in Chiapas* in his new gallery *Copal*.[20] After the celebration, he wandered in the plaza to 'be caught in a walking dream', as he confessed. Masked and armed men and women had taken over the city. Turok took some photographs of the Zapatistas marching on San Cristóbal's streets, arguably the only documents of this historical event. These photographs were not only circulated widely in the following months, but also became some of the most iconic photographs of the rebellion.

These last photographs decisively shaped Turok's understanding of the indigenous communities, and his self-reflection on his practice, as well as the viewers' reception of the project. An interesting example of a photograph that contributed to Turok's growing consciousness is the fifth photograph of the collection, entitled *The Church of San Andrés*. In this photograph, the interior of the church is decorated with flowers, and the people who are kneeling to pray are taken from a high viewpoint. The religious subject matter is highlighted by the striking light that enters from an invisible window, creating a mystical atmosphere. The photograph was taken during the early stages of the Zapatista rebellion. Turok explains that he photographed the fiesta of the patron saint San Andrés at the invitation of the religious official. This invitation caught him by surprise – as he states – since the indigenous people objected to him photographing their religious spaces. Only later did he understand that the community gave him this permission for fear of the violation of their churches as a punishment for their involvement in the invasion of San Cristóbal. As he declared, 'I did not understand their generous invitation, but a few months after the fiesta the inevitable happened: the Mexican army, in February of 1995, systematically began dismantling campesino organisations and intimidating the civil population'.[21]

In this statement, Turok vividly sums up the political awareness of a new generation of photographers, whose practices signalled critical distance from past photojournalistic practices closely interrelated with the quasi-official press.[22] The Zapatista rebellion is just one defining moment in the circle of political resistance that followed the Tlateloclo massacre in Mexico City in 1968, which had a great impact on this generation. The increasing documentation of political resistance is, according to John Mraz, the most outstanding evidence of the recent profound changes that Mexican photojournalism has undergone.[23] The massacre in Tlateloclo Plaza on 2 October 1968 was decisive in this respect, not only revealing the repressive and undemocratic Mexican governance internationally, but most importantly, generating a general consensus about the necessity for a more democratic and free press in Mexico. The gradual opening up of the press and the founding of two dailies, namely *Unomásuno* and *La Jornada*, in the aftermath of 1968 was of vital importance.[24] Founded in 1977 and 1983 respectively, both these dailies fostered serious photojournalism and shifted the focus of interest from official politics, the president and the upper class to images of social groups that had been seriously neglected, such as women, ordinary people, indigenous communities and people opposing the political and social status quo. During the 1980s, images of resistance, such as the teachers' movement or the workers' demonstrations against strict economic policies on May Day in 1984, became more habitual in the press. The Zapatista rebellion pushed this generation of photographers to deal with a pressing political issue taking place not in the urban space of the metropolis, but at the periphery of the country.

Antonio Turok, Pedro Valtierra, Víctor León, Rogelio Cuéllar and Raúl Ortega are some of the most important representatives of this new generation of photojournalists. Their practices differ from past practices in their growing freedom of expression and in the inclusion of photographs of ordinary people and marginalised communities, including women and indigenous people; the publication of critical political imagery, especially critical images of the PRI's political domination, mainly in the pages of *La Jornada*, and extraordinary critical imagery of the police and a representation of resistance.[25] The inclusion of photographs of the Zapatistas in the exhibition catalogue of the *Mexican Bienal de Fotoperiodismo* (The Mexican Biennial of Photojournalism) held in the *Centro de la Imagen* (Centre of the Image) in Mexico City is evidence of this tendency.[26] Raúl Ortega's oft-reproduced photograph of Subcomandante Marcos (figure 4) and Pedro Valtierra's iconic photograph of the indigenous women resisting the Mexican army are published along with photographs of Chiapas and the Zapatistas taken by Darío López Mills, José Carlo González and Ernesto Muñoz.

Turok's photographs of Zapatistas in the collection form the viewers' perception of these indigenous people, who have been portrayed rather stereotypically in the largest part of the book. In the latest photographs of the collection, the indigenous people feature as active agents acting towards political change. In one of the best-known photographs, a young Zapatista in a military uniform in the foreground of the photograph points his gun out towards the photographer and, therefore, the viewer (figure 15). The photograph was taken as a document of the Zapatistas marching in San Cristóbal, and in the background more Zapatistas are visible, seemingly unaware of the photographer's presence. The Zapatista in focus directly looks at the camera with a rather aggressive gaze. The photographer perceived this as a threat to his efforts to document the taking over of the city. In his words, 'a young rebel pointed his weapon directly at my heart. He was challenging me, forcing me to see that we were opposites, and, for good or ill, he and his comrades had decided to take the final road'.[27] The photographer's description manifests that he positions himself opposite to them, an outsider to their cause. While the moment captured reinforces our viewing the Zapatistas as a military force, the fact that most of the Zapatistas in the background do not carry any guns (nor do they seem to be aggressive) opens up questions about the way the Zapatistas are portrayed in this collection, in particular given that the photograph was widely disseminated and often considered as a symbol of the takeover of the city and the beginning of the movement.

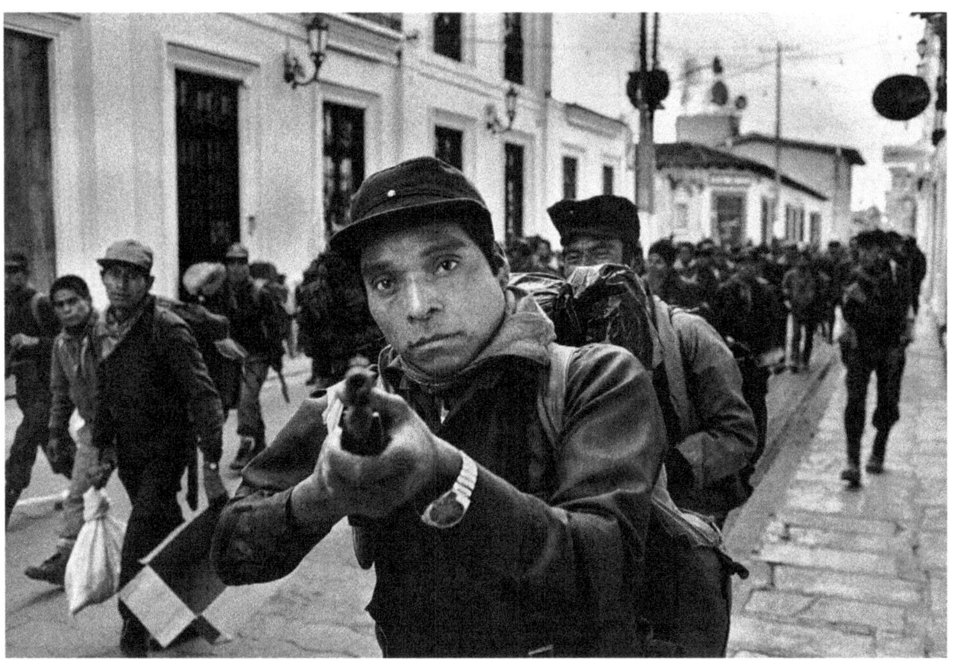

15 Antonio Turok, *Año Nuevo en San Cristóbal* (New Year in San Cristóbal), 1994 (© Antonio Turok)

There is a striking visual emphasis on the military character of the movement which becomes obvious in another photograph, a portrait of a female Zapatista, with her face partly hidden by her balaclava and partly by her gun (figure 16). The female Zapatista gazes directly into the camera in a similar way as the previous photograph, although many fewer characteristics can be picked out given that the balaclava and the gun obscure some of her face. Nevertheless, it is the close-up portrait that allows the viewers to distinguish the individual characteristics. Unlike the male Zapatista, who is caught while walking, this woman seems to be posing for the photographer, a gesture that does not necessarily point towards their antagonism. Turok's decision to photograph a woman Zapatista is interesting as it chimes with the website's proliferation of photographs of women involved in the struggle and participating actively in democratic meetings.

This emphasis on the military character of the movement has a twofold explanation: first, the initial *foco* character of the movement and, second, the potential difficulty of a middle-class white Mexican citizen comprehending the Zapatista struggle. The latter seems to be in the spotlight, given that the Zapatistas

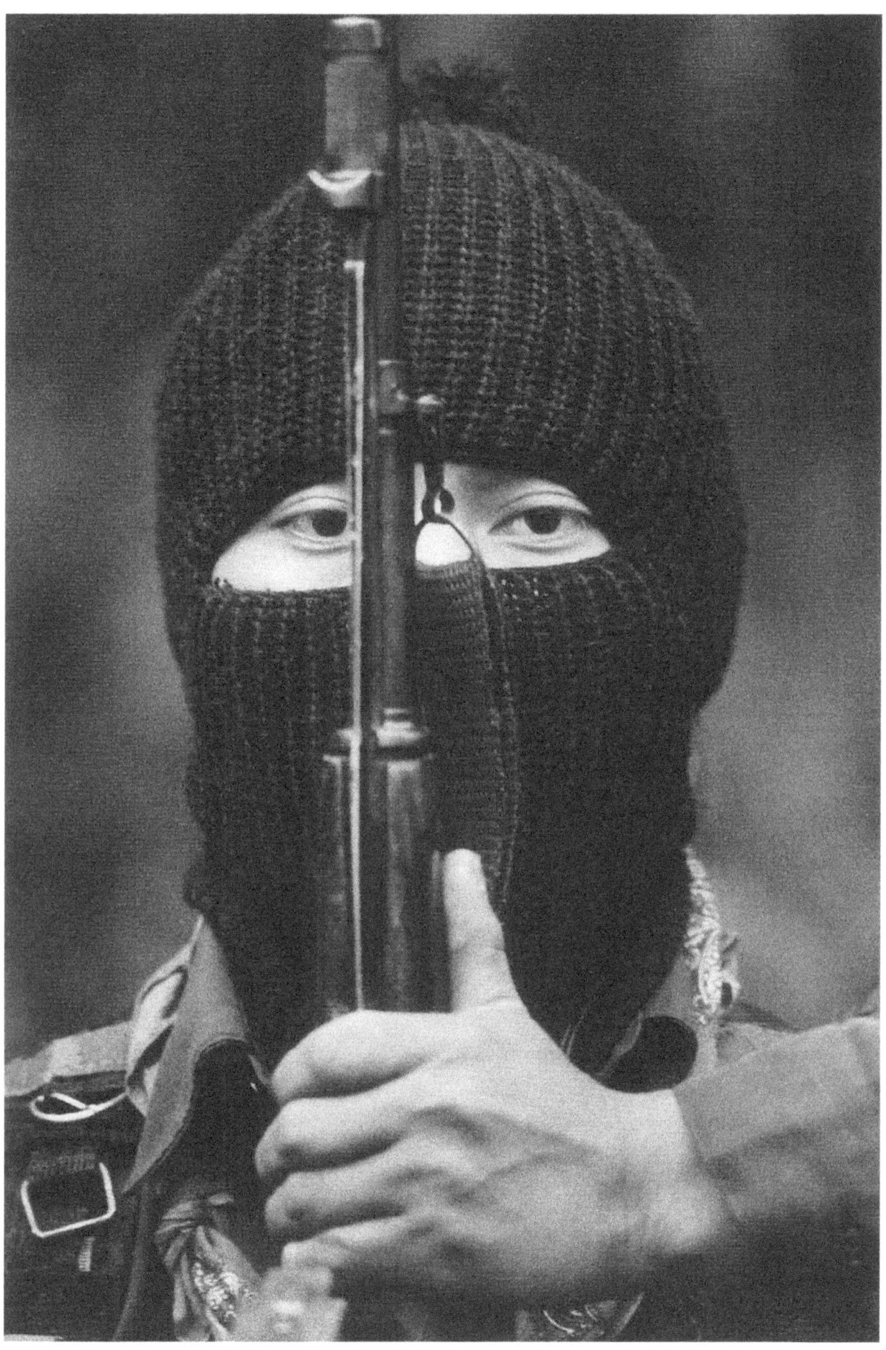

16 Antonio Turok, *Mujer Zapatista* (Zapatista Woman), 1994 (© Antonio Turok)

decided on a ceasefire and denounced guerrilla warfare as early as 1995, while the book was published in 1998. Within four years of the beginning of the uprising, EZLN communicated its goals and tactics mainly through the internet, which clearly transcended the narrow military character of older guerrilla movements. The book does not engage with these ideas, but rather insists on representing the EZLN as an armed force. Turok closes his introductory essay with a description of the devastation which followed the takeover of San Cristóbal:

> For twelve days the rebels waged intense battles, then retreated to their villages. Orphans and widows count the dead and wounded on both sides. In the wake of open conflict arose old grudges, random violence, anarchy. The faceless ones subsist in the treeless forest, wait in the Place of shadows. Both sides still walk in shame.[28]

This account of the destruction only gives the short-term outcomes of the first battles between the Zapatistas and the army, highlighting the mutual damage of such a conflict. The attribution of responsibility to both sides indicates a failure to engage with the deeper origins of the Zapatista struggle, a decision that contradicts his own visual decisions.

Two of the photographs of dead children in the book depict quite clearly the poverty and misery in Chiapas. The first one, entitled *El Angelito* (Little Angel), depicts a funeral procession of a child and the second, entitled *Niña Muerta* (Dead Girl), portrays a small girl in her coffin (figure 17). In the latter photograph, the dead girl is dressed in torn fabric, the coffin looks cheap and the barefoot children present in the background wear torn clothes. On the next page, a photograph of a woman lying on a bed and surrounded by children and an old woman is entitled *Tuberculosis* and is dated 1995. While *El Angelito* is positioned among photographs depicting dancers and scenes from the circus, the two other photographs are within the last fifteen photographs of the collection. While these images may be read as a direct reference to poverty and exploitation in Chiapas for the informed readers, Turok does not directly acknowledge them as reasons for the uprising. Marginalisation seems to be considered just part of their human condition, which cannot be a sufficient reason for disobedience, unrest and revolt. In fact, the basic political, social and economic realities in Chiapas go unacknowledged.

The uprising itself is depicted through a few images of individuals, neglecting the fact that it is the whole community in insurrection. The only photograph of a gathered crowd depicts a man speaking right in the middle of the crowd.

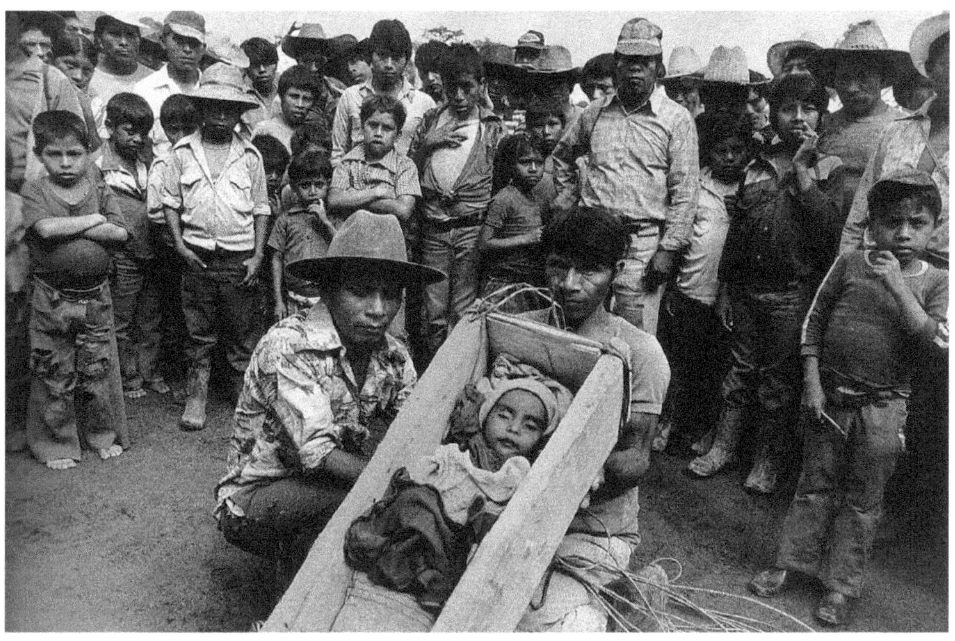

17 Antonio Turok, *Niña Muerta* (Dead Girl), 1982 (© Antonio Turok)

The photograph entitled *Guatemalan Refugees* depicts Mayan communities, who, repressed during the intense guerrilla warfare in Guatemala, moved to Chiapas. Turok, Marta Zarak and José Ángel Rodríguez photographed this migratory phenomenon between 1980 and 1983 under sometimes dangerous conditions, but they have not published this work in its entirety.[29] While this photograph is included in the last fifteen photographs, there is no clear link between it and the photographs of the rebels.

This emphasis on individualism is also characteristic in the scenic portrait of Subcomandante Marcos (figure 18). Marcos in his typical military outfit is photographed in the mountains, surrounded by wild nature. He is positioned right in the middle of the frame, photographed in profile and deep in thought, while the foggy atmosphere of the jungle adds to his melancholic gaze. Around him, masked Zapatistas holding guns seem to protect the Subcomandante. The difficulty of dealing with collectivity results in creating emblematic images, such as the one of Marcos, that stand for the political uprising and point to the difficulty of creating a characteristic portrait of a whole community in insurrection. The photograph acquired iconic status and was repeatedly reproduced, not only on various websites and media, but also in a photographic exhibition entitled

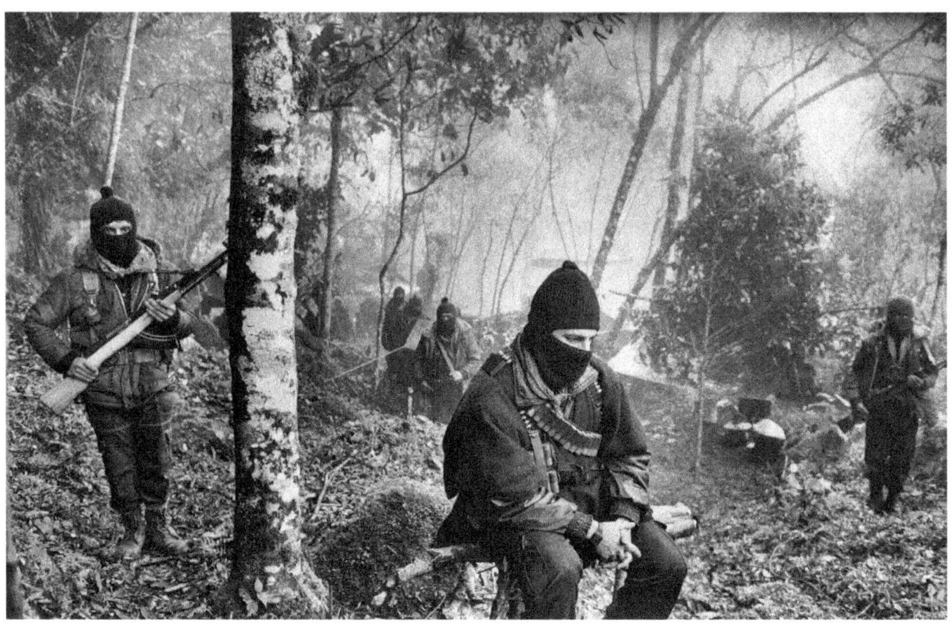

18 Antonio Turok, *Subcomandante Marcos* (Subcomandante Marcos), 1992 (© Antonio Turok)

69 *Miradas Contra Polifemo*, which marked the tenth anniversary of the Zapatista movement, along with several photographs taken by various photographers focusing on the democratic nature of the movement, the active participation of women and the conscious decisions of the communities against military action.[30] One then has to ask in what way photographic representations of these communities by new photojournalists – in our case Antonio Turok's photographs – can contribute to our understanding of the specific conditions of their life. De Mendiola maintained that these new representations are not particularly different from older stereotypical ones. Instead, contemporary practices tend towards a homogenisation of the indigenous communities. As an example, contemporary photographic anthologies, such as *El Ojo de Vidrion: Cien Años de Fotografía del México Indio* deny their ethnic and social heterogeneity.[31] Mendiola commented that, 'interestingly enough, Mexican photography of the past twenty-five years is particularly resonant with a kind of ethnographic visual representation marked by exoticism and racist underpinnings'.[32]

Following this line of thought, one could argue that Turok's photographs of the communities of Chiapas just reproduce stereotypical perceptions about the modernised metropolis and the marginalised peripheries of the Western world.

While this may be true to a certain extent, one should not neglect the fact that practices like Turok's opened up a new photographic space available to the indigenous people of Mexico, which put an end to their visual marginalisation. The recognition that occurs on a visual level does not necessarily mean a profound understanding of the political, social and economic conditions of their life in Chiapas. The now well-known criticism of the politics of representation is of great relevance here; despite their intentions, these practices can deal only with appearances, excluding any analysis of societal structures and political causes and congealing into an image that is in effect the result of history and politics.[33] It is fundamental to highlight that in none of these cases was the indigenous people in control of the means of production or dissemination of the visual imagery. In the aforementioned case, the disenfranchised rural communities, not themselves having the means or even the motives for self-representation, were represented by some more powerful individuals for the gaze of the politically and socially powerful, whether this is a Western or a middle-class urban Mexican audience. The objectification of the photographic subjects secures the otherness of the other and transforms the spectators into mere voyeurs. In the case of the indigenous people in Mexico, as is the case for most minority groups, the difficulties (as well as the possibilities) of self-representation can be seen as the cultural equivalent to the struggle for political visibility and enfranchisement. The historical exclusion of the rural indigenous communities from Mexican political discourse was underscored by the movement, which attempts to mend traditional injustices against the indigenous communities and asks for a truly inclusive democracy equivalent to the multicultural nature of Mexican society. Within these efforts, one can trace their attempt to make room for the indigenous people to actually engage in an act of autonomous self-representation.

It is no accident that in the first electoral campaign after the outbreak of the uprising, the government efforts to integrate the indigenous people into Mexican official politics exceeded the political level to embrace the visual. During the summer of 1994, the PRI launched its electoral presidential campaign with the slogan 'Ven y tómate la foto' (come and take a photo of yourself).[34] The slogan, which dominated the public space and the mass media of Mexico, invited every citizen to take an automatic colour photographic portrait of him/herself. The novelty of including a photograph of the voter in the electoral campaign can be perceived as reassurance about the theoretical transparency of the elections. Marina Pérez de Mendiola interprets the governmental strategy as an attempt to engage the electoral body in full political participation. As she argues:

The slogan conveys the idea that this spontaneous, mechanical portrait will bring recognition of social integration and civil identity. This initiative also aims to convince historically and geographically marginalised groups that, in Mexico, governmentality will no longer be exercised without a certain measure of self-restraint, that is to say, without asking 'why must one govern and what ends should (government) pursue with regard to society in order to justify its existence?'[35]

The automatic self-portrait, therefore, gives the Mexican citizens the illusion that they can all be 'seen', 'heard' and 'taken into account'. This illusion is mostly based on the wrong perception that since someone takes the photograph, he/she can also control its circulation and, therefore, its perception.

While one should be aware of the difference between the illusion of participation and visibility with participation and visibility per se, the governmental efforts to encourage neglected groups of the Mexican population, and especially the indigenous people, to play an active political role, giving them access to visibility, can only be seen as a result of the Zapatista uprising and their increasing visibility in the public sphere. Nevertheless, one should not underscore that the visuality through the publication *Chiapas: The End of Silence* may be one first step towards their political emancipation. While such a documentary project is not without limitations, it does open critical questions for an understanding of the deeper social, economic and political conditions, the necessity of the Zapatista struggle and the need for change.

Notes

1 Y. LeBot, *Subcomandante Marcos: El Sueño Zapatista* (Barcelona: Plaza & Janés, 1997), p. 21.

2 A. Turok, *Imagénes de Nicaragua* (Mexico City: Casa de las Imagénes, 1988).

3 A. Turok, *Chiapas: The End of Silence* (New York: Aperture, 1998).

4 J. Mraz explains that the economic interests of the owners of the Mexican press were and are still directly correlated with the political party in power, the Partido Revolucionario Institucional (Institutional Revolutionary Party, PRI). The PRI is the political party that monopolised political power in Mexico from 1928 to 2000. J. Mraz, 'The New Photojournalism of Mexico 1976–1998', *History of Photography*, 2: 4 (1998), pp. 313–65.

5 R. Blanco Moheno, *Memorias de un Reportero* (Mexico City: Libro-Mex Editores, 1965), p. 294, as quoted in J. Mraz, *Nacho López: Mexican Photographer* (Minneapolis, MN: University of Minnesota Press, 2003), p. 35. For a discussion of the photography of official politics in Mexico in the late nineteenth and early twentieth century, see: J. Mraz, 'Photographing Political Power in Mexico', in W. G. Pansters (ed.), *Citizens of the Pyramid:*

Essays on Mexican Political Culture (Amsterdam: Thela Latin America Series, 1997), pp. 147–80.

6 Museum of Modern Art, *Tierra y Libertad!: Photographs of Mexico 1900–1935* (Oxford: Museum of Modern Art, 1985), p. 7.

7 J. Mraz, 'The New Photojournalism of Mexico 1976–1998', p. 315.

8 Some photographs from the famous Casasola Archive were exhibited in the Museum of Modern Art Oxford in 1985. Museum of Modern Art, *Tierra y Libertad!: Photographs of Mexico 1900–1935*. Also, see: I. Gutiérrez Ruvalcaba, 'A Fresh Look at the Casasola Archive', *History of Photography*, 20: 3 (1996), pp. 191–5; J. Mraz, 'Foto Hermanos Mayo: A Mexican Collective', *History of Photography*, 17: 1 (1993), pp. 81–9; N. López's work, see: J. Mraz, *Nacho López: Mexican Photographer*, pp. 7–8; H. García, *Escribir con Luz: Héctor García* (Mexico City: Fondon de Cultural Económica, 1985).

9 M. Pérez de Mendiola, 'Mexican Contemporary Photography: Staging Ethnicity and Citizenship', *Boundary 2*, 31: 3 (2004), pp. 131.

10 T. Ziff, *Between Worlds: Contemporary Mexican Photography* (London: Bellew Publishing, 1990), p. 13.

11 C. Naggar and F. Richtin, *México Through Foreign Eyes, 1850–1990* (New York and London: W.W. Norton & Company, 1993), p. 15.

12 J. Mraz, *Nacho López: Mexican Photographer*, p. 2.

13 Ibid., p. 151.

14 A. Turok, *Chiapas: The End of Silence*.

15 Ibid.

16 F. Álvarez Quiñones, 'Tonyalux Turok: Wild Turkey in the Darkroom', in Antonio Turok, *Chiapas: The End of Silence*, n. p.

17 M. Rosler, 'In, Around and Afterthoughts (On Documentary Photography)', in R. Bolton (ed.), *The Contest of Meaning: Critical Histories of Photography* (Cambridge, MA: The MIT Press, 1992), p. 309.

18 A. Sekula, 'The Traffic in Photographs', *Art Journal* (1981), p. 15.

19 A. Turok, *Chiapas: The End of Silence*, n. p.

20 Ibid.

21 Ibid.

22 J. Mraz, 'The New Photojournalism of Mexico 1976–1998', pp. 313–65.

23 Ibid.

24 Ibid.

25 Ibid.

26 Centro de la Imagen, *1a, 2a, 3a, 4a Bienal de Fotoperiodismo* (Mexico Conaculta: Centro de la Imagen, 2001).

27 Ibid.

28 A. Turok, *Chiapas: The End of Silence*, n. p.

29 O. Debroise, *Mexican Suite: A History of Photography in Mexico* (Austin, TX: University of Texas Press, 1994), p. 161.

30 An article about this exhibition was written by Subcomandante Marcos and was published in *La Jornada* in 2003. See: Subcomandante Marcos, 'Ver al Zapatismo es Mirar al Fuego y la Palabra', *La Jornada* (27 November 2003).

31 For a discussion of this collection as an indicative example of the 'identical filiation of all

indigenous communities' and the representation of them according to stereotypes, see: R. González Rudo and J. Velez Storey, *El Ojo de Vidrion: Cien Años de Fotografía del México Indio* (México Bancomext, 1999), as quoted in Pérez de Mendiola, 'Mexican Contemporary Photography: Staging Ethnicity and Citizenship', pp. 135–44.

32 Ibid., p. 133.

33 M. Rosler, 'In, Around and Afterthoughts (On Documentary Photography)'; A. Sekula, 'Dismantling Modernism, Reinventing Documentary: Notes on the Politics of Representation', in P.Holland, J. Spence and S. Watney, *Photography/Politics: Two* (London: Comedia, 1986); A. Solomon-Godeau, 'Who Is Speaking Thus?', in *Photography at the Dock: Essays on Photographic History, Institutions and Practices* (Minneapolis, MN: University of Minnesota, 1997).

34 M. Pérez de Mendiola, 'Mexican Contemporary Photography'.

35 Ibid., p. 126.

<h1 style="text-align:center">9</h1>

Joel Sternfeld's anti-photojournalistic images of Genoa

J OEL Sternfeld's *Treading on Kings: Protesting the G8 in Genoa* is a series of twenty-seven formal portraits, which form the basic body of a book, published on the occasion of an exhibition of Sternfeld's project at the White Box Gallery in New York.[1] The photographs were taken during the anti-globalisation protests in Genoa in 2001, and document the diversity of participants in the transnational movement against neoliberal globalisation. The movement, which took to the streets in Seattle, Prague, Porto Allegre, Quebec and Genoa and is known by various names such as 'anti-corporate movement', 'anti-capitalist movement', 'global justice or fair trade movement', 'a movement for a globalisation of rights', was far from homogenous: it brought together people from across the globe, who shared different ideological and cultural backgrounds, and often had diverse understandings of its processes, alternative visions, strategies and tactics. Workers and their unions, small farmers and their organisations, consumers, environmentalists, students, women, the unemployed, indigenous people or religious believers, just to name but the most important, challenged decisions taken by global meetings such as those of the G7, G8, World Bank and the World Economic Forum.

Sternfeld documented the protests in Genoa and produced a body of work which focused on the resistance to the limits of globalisation, as manifested on the streets of Genoa in 2001. This chapter examines Sternfeld's photobook, highlighting the interrelationship between the visual and the textual in the book. It studies Sternfeld's strategy in relation to contemporary photographic projects that privilege straightforward pose and strict composition of portraits, and questions the relationship of the project with earlier documentary and photojournalistic practices.

Revisiting or breaking with past practices?

The main body of the book consists of portraits of participants, activists who travelled to Genoa to protest against the policies of the eight richest countries of the world. Each photograph, on the right page, depicts usually one participant per picture. The subjects centrally placed in the photographs, look straight at the camera, and therefore the photographer and the viewer. Their posing in front of the camera shows not only their awareness of the camera's presence, but most importantly self-representation. Although there is a deliberate emphasis on the diverse characteristics of age, gender and ethnicity among the subjects, young people take up a big part of the book (plate 11).

The activists' reported statements, on the left page of the portrait, vary from statement to statement, from describing feelings and intentions to long explanatory texts arguing against capitalism, economic inequalities and exploitation of the poor countries and ecological destruction. The statements record the participants' beliefs and incentives to travel to Genoa, indicating the movement's diversity. Nevertheless, what most of them share is an emotional response, at times strong, to the injustices of the capitalist system. The underlying emphasis on the right causes of the protest is not only evident in the texts, but also in the introductory passage chosen by Sternfeld. The quoted text taken from Henry the Fourth by William Shakespeare reads:

> O gentlemen! the time of life is short;
> To spend that shortness basely were too long,
> If life did ride upon a dial's point,
> Still ending at the arrival of an hour.
> And if we live, we live to tread on kings;
> If die, brave death, when princes die with us!
> Now, for our consciences, the arms are fair,
> when the intent of bearing them is just'.[2]

The principle of the justice is omnipresent not only on the book's title taken from the passage above, but also throughout the book.

The first portrait of the series shows a young woman dressed in a red T-shirt and wearing a sticker on her top that reads: 'no to violence, no to debt, drop debt'. The participant poses against the neutral background of the sky and leaves us with little choice but to focus on her facial expression – sad, perhaps even frustrated. Her statement on the left page gives the reason for her activism, while her disappointment is also reflected in her words:

> I'm concerned about the world. I don't want to sound too pessimistic, but it seems like everything is falling to pieces. This is the first march I've ever joined, but I came because I felt it was important to come.[3]

In another portrait, a young man in a T-shirt with a declaration against the embargo imposed on Cuba stares at the camera angrily. His statement, short but strong, reads: 'Rage. Three billion people feel rage'.[4] The protester poses within the demonstration, as one can tell from the other people visible in the background.

One of the strongest photographs of the series depicts a man who poses next to a poster of the campaign against the ecological disaster of Bhopal (plate 12).[5] The US multinational company's leak of toxic gas killed thousands of residents of the Indian city, Bhopal, in 1984. The hideous picture of the burial of a dead baby became a recognisable symbol of the catastrophe and the following campaign. The man in Sternfeld's picture is photographed next to the campaign posters bearing that photograph. Although the man is not centrally placed in Sternfeld's photograph and his body is directed towards the posters, his gaze is directed back to the camera. The title of the poster, 'The real face of globalisation', reads as a strong response to the cruelty of the photograph. The statement on the opposite page raises issues, relevant not only to Bhopal but globally, such as ecological catastrophe, human devastation, lack of justice and corporate irresponsibility. This is only one of the cases where smaller causes and organisations find shelter in the wider movement. While this man is dedicated to a specific cause, other participants' motivations appear looser. In another photograph, the young boy in the black top, staring at the camera in a rather enigmatic way, does not look angry. Instead, his gaze reveals a youthful brightness. He travelled all the way to Genoa to protest against exploitation, injustice and insufficient democratic government. But as he humorously admits, he also travelled there for the lasagne.

The integration of text and image is extended through the two long essays written by Alexander Stille and Stefania Galante. In fact, the book opens with the essay written by Stille, a journalist and author. His essay entitled *Violence at Genoa – A 'Question of Detail?'* is a detailed account of the events in Genoa focusing primarily on the issue of violence. The text also provides important information about the preparation of Genoa for the summit and the police raid on the Diaz School. A personal account of the events at Diaz written by Galante, a doctoral student in historical studies and sociology and one of the activists who spent the night at Diaz School during the police raid, gives details about the violent police, the torture and the imprisonment of many demonstrators and is published at the end of the book.

The collaboration of Sternfeld with Stille and Galante and the inclusion of quotations next to the photographs is a mode that has been revisited many times throughout the twentieth-century history of photography. More precisely, the format of the book directly refers to a long documentary tradition resembling, in particular, the 1930s' American documentary photobooks. Indicative examples of the close collaboration between a photographer and a writer are *An American Exodus* (1939), a very successful photobook of the period which was the result of the collaboration of the photographer Dorothea Lange and sociologist Paul Schuster Taylor and *You Have Seen Their Faces*, initially published in 1937, which inaugurated the collaboration of the photographer Margaret Bourke-White and her husband Erskine Caldwell in the role of the creative writer.[6] In both cases, the essays contextualised the photographs and formed the interpretive background. The combination of visual and textual information also takes place on a more direct level, that of direct juxtaposition of photographs and captions or small texts. Lange and Taylor decided to caption the photographs with statements by the migrating farmers. Next to the photographs appeared 'what people said, not what we think might be unspoken thoughts'.[7] On the other hand, Caldwell and Bourke-White gave their own captions to the photographs of sharecroppers, quoting 'people saying things they never said'.[8] The underpinning idea of framing the photographs with an analysis and documentation of the beliefs of the people photographed remains very similar. Many of these American documentary photobooks achieved high popularity and commercial success, and nowadays are considered classical representations of 1930s America. *Treading on Kings* shares with them some characteristics such as the close combination of textual and visual documentation, the adaptation of this format as a result of the successful collaboration of a photographer and a writer, and the highly explicit political content.

Nevertheless, criticism of the 1930s documentary projects focused on the subjects being presented as mute victims and the imposition of the photographer's ideas on them; the class inequalities between the photographers and their subjects and even further between the subjects and their audiences; the transformation of the subjects depicted into objects of knowledge; the lack of any objective content in these projects; the interpretation of these documentary projects as expressions of liberal consensus according to which poverty is shown as a result of natural disasters and misfortune rather than as a result of the intrinsic character of the predominant economic and social system. Or as Martha Rosler put it in words in one of the most influential critiques of documentary photography: 'poverty and oppression are almost invariably equated with misfortunes caused by natural disasters: casualty is vague, blame is not assigned, fate cannot be overcome'.[9] Rosler's critique among others that surfaced during the 1980s, including Allan Sekula's, John Tagg's and Victor Burgin's – to name only the most prominent – targeted the ideological claims for documentary photography's neutrality and revealed its structural limitations to disrupt the ideological constraints imposed by the social democratic version of state corporatism in the period of the New Deal in the United States.[10]

Despite Sternfeld's obvious and likely deliberate reference to this tradition, much of this criticism could not be applied to his project, which lacks the power relations ascribed to these early documentary projects. In fact, most of the subjects are not strongly differentiated from the photographer or their likely viewers. Sternfeld, as well as the potential viewers of these photographs, are middle-class Western citizens, as are a majority of the participants in these demonstrations. Given the high cost of travelling to Genoa for non-European citizens, a quite large number of the demonstrators are Westerners. This is not to argue against the multiculturalism and class diversity of the anti-capitalist demonstrations, in which people from different social, cultural and economic backgrounds participate, but to state that the power relations inscribed in the 1930s documentary projects cannot apply to Sternfeld's project.

Bourke-White dramatised her subjects, photographing farmers from low camera angles, taking close-ups of her subjects, juxtaposing them with the sky and not their agricultural environment.[11] In contrast, the way that the subjects pose for Sternfeld, their direct gaze into the camera, shows a relationship of equality between the photographer and the photographed. There is a strong sense throughout the project that there is an emphasis on the personalities of the participants, evident in their personal statements published in the book. This is justified by the decision of the photographer not to portray any big groups or mass demonstrations. This decision seems to be at odds with journalism's obsession with the masses and the violent subject and the official political perception of the demonstrations as an amorphous mass.

There is a break, too, with another long tradition, that of the street photography that has its roots in the first half of the twentieth century. Street photography's fragmented and dispersed history became associated with such diverse practices as those by Jacques-Henri Lartigue, Brassaï, Henri Cartier-Bresson, Walker

Evans and Robert Frank, to name a few of the most influential photographers of the genre.[12] Street photographers took as their subject the life of the street and attempted to capture its instantaneity, motion, its details and peculiarities. Many times, they have been characterised as 'innocent bystanders', witnesses to an event almost by chance. For this reason, contemporary theorists have criticised the genre for 'loss of specificity or scrupulousness', which lacked the 'desire to change social realities' and the practitioners for being devoid of any 'sense of the social' and, therefore, being transformed into mere voyeurs.[13]

In *Treading on Kings*, Sternfeld took the street as his medium. The majority of the photographs are taken in the streets of Genoa with the exception of the two photographs taken indoors at the Diaz School. The striking difference with traditional street photographic practices is that the streets of Genoa were devoid of their everyday life. In fact, the centre of the city was shut down and divided into three zones, the red, blue and yellow zones, during the summit of the eight leaders. The red zone was around the Ducal Palace where the summit was accommodated and was protected with wire fences from the protesters. The yellow and blue zones of the city were given to the protesters, but normal transportation was stopped and many shopkeepers and coffee owners shut their shops and cafes for fear of them being destroyed by the 'violent demonstrators'. The creation of red areas that demonstrators could not approach, broadened the police strategies for the defence of the summit meeting places. These red areas acquired symbolic meanings for the demonstrators and can be perceived as 'metaphors for an economic model that exiles millions to poverty and exclusion'.[14]

Obviously, the conditions on the streets of Genoa did not resemble their customary life and therefore Sternfeld had to work in different conditions from those in which earlier street photographers had worked. While his preference for photographing on the street may have put him in similar circumstances to other street photographers, such as the street as location where the events unfolded, the spontaneity and motion of a demonstration and the peculiarities of the street life as it unfolds in a demonstration differentiate his practice from earlier practitioners. However, Sternfeld deliberately chose not to look for random images of the demonstrations as they were unfolding on the streets, but instead he carefully chose his subjects posing against urban backgrounds. His decision distances him from the almost random shooting of preceding representatives of the genre, as well as from their inability to define their subjects and their 'apparent aimlessness and an attraction to drift'.[15]

Anti-photojournalism's relation to violence

Sternfeld's avoidance of spontaneous shooting on the streets of Genoa is based on anti-photojournalistic principles. This distance from the tradition of photojournalism and its obsession with the worthwhile picture that would make headlines was also highlighted by the curators at the White Box Gallery. In their press release, the curators emphasised that Sternfeld's approach to the events in Genoa greatly differed from the great majority of photojournalists who covered the summit, spending their time in the air-conditioned Magazzini di Cotone – temporarily converted into a significant broadcast studio – dining on pasta generously provided by the sponsor Barilla and gathering the official briefings of the summit. Similarly, his practice was entirely different from the photographers who wandered in the red and yellow zones looking for the moment of high violence that would make impressive headlines. Instead, Sternfeld was motivated by the question: 'What did the banner-waving, song-singing, globally-wired "anti-global protesters" actually want?'[16]

Sternfeld's anti-photojournalistic concerns remind us of the critique that Allan Sekula also exercised on the genre. In his project *Waiting for the Tear Gas [White Globe to Black]*, Sekula photographed the five days of protest against the WTO in Seattle in 1999. A part of his series of photographs was published in a collective book entitled *Five Days that Shook the World: Seattle and Beyond*, which consists of accounts of the Seattle demonstrations and movement's goals and objectives.[17] Sekula's photographic sequence captures the crowd that protested in Seattle, of all ages, dressed up or naked, trade union activists or feminists, 'people waiting, unarmed, sometimes deliberately naked in the winter chill, for the gas and the rubber bullets and the concussion grenades'.[18] Zanny Begg, in her thoughtful account of Sekula's project, argues that Sekula provides an image of the crowd not as an 'angry mob being manipulated or led from outside' or a 'unified group of people who can be spoken for by a higher body' but as a 'self-organising collection of singularities'.[19] This emphasis on the counterforce of neoliberal globalisation, the 'multitude', which seeks to construct 'another world' is indicative of Sekula's photography, and its close relationship to the social and political reality, which is also manifested in his other contemporary projects.[20]

Although Sekula photographed the evolution of the demonstrations, as many photojournalists definitely did, he clearly defined his practice as anti-photojournalistic. Sekula moved with the flow of the demonstration with 'no flash, no telephoto lens, no gas mask, no auto-focus, no press pass and no pressure to grab at all costs the one defining image of dramatic violence'.[21] The photographer, in this case, becomes an integral part of the crowd, following the demonstration and being subjected to the police's tear gas. The small 35mm camera, the available light and lack of digital manipulation of the colours cast by the street lights resulted in photographs of low technical qualities, a new way of employing a 'strategy of de-skilling' as central to his critical realism.[22]

Sternfeld employs a similar anti-photojournalistic mode, not as much as in the technical features, in which he obviously takes a different strand from Sekula, but in his approach to any defining images of dramatic violence favoured by photojournalists. It is exactly the way that Sternfeld decided to treat the issue of violence that places him in total opposition to any photojournalistic project. Violence is nevertheless the focal point of his book, omnipresent in Stille's account of the events and implicit in most of the photographs of the book. Three of the five opening photographs and two of the four closing photographs depict the results of two peak moments of violence during the demonstrations: the violent night raid of the Italian carabinieri on the Diaz School; and the shooting of the young protester Carlo Giuliani by the police. Choosing to photograph the consequences of these two events, Sternfeld extends his critique to two major issues of photojournalism: the dramatisation of specific events and the omission of others. In fact, the violence in the Diaz School either never made it to the news, simply because the journalists were never there – questioning the omnipresence of the journalists and the intentionality on behalf of the police – or was mistakenly reported by newspapers such as the *Daily Mail*, as explained in part II. The raid became known only through the stories and personal reports that activists posted on websites, blogs and more specifically on the Indymendia network. Almost seven years later Nick Davies in his article in *The Guardian* brought again the story to the fore, as well as its main protagonists, who still seek justice, while the police officers responsible for the raids evade disciplinary and criminal charges.[23]

According to these stories, on the night of Saturday, 21 July, policemen invaded the Diaz School, a dormitory for peaceful activists and the Indymedia centre. The police showed inexplicable violent behaviour towards protesters who were asleep or about to sleep and destroyed computers, video equipment and printed material in the Indymedia centre. Sixty demonstrators were injured and ninety-three were arrested and mistreated by the police, who humiliated the protesters, sprayed them with irritants, forced them to stand for hours and compelled them to recite Fascist slogans and songs. Galante vividly describes the moment that the policemen entered the school. According to her:

They run towards us, unleashed, and start violently beating inert people who embrace each other in a desperate hope of escaping what is to come. They run towards those who, with their arms raised in gestures of peace and submission, are hoping to reason with madness. Before my eyes, there is a massacre occurring, and nothing can be done. Soon, blood is everywhere: heads, arms, legs, the walls, the floor.[24]

The destruction, disorder and chaos during the raid were never depicted on the mainstream media. Sternfeld visited the site many hours after the events and tried to reconstruct pictorially what had happened.

The two opening photographs taken in Diaz School, where many demonstrators camped during the demonstrations, depict destruction: a smashed door and stains of blood on the floor of the school (plate 13). What is interesting is that the captions that follow both pictures explicitly connect the destruction with the police behaviour. The captions read 'A door in Armando Diaz School after the police raid, Genoa, 21 July 2001' and 'The fifth floor of the Armando Diaz School after a police raid, Genoa, 21 July 2001'.[25] In contrast, in a photograph of a smashed window, the caption states only 'A storefront on Corso Torino, 19 July 2001'. In the photograph, some stones and a bottle on the front pavement are also visible, but there is no textual reference to the perpetrators of the deed – unlike with the previous two photographs that depict the results of violence performed by the policemen, Sternfeld does not make clear who was responsible for the violence. The decision to highlight the police's violent behaviour contradicts the established stereotypes of violent protesters as constructed by the mainstream mass media and indicates the clear political statement that underlines the whole book.

The closing photographs overtly refer to the shooting and death of the young protester Carlo Giuliani, another result of the extensive use of violence by the carabinieri. Nevertheless, Sternfeld comments on Giuliani's death in a very different way from the mainstream press, which made the photographs of his dead body front page news. This deliberate choice can be perceived as a comment on the dramatisation of news photography, which most of the time leads to a certain degree of apathy, the transformation of 'threat into fantasy, into imagery' and the reassurance that 'it is them, not us'.[26] Martha Rosler, who brilliantly described what effect dramatic imagery may have on viewers, has concluded: 'One can handle imagery by leaving it behind'.[27] Instead, Sternfeld showed that for many people – including himself – Giuliani's death is not something that they leave behind. The photograph that shows a kneeling man in front of a stain of Giuliani's blood on a Genoa street points in this direction. It is easily understandable that the death of this young activist may have had absolutely different impacts on the citizens who received the news in their homes through the mass media and the citizens who had also travelled to Genoa and participated in the demonstrations for similar reasons to Giuliani's. Remembrance of Guiliani and his tragic death has been significant among activists. To the same end, the accompanying caption of the last photograph in the series highlights the importance of his death for the movement: 'You think that you killed him but he lives on us.'[28]

Police violence then becomes the central point of the book, and frames all the portraits. Alexander Stille argues that violence was the keypoint in the way that the summit and the events around it were understood. As he argued:

the genesis of and the responsibility for the violence in Genoa is complex, and the way in which the summit unfolded tells a strange story about the nature of democracy, governance and dissent in the age of globalization and modern communications technology.[29]

It is true that the events in Genoa became synonymous with violence for the mass media and the dominant political circles. Stille pointed out that the violence was performed by a small part of the movement. As he explains 'There were an estimated 250,000 to 300,000 demonstrators in Genoa of whom, according to various estimates, between 500 to 5,000 were violent'.[30] Sternfled's avoidance of depicting any violent behaviour on behalf of the activists is distinctive. He seemingly sides with the majority of non-violent protesters who might otherwise be marginalised in the daily struggle for media coverage, leaving aside the part of the movement that responds to the media spectacle by staging spectacle.[31] These 'image events' for dissemination in the mainstream mass media are performed by a rather small part of the movement, mostly identified with small groups of young protesters such as the Black Block. The symbolic violence performed by such groups has been stigmatised by the majority of the groups that seek to develop non-violent tactics 'both in principle (seen as a form of accepting the violence of the system and even more as a behaviour akin to war) and for their practical effects in isolating protest'.[32]

Sternfeld's references to violence are also evident in his series of portraits. There are portraits of injured protesters followed by their reports of the performed violence. One portrait is of a man who turned his back to the camera, the only portrait in the series in which the subject does not confront

150

the camera. Through his statement, he touches upon two very important issues: the violence against the journalists, but even more importantly the legitimisation of this violence. After the description of assaults he received by the police the young man declares:

> Today, Tuesday, I went to see a lawyer, who advised me not to report the carabinieri because, even if I have two witnesses, the police could either come to my home and beat me or say that they remember seeing me throwing stones, setting fires or doing other things that could land me in jail. And this was said by my lawyer.[33]

The legitimisation of the police's violence is an issue that Slavoj Žižek discusses in regard to the way that the US authorities treat the Guantánamo prisoners. According to Žižek, their behaviour is in 'a kind of in-between legal status', since they act as a legal power, but without being controlled and limited by the law.[34] It is the same when the authorities which inflict violence on peaceful protesters act as a legal power, but are not subjected to the law. According to Žižek, 'the paradox here is that of an empty space, a dead zone, that exists within the domain of the law but is not itself subject to the rule of law'.[35] The status of *homo sacer* of the prisoners, that is that although they are biologically alive they are deprived of any legal rights, leads to the tolerance and, finally, the legitimisation, of violence. The sustainability of this tolerance and legitimisation of violence is totally independent of the existence of an invisible threat, an omnipresent enemy. The protesters were seen as a forthcoming threat for the city of Genoa with politicians and Prime Minister Berlusconi predicting scenarios of violent protesters and danger in the city. Under these circumstances, the police violence appears expected, if not justified. But as Žižek points out:

> only by rejecting in principle the notion that torture is permissible even in dire circumstances (while knowing that we resorted to it in precisely such circumstances) can we retain the requisite sense of guilt and awareness of the inadmissibility of what we did.[36]

This rejection of the notion of violence becomes even more important when we have to deal with the murder of a young protester. The book closes with a very strong photograph of Giuliani's family, his parents and his sister sitting on the stairs of a historical building of Genoa. The accompanying comment reads:

> Nothing is worth the life of a child. Nothing can bring him back to life for us – or for the young people like him. For this reason, we call for peace – a refusal of violence. We ask for the feelings of Peace, Tolerance and Solidarity to be the authentic values in which people recognize themselves, in order that the absurd death of Carlo should not become more absurd and useless.[37]

Their comment underlines the importance of the negation of any kind of violence and is indicative of the growing criticism of violence within the movement, which in fact increased after the events of Genoa.

A contemporary photographic practice

Although the book format, with the emphasis on visual and textual interaction, revisits twentieth-century documentary projects, the project's exhibition in the White Box gallery in New York raises interesting questions about the project's affinity to other contemporary art projects. In line with contemporary advances in photography, Joel Sternfeld's technique alludes to contemporary photographic trends. In a similar way to his book *American Prospects*, his subjects' full awareness of the presence of the camera, their straightforward pose, the strict composition of his photographs and the sequence of the portraits seem to perfectly fit into what Julian Stallabrass described as one of the most prominent and established trends in contemporary art photography.[38] This prominent strand, which includes among others the work of Rineke Dijikstra, Jitka Hanzlova, Thomas Ruff, Céline van Balen and Gillian Wearing, depicts people in uniform series, in which the subjects normally centrally placed, remain still in front of the camera, 'showing little or no activity other than self-representation'.[39] Stallabrass argues that these projects privilege formality, standardisation, frontality and centeredness in a quasi-ethnographical mode and raises interesting questions about the representation of identity and difference in the globalised art world. The solitary character of most of the subjects in these projects, and in particular in Dijikstra's well-known large format portraits, their detachment from their social environment, and the affinity of their self-representation to predominant images of the fashion industry, as well as the identification of the subject and the viewer only at the level of the image, are intrinsic features of these images which 'describe and also enact a world in which people are socially atomised, politically weak and are governed by their place in the image world'.[40]

Sternfeld apparently chooses, but does not instruct his subjects – in a way similar to that of Dijkstra and Ruff – and the result is not an isolated and powerless subject, whose image is just another commodity subject to the same logic of the market that all the commodities in the contemporary neoliberal economy undergo. In direct contrast to the Dijkstra's and Ruff's large format portraits destined to meet the requirements of the contemporary museum logic, Sternfeld chose medium-size prints juxtaposed with text for the exhibition, replicating the same format of his book. The specificity of the subjects' statements, which bring to the fore concerns about the loss of culture and values, economic inequalities and exploitation of the poor countries, poverty, consumerism, exploitation, sexism,and ecological destruction leaves little space not to encounter these subjects as active political subjects. The framing of the portraits with the photographs of the Diaz School and the photographs about Carlo Giuliani provides the right framework to read them politically. Having taken a critical stance towards the stereotypical mass media representations of protesters as a violent mass, the project refashions the combination of photography and text – common in traditional documentary projects – to represent its subjects as active political subjects. This choice contradicts other contemporary photographic projects, with which Sternfeld's project shares common technical and aesthetic qualities.

The question remains why Sternfeld insisted on the use of the portrait as the most eloquent representational mode given its use in contemporary art photography. This choice may also seem to be an oxymoron, if one considers the anti-photojournalistic claims of the project. It is, in fact, photojournalism's general fondness for choosing representative individuals to stand in for the news story; these individuals often representing collective social action.[41] This focus on the individual that disables the reader to relate the individual story with the social conditions that underpin the situation also characterised the documentary projects of the 1930s.

Sternfeld's choice seems deliberate in his effort to displace the crowd from view. The individual portraits can therefore be seen in contrast with stereotypical representations of the crowd, in particular with 'emblematic' and the 'oceanic' images of masses of individuals as modes of imagining the body politic.[42] The photographic portrait seems then the most eloquent choice to visualise the constructive differences of the people who participate in the movement Trent. These differences remain different even when the people meet together in the anti-G8 demonstrations to create common power. This multiplicity of singularities, which Hardt and Negri defined as 'multitude', differed severely from earlier social formations of the crowd and mob in its lack of passivity and centralised leadership.[43] Sternfeld's project is a serious effort to represent the multitude visually.

While these portraits are restricted in the art gallery and, therefore, their potential to challenge the dominance of TV and photojournalistic images that shape public opinion about protest is not without limitations, they are unique in their effort to bring to the museum an iconography of protest and activism pushed to the margins of artistic production. Seen along with new critical artistic formations, collective artistic work and critical photographic projects – arguably seen as the result of the considerable impact that the emergence of the 1990s movements against neoliberal globalisation had on contemporary artistic and photographic practices – Sternfeld's project raises interesting questions not only about the engagement of photography with activism and anti-globalisation politics, but also about the position of contemporary art in a continuously changing globalised world.

Notes

1 J. Sternfeld, *Treading on Kings: Protesting the G8 in Genoa* (Göttingen: Steidl Publishers, 2002).

2 William Shakespeare, Henry the Fourth, Part I, as quoted in Sternfeld, *Treading on Kings*, n. p.

3 Sternfeld, *Treading on Kings*, pp. 20–1.

4 Ibid., pp. 34–5.

5 For more information about the international campaign for justice in Bhopal, see: www.bhopal.net/.

6 D. Lange and P. Schuster Taylor, *An American Exodus* (New Haven and London: Yale University Press, 1969); E. Caldwell and M. Bourke-White, *You Have Seen Their Faces* (Athens and London: The University of Georgia Press, 1995).

7 The quote is from the introduction written on 1 August 1939 by Dorothea Lange and Paul Schuster Taylor. See: Lange and Schuster Taylor, *An American Exodus*.

8 W. Stott, *Documentary Expression and Thirties America* (London, Oxford, New York: Oxford University Press, 1973), p. 21.

9 M. Rosler, 'In, Around and Afterthoughts (On Documentary Photography)', in R. Bolton (ed.), *The Contest of Meaning: Critical Histories of Photography* (Cambridge, MA: The MIT Press, 1992), p. 307.

10 V. Burgin (ed.), *Thinking Photography* (London: Macmillan, 1982); A. Sekula, *Photography Against the Grain* (Halifax: Press of the Nova Scotia College of Art and Design, 1984); J. J. Tagg, *The Burden of Representation: Essays on Photographies and Histories* (London: Macmillan Education, 1988).

11 A. Tranchenberg, *Reading American Photographs* (Chapel Hill, NC and London: The University of North Carolina Press, 1991), p. 117.

12 For a comprehensive history of street photography, see: C. Westerbeck and J. Meyerowitz, *Bystander: A History of Street Photography* (Boston, New York and London: Bulfinch Press, 2001).

13 M. Rosler, *Decoys and Disruptions: Selected Writings, 1975–2001* (Cambridge, MA and London: The MIT Press, 2004), pp. 226–8.

14 N. Klein, *Fences and Windows: Dispatches from the Front Lines of Globalisation Debate* (London: Flaming, 2002), p. xxv.

15 R. Ferguson, 'Open City: Possibilities of the Street', in B. Bowman (ed.), *Open City: Street Photography Since 1950* (Oxford: Museum of Modern Art Oxford, 2001), p. 10.

16 Exhibition Press Release, www.whiteboxny.org/home.html (accessed 10/11/2007).

17 A. Cockburn, J. St Clair and A. Sekula, *Five Days that Shook the World: Seattle and Beyond* (London, New York: Verso, 2000).

18 A. Sekula, 'Waiting for Tear Gas', in Cockburn *et al.*, *Five Days that Shook the World*, p. 121.

19 Z. Begg, 'Recasting Subjectivity: Globalisation and the Photography of Andreas Gursky and Allan Sekula', *Third Text*, 19: 6 (2005), p. 632.

20 A. Sekula, *Fish Story* (Düsseldorf: Richter, 1995).

21 Cockburn *et al.*, *Five Days that Shook the World*, n.p.

22 S. Edwards, 'Commons and Crowds: Figuring Photography from Above and Below', *Third Text*, 23, 4, July 2009, pp. 447–64.

23 N. Davies, 'The Bloody Battle of Genoa', *The Guardian*, 17 July 2008 (online, accessed 10/06/2012).

24 Sternfeld, *Treading on Kings*, pp. 74–5.

25 Ibid., pp. 14–15.

26 Rosler, 'In, Around and Afterthoughts (On Documentary Photography)', p. 306.

27 Ibid., p. 306.

28 Sternfeld, *Treading on Kings*, p. 83.

29 Ibid., p. 2.

30 Ibid., p. 1.

31 K. Deluca, J. Peeples, 'From Public Sphere to Public Screen: Democracy, Activism and "Violence" of Seattle', *Critical Studies in Visual Communication*, 19:2 (2002), p. 134.

32 D. della Porta, M. Andretta, L. Mosca and H. Reiter (eds), *Globalization from Below: Transnational Activists and Protest Networks* (Minneapolis, MN: University of Minnesota Press, London, 2006), p. 3.

33 J. Sternfeld, *Treading on Kings*, p. 66.

34 S. Žižek, 'Biopolitics: Between Abu Ghraib and Terri Schiavo', *Art Forum International*, 44: 4 (2005), p. 270.

35 Ibid.

36 Ibid.

37 J. Sternfeld, *Treading on Kings*, p. 80.

38 J. Stallabrass, 'What's In a Face? Blankness and Significance in Contemporary Art Photography', *October*, 122 (2007), pp. 71–90.

39 Ibid., p. 73.

40 Ibid., p. 75.

41 R. Hariman and J. L. Lucaites, *No Caption Needed: Iconic Photographs, Public Culture and Liberal Democracy* (Chicago and London: The University of Chicago Press, 2007), p. 90.
42 J. T. Schnapp and M. Tiews (eds), *Crowds* (Stanford, CA: Stanford University Press), 2006.
43 M. Hardt, 'Bathing in the Multitude', in Schnapp and Tiews (eds), *Crowds*, pp. 35–40.

Conclusion

T H E global wave of mobilisations that emerged in the late 1990s and challenged the dominance of neoliberalism bore considerable similarities with the student and worker opposition to the dominant political order in France in 1968. While May '68 and the anti-globalisation movement were symptoms of and were formed by specific historical and socio-political conditions, they both interrupted periods of prosperity for Western capitalist societies, challenging the stability of the dominant system. The two movements also shared common elements in terms of their social composition, organisation and direct demands. The enthusiastic calls for democracy, justice and human rights and the broad attack on capitalism, its injustices and inequalities can been found in both movements. Furthermore, a loose decentralised organisation, a lack of strict leadership, a rejection of authoritarianism and any kind of hierarchy signalled a rupture with the old forms of organisation. These principles were put into practice in anti-hierarchical assemblies in the occupied Sorbonne in 1968 as well as in the Zapatistas 'Encuentros' and the European and World Social Fora at the turn of the millennium.

Photography's centrality in these movements' formation, sustainability, reception and outcome has been extraordinary. Looking at photography's circulation within different contexts, following its usage by different individuals and groups for different purposes becomes crucial within the context of the struggles against capitalism. It is the central argument of this book that these struggles transcended the economic and political level and were extended to a representational level. The book followed the circulation of these images from the mainstream mass media to the activists' communication channels, and, finally, to photobooks and exhibition displays. Echoing Benjamin's belief in the democratic potential of the medium and its instrumental role in a radical critique of bourgeois society, due to its inherent reproducibility and accessibility to a wider public, the book examined the photographic production, not only by professional photographers but also by amateurs, activists themselves in control of their own representation and in construction of historical counter-narratives.[1] Following the activists' efforts to use the medium in their construction of their own histories and taking into account that these histories 'bear the scars of capitalism' and are not so easily disentangled from their role within the framework of capitalist order, as Adorno put it in his now famous critique of Benjamin's aforementioned text, the book examined these photographs as bearers of both the innovations and the contradictions inherent in the movements.[2]

The two movements occurred in different media ages. In 1968, de Gaulle's government was in total control of all the media, including television and newspapers. As a result, transistor radios became the most popular means of communication. The photographs disseminated in mainstream press shifted between images of an amorphous crowd to images of a leader exemplified in photographs of Cohn-Bendit. Both representations were problematic, since they failed to represent the movement's innovations, including the different social subjects involved in the struggle and its anti-hierarchical character. In the case of *L'Humanité*, the focus on stereotypical configurations of the workers' occupations in factories indistinct from representations of the labour movement overshadowed the novelties of the new struggle.

In the 1990s, the concentration of media ownership, the elimination of small and localised media, as a result of the expansion of the multinational corporations' market practices in every economic sphere, and the dependence on advertising as the primary source of funding, impacted on the hierarchy in mainstream media for news. News related to mainstream politics, to political, governmental and corporate institutions or to celebrities, sex and violence has been habitually prioritised.[3] Their oligopolistic structure, their strong political ties and their prioritising of 'all the news that's fit to sell' have determined their news agenda.[4] News about activist groups and organisations challenging dominant politics, big corporations' ethics, consumerism and the subsequent destruction of the environment is pushed to the margins of news reporting.[5] This is overturned when photographs of protest violence are deemed 'newsworthy'. The coverage of the anti-G8 demonstrations in Genoa has been characteristic in this respect. The extreme violence of the police and the killing of the young protester Carlo Giuliani provided the Western dailies with photographs of chaos, destruction and violence. The 'framing' of these photographs within editorial content, followed by captions, titles, articles and other images of the world, highlighted the protesters' violent behaviour, playing an instrumental role in creating particular stereotypes about anti-capitalist protest, political participation and social dissent.[6] It is this media's obsession to portray social movements in conventional and preconceived visual terms that has been profoundly challenged by the Zapatistas and, in particular, their spokesperson Subcomandante Marcos. Marcos's conscious efforts to re-appropriate the easily recognisable images of the revolutionaries Zapata and Che Guevara and to create a particular image for the media spectacle has subverted the mass media's endeavour to pigeonhole new struggles into preconceived visual narratives.

It is worth noting that in all aforementioned cases, real editorial choices have been diminished to choices based on newsworthy-ness, according to which the movements' leaders join the pantheon of show-business celebrities, and the dead body of a protester makes the front pages. Ethical issues about showing the body of a dead young man on the front pages of a newspaper are sacrificed to the logic of the market. The real causes behind these protests are hidden in accounts about the protest violence and pejorative characterisations of the protesters, whose anti-corporate and anti-consumerist ideology is clearly incompatible with the mainstream press's profit orientation, its shared interests with huge corporations and its dependence on advertisers. Within this framing, photographs of peaceful protesters, anti-hierachical and democratic meetings fall into the 'black hole' of news making.

On the other side of this representational conflict, activists' communication systems promote an alternative visual story. In the student newspapers in 1968 and in the websites of Zapatistas and the anti-globalisation movement, a fusion of photographic practices is chosen by activists themselves to offer an alternative visual story. The emphasis on photographs of democratic, anti-hierarchical meetings at the Sorbonne during May '68 and the democratic assemblies in Chiapas villages, on images of carnival, joy and dance in the J18 and on the numerous photographs of indigenous women in active roles within the EZLN are symptomatic of the movements' efforts to highlight the innovations of the movements. In all these efforts, photography plays a crucial role in creating a counter-narrative of protest, although the fact that they may be buried in state and library archives – as in the case of May '68 – renders these counter-narratives less accessible to a wider public.

In the more contemporary cases, new technologies and the internet opened up new communicative possibilities to promote these alternative stories to the public sphere. Indymedia, born concurrently with the new movement in Seattle in 1999, used and produced Free Software publishing systems to allow activists and journalists to upload their own reports, photographs, videos and stories.[7] Following the motto 'Don't Hate the Media-Become the Media', Indymedia offered an alternative to corporate media's coverage of the new movement.[8] Several other websites and blogs followed Indymedia's example and expanded to such an extent that anyone can self-publish their texts or photographs offering new ways for both dissemination and preservation of protest photographs. The editorial choices and the distribution systems that deliver these photographs to the audience are heavily reliant on the activists, equating looking at these photographs with looking at the self-reflection of the movement. This self-reflection did not only highlight the movements' novelties, but often revealed their struggles' weaknesses related to their function within a prevailing capitalist order.

Distinctive in the use of photography by activists has also been a renewed belief in the evidential status of photography. In the murder of the young activist Giuliani by the Italian carabinieri and the torture of peaceful protesters by the police at the Diaz School during the demonstrations in Genoa, photography's evidential status was revisited by activists who sought justice. Photographs were central on the activists' websites and blogs in an attempt to make these stories known to the wider public, and they acted as evidence in the juridical debates to the advantage of the activists. Activists re-appropriated photojournalistic snapshots of Guiliani's shooting to support their case and collated thousands of amateur snapshots and footage to sustain their appeal against the Italian police force in the case of the raid on Diaz School.

While the photographs published in ephemeral media, both mainstream and activist, are destined to be forgotten after the end of the events, some photographs have a more enduring life. Displayed in exhibitions or published in photobooks, these photographs are responsible for how these movements are remembered after the echo of the events has faded away. Photographs of May '68 became the museum's special object of study, only when they were already 'dead' objects and the observers could not identify with them any longer.[9] Part of commemorating the events of 1968, these displays brought to the fore a romanticised image of spontaneous revolt of the youth, which decisively contributed to the rise of the individual, obscuring the radical collective nature of the events.

The photobooks and exhibition displays of the Zapatistas and the anti-globalisation movement, exemplified in Antonio Turok's and Joel Sternfeld's photography, point to projects that were only made possible as a result of the impact of the anti-globalisation movement on artistic and photographic production. Towards the end of the twentieth century, web-based initiatives, such as RTMark, Etoy and Rhizome and interventions by groups and collaborations that challenged the profit-oriented ethos of the contemporary art market, merging political ends with cultural means, can be deemed as the direct effects of the anti-globalisation movement on the art world. Some of them have been directly involved with contemporary movements, such as the Electronic Disturbance Theatre (EDT), which organised virtual sit-ins and FloodNet in support of the Zapatista struggle.[10] Directly connected to attempts at social transformation, these artistic practices challenged the dominant political status quo and the gallery system, even if their impact has not been sustained longer than the impact of the struggles they were involved with. Seen within this context, Turok's and Sternfeld's projects brought into the gallery space and the photobook an iconography of activism pushed to the margins of artistic production by longstanding interdictions. This visual recognition of neglected political subjects – be they indigenous people of Chiapas or activists from all over the world – may not necessarily be followed by political recognition, but it without doubt opens the way to imagining a new body politic, which does not comply with the stereotypical images promoted by the mainstream discourse.

Within the last couple of years, photographs of people protesting across the globe from Egypt to New York and from Greece to the United Kingdom have bombarded the public domain, bringing to the fore thorny questions pertinent to this book, that is questions regarding the role of photographs in constructing mainstream and alternative narratives about social protest and resistance to the dominant system. The centrality of photographic images within these comtemporary social and political struggles raises questions about photography's ability to shape or change public opinion, generate public discussion and stimulate acts of solidarity actions across the world. The images of the massive demonstrations of the Arab Spring and the indignant movements in Spain and Greece were disseminated widely and became a source of inspiration for protesters in the Occupy movements, which sprang in several cities across the globe. This new generation of activists extended the use of the internet, initiated by the 1990s anti-globalisation struggles, to include Facebook, Twitter, Google Images and Flickr among others in order to disseminate their messages widely, built coalitions and communicated with other struggles. The use of photographs within these various platforms of counter-information has been pivotal. This new wave of resistance is at the moment unforseen but not unannounced. Preguntando Caminamos (Asking We Walk).

Notes

1 W. Benjamin, 'The Work of Art in the Age of Mechanical Reproduction', in Harry Zohn (trans), *Illuminations* (New York: Schocken Books, 1969).

2 T. Adorno, 'Letters to Walter Benjamin', in T. Adorno, W. Benjamin, E. Bloch, B. Brecht and G. Lukács, *Aesthetics and Politics* (London and New York: Verso, 2007), pp. 120–6.

3 Among the most influential studies of the profound changes of the mass media are: B. Bagdikian, *The Media Monopoly* (Boston, MA: Beacon Press, 1992); E. S. Herman and N. Chomsky (eds), *Manufacturing Consent: The Political Economy of the Mass Media* (New York: Pantheon Books, 1988).

4 J. T. Hamilton, *All the News That's Fit to Sell: How the Market Transforms Information to News* (Princeton, NJ: Princeton University Press, 2004).

5 W. de Jong, M. Shaw and N. Stammers (eds), *Global Activism, Global Media* (London: Pluto Press, 2005), p. 6.

6 For an interesting study about how the media 'frame' the protest activity and produce meanings for a wide public, see: T. Gitlin, *The Whole World is Watching: Mass Media in the Making and the Unmaking of the New Left,* Press (Berkeley, CA: University of California Press, 1980).

7 www.indymedia.org (accessed 24/05/2006).

8 D. Kidd, 'Indymedia.org: A New Communications Commons', in M. McCaughey and M. D. Ayers (eds), *Cyberactivism: Online Activism in Theory and Practice* (New York and London: Routledge, 2003), p. 49.

9 T. W. Adorno, 'Valéry Proust Museum', in Samuel Weber and Shiery Weber (trans), *Prisms* (London: Neville Spearman, 1967), pp. 173–86.

10 C. Fusco and R. Dominguez, 'Electronic Disturbance', in G. Tawardos (eds), *Changing States: Contemporary Art and Ideas in an Era of Globalisation* (London: Institute of International Visual Arts, 2004), pp. 150–5.

Index

EU authorised representative for GPSR:
Easy Access System Europe, Mustamäe tee 50,
10621 Tallinn, Estonia
gpsr.requests@easproject.com

www.ingramcontent.com/pod-product-compliance
Ingram Content Group UK Ltd.
Pitfield, Milton Keynes, MK11 3LW, UK
UKHW062135150726
7214IPUK00024B/416